ASYMMETRIC TRADE NEGOTIATIONS

The International Political Economy of New Regionalisms Series

The International Political Economy of New Regionalisms series presents innovative analyses of a range of novel regional relations and institutions. Going beyond established, formal, interstate economic organizations, this essential series provides informed interdisciplinary and international research and debate about myriad heterogeneous intermediate level interactions.

Reflective of its cosmopolitan and creative orientation, this series is developed by an international editorial team of established and emerging scholars in both the South and North. It reinforces ongoing networks of analysts in both academia and think-tanks as well as international agencies concerned with micro-, meso- and macro-level regionalisms.

Asymmetric Trade Negotiations

Edited by

SANOUSSI BILAL
European Centre for Development Policy Management (ECDPM),
The Netherlands

PHILIPPE DE LOMBAERDE
United Nations University Institute on Comparative Regional
Integration Studies (UNU-CRIS), Belgium

DIANA TUSSIE
Facultad Latinoamericana de Ciencias Sociales (FLACSO) and
Latin American Trade Network (LATN), Argentina

Routledge
Taylor & Francis Group

LONDON AND NEW YORK

First published 2011 by Ashgate Publishing

2 Park Square, Milton Park, Abingdon, Oxon OX14 4RN
711 Third Avenue, New York, NY 10017, USA

Routledge is an imprint of the Taylor & Francis Group, an informa business

First issued in paperback 2016

British Library Cataloguing in Publication Data
Asymmetric trade negotiations. -- (The international
  political economy of new regionalisms series)
  1. Commercial treaties. 2. Commercial treaties--Case studies.
  I. Series II. Bilal, Sanoussi. III. Lombaerde, Philippe De.
  IV. Tussie, Diana.
  382.9-dc22

Library of Congress Cataloging-in-Publication Data
Bilal, Sanoussi.
  Asymmetric trade negotiations / by Sanoussi Bilal, Philippe De Lombaerde and Diana Tussie.
      p. cm. -- (The international political economy of new regionalisms series)
  Includes bibliographical references and index.
  ISBN 978-1-4094-3406-1 (hardback)
  1. International trade. 2. Negotiation in business. 3. International economic
relations. I. Lombaerde, Philippe De. II. Tussie, Diana. III. Title.

  HF1379.A89 2011
  382'.9--dc22

                                                                        2011016482

ISBN 978-1-4094-3406-1 (hbk)
ISBN 978-1-138-26156-3 (pbk)

Contents

List of Figures, Tables and Boxes

Boxes

List of Contributors

Fernando Barberi is a Consultant (Bogotá, Colombia).

Andrea C. Bianculli is a Postdoctoral Researcher at Institut Barcelona d'Estudis Internacionals (IBEI) (Barcelona, Spain).

Sanoussi Bilal is the Head of the Economic and Trade Cooperation Programme at the European Centre for Development Policy Management (ECDPM) (Maastricht, The Netherlands).

Mercedes Botto is a Senior Researcher at the Department of International Relations at Facultad Latinoamericana de Ciencias Sociales (FLACSO), Argentina, where she heads the Research Program on International Economic Institutions.

Santi Chaisrisawatsuk is Assistant Professor and Director of the Centre for International Economics and Development Studies (CIEDS), School of Development Economics, National Institute of Development Administration (NIDA) (Bangkok, Thailand).

Ludo Cuyvers is Professor of International Economics and Chairman of the Centre for ASEAN Studies, University of Antwerp (Belgium); Professor extraordinary, Faculty of Economics and Management Sciences, North-West University, Potchefstroom Campus (South Africa).

Philippe De Lombaerde is Associate Director at the United Nations University Institute on Comparative Regional Integration Studies (UNU-CRIS) (Bruges, Belgium).

Luis Jorge Garay is Associate Research Fellow at the United Nations University Institute on Comparative Regional Integration Studies (UNU-CRIS) (Bruges, Belgium) and International Consultant.

Rita Giacalone is Professor of Economic History, Economics Department, Universidad de Los Andes (ULA), Coordinator of the Research Group in Regional Integration (GRUDIR), and Researcher of the Centre of Agribusiness Studies (CIAAL) (Mérida, Venezuela).

Wisarn Pupphavesa is Advisor at the Thailand Development Research Institute Foundation (TDRI) (Bangkok, Thailand).

Marcelo Saguier is a Senior Researcher at the Department of International Relations at Facultad Latinoamericana de Ciencias Sociales (FLACSO/Argentina) and a Research Fellow at Argentina's National Science and Technology Research Council (CONICET).

Timothy M. Shaw is Professor and Director at the Institute of International Relations, University of the West Indies (UWI) (St. Augustine, Trinidad and Tobago).

Diana Tussie directs the Department of International Relations at the Argentine campus of the Facultad Latinoamericana de Ciencias Sociales (FLACSO), and is founding director of the Latin American Trade Network.

Stephen Woolcock is Lecturer, Programme Director of the Masters in International Political Economy, and Head of the International Trade Policy Unit at the London School of Economics (UK); and Associate Research Fellow at the United Nations University Institute on Comparative Regional Integration Studies (UNU-CRIS) (Bruges, Belgium).

Acknowledgements

This book project was made possible thanks to the support of the United Nations University Institute on Comparative Regional Integration Studies (UNU-CRIS) (www.cris.unu.edu).

The editors are grateful to Ajsela Mašović and Liesbeth Martens for their outstanding job in revising and formatting the manuscript, to Lurong Chen for his help with data gathering, and to Director Luk Van Langenhove, all at UNU-CRIS.

We are also thankful to IPENR series editor Timothy Shaw of the University of the West Indies, and to Margaret Younger and colleagues at Ashgate.

San Bilal, Philippe De Lombaerde and Diana Tussie, Editors

List of Acronyms

ABF	Americas Business Forum
ACP	African Caribbean and Pacific Group
ACS	Assocation of Caribbean States
AEC	ASEAN Economic Community
AER	Amity and Economic Relations
AfT	Aid for Trade
ALBA	Bolivarian Alternative for the Americas
ANDI	National Business Association of Colombia
	Asociación Nacional de Empresarios de Colombia
APEC	Asia-Pacific Economic Cooperation
ASEAN	Association of South East Asian Nations
ASEM	Asia-Europe Meeting
ATP	Andean Trade Promotion
ATPA	Andean Trade Preference Act
ATPDEA	Andean Trade Promotion and Drug Eradication Act
AUI	ASEAN-US Initiative
BCG	Boston Consulting Group
BNC	Bi-regional Negotiations Committee
CAFTA	Central American FTA
CAN	Andean Community
CAP	Common Agricultural Policy
CARICOM	Caribbean Community
CARIFORUM	Caribbean Forum
CCSCS	Coordinating Group of Trade Unions of the Southern Cone
	Coordinadora de Centrales Sindicales del Cono Sur
CEMAC	Communauté Economique et Monétaire de l'Afrique Centrale
CFATF	Caribbean Financial Action Task Force
CGD	Center for Global Development
COCEGA	General Confederation of Agricultural Co-operatives in the European Union
COMESA	Common Market for Eastern and Southern Africa
COPA	Committee of Professional Agricultural Organisations
CRTA	Committee on Regional Trade Agreements
CSO	Civil society organisation
CUFTA	Canada United States Free Trade Agreement
DC	Developing Countries
DDA	Doha Development Agenda
DEA	Drug Eradication Act

DG	Directorate General
DR	Dominican Republic
DRC	Democratic Republic of Congo
DSS	Dispute Settlement System
EAC	East African Community
EAI	Enterprises for ASEAN Initiative
EBA	Everything But Arms
EC	European Commission
ECLAC	United Nations Economic Commission for Latin America and the Caribbean
ECOWAS	Economic Community of West African States
EDF	European Development Fund
EEC	European Economic Community
EFTA	European Free Trade Association
EMIFCA	Interregional Framework Cooperation Agreement
EPA	Economic partnership agreement
EPADP	Economic partnership agreement development program
ESA	Eastern and Southern Africa
ETUC	European Union Trade Confederation
EU	European Union
FAO	Food and Agriculture Organisation
FDI	Foreign Direct Investment
Fedecamaras	Federation of Chambers of Commerce of Venezuela
FTA	Free Trade Agreement
FTAA	Free Trade Area of the Americas
FTC	Federal Trade Commission
GATS	General Agreement on Trade in Services
GATT	General Agreement on Tariffs and Trade
GI	Geographic Indicators
GPA	Government Procurement Agreement
GSP	Generalised System of Preferences
HCP	Hemispheric Cooperation Program
HSA	Hemispheric Social Alliance
IBSA	India, Brazil and South Africa
ICE	Institute of International Trade
IEPA	Interim Economic Partnership Agreement
IMF	International Monetary Fund
INN	International Non-proprietary Names
INVIMA	Instituto Nacional de Vigilancia de Medicamentos y Alimentos
IPR	Intellectual Property Rights
LAC	Latin American Country
LDC	Least Developed Country
LMG	Like Minded Group
MEBF	MERCOSUR-European Business Forum

MERCOSUR	Southern Common Market
MFN	Most Favoured Nation
MNCs	multinational companies
MOU	Memorandum of Understanding
NAFTA	North American Free Trade Agreement
NAM	Non-Aligned Movement
NG	Negotiating Group
NGO	Non-Governmental Organisation
NTB	non-tariff barriers
OAS	Organization of American States
OECD	Organisation for Economic Cooperation and Development
OECS	Organization of Eastern Caribbean States
ORRC	other regulatory restrictions of commerce
PACP	Pacific ACP Group
PDVSA	Petróleos de Venezuela S.A.
PICTA	Pacific Island Countries Trade Agreement
PNG	Papua New Guinea
RECALCA	Red Colombiana de Acción frente al Libre Comercio y el ALCA
REIH	Red Empresarial para la Integración Hemisférica (Business Network for Hemispheric Integration)
RMALC	Mexican Network of Action Against Free Trade
RPTF	Regional Preparatory Task Forces
RSA	Republic of South Africa
S&D	Special and Differential treatment
SACU	Southern Africa Customs Union
SADC	Southern African Development Community
SAFTA	South American Free Trade Agreement
SAT	substantially all trade
SCC	Subcommittee on Cooperation
SCO	Shanghai Cooperation Organization
SME	Small and Medium-sized Enterprise
SPS	Sanitary and Phytosanitary measures
TBT	Technical Barriers to Trade
TDCA	Trade, Development and Cooperation Agreement
TG	Technical Group
TNC	Trade Negotiations Committee
TPA	Trade Promotion Agreement
TRIM	Trade Related Investment Measures
TRIPs	Trade Related Intellectual Property rights
TRQ	Tariff Rate Quota
TUSFTA	Thailand-US Free Trade Agreement
TWN	Third World Network
UN	United Nations
UNDP	United Nations Development Programme

US	United States
US-CAFTA-DR	US-Central America FTA-Dominican Republic
USSFTA	US-Singapore FTA
USTR	United States Trade Representative
Venamcham	Venezuelan-American Chamber
WAEMU	West African Economic and Monetary Union
WEF	World Economic Forum
WTO	World Trade Organisation

Chapter 1

The Sweep of Asymmetric Trade Negotiations: Introduction and Overview

Diana Tussie and Marcelo Saguier

Introduction

Trade always raises the old question of who gets what. Despite pretensions to 'global' scope and relevance, the multilateral trade system covered a highly specific and asymmetric set of rules which served the interests of global business. The extent of 'global' applicability of its central rules and the fairness of processes was always open to considerable question.[1] The evolution of global trade regulation must be seen as the result of a history of political bargains among states of differing power capabilities. Each bargain struck put in place a new layer of regulation that creates economic opportunities for global interests (in industrial countries and sectors) while narrowing or offering less opportunities for others (in developing countries and sectors).

The trading system was composed of rules and institutions which reflect the broader US-led arrangement of strategic alliances in a permanent tension with the East-West and North-South binary axes. The United States, with its willing quasi-hegemonic allies in Western Europe, promoted and supported the General Agreement on Tariffs and Trade (GATT) because under the GATT's consensus rule its own power was maximised. GATT members operated on the basis of a negative consensus rule. This meant that unless a member objected decision consensus was assumed. Powerful players like the US or the European Union (EU) could better absorb the costs of denying consensus, more credibly threaten objecting to a consensus and find more ways to exert pressure in order to reach consensus.

When the World Trade Organisation (WTO) was born, a new era of rule of law was believed to have come into being. Yet, the growing coverage and rule orientation of the WTO also meant that cohesion was lost. Consensus became harder to reach amongst the ever growing number of entrants with less accepting views and interests of their own. The diversity of goals and interests currently at stake and the resulting newly forged crisscrossing alliances changed the character

---

1 The scope for asymmetric provisions and asymmetric interpretations is discussed in Woolcock in this volume (Chapter 2).

of the institution.[2] This was especially the case after the Cancun Ministerial in 2003 when the South showed that collectively they could muster the power to block consensus, endangering the underlying structure of power in the WTO. To be sure, negotiations were derailed and continue to go on seemingly forever without result; but the process of creating norms continued.

A period of slow motion was opened in which developed countries found new ways for extending some rules and evading others; a network of bilateralism agreements spread swiftly; and new binary distinctions were construed.[3] With the world's major trading power playing a trade game based on securing preferences, other trading nations saw little option but to follow suit and secure preferential deals for themselves. The upshot was a dramatic rise in the number of North-South regional trade agreements which we assert to be asymmetrical in nature.

The Oxford English Dictionary defines asymmetry as a state in which there is a disproportionate correspondence between parts. Though asymmetries are rampant and varied, we are interested in circumstances of significant disparity between contending parties where there is no consideration of such disparity or a fair chance of matching up forces in the process. Interdependent economic relations may be relatively asymmetrical from time to time. However, in these circumstances the interactions, and its outcomes, have a chance of being equally distributed and both parties are more or less equally vulnerable to the positive and the negative effects or threats of eventual discontinuations.

In contrast, the nature of asymmetry in the cases we study is such that not only the threat of discontinuation is disproportionate but that such discontinuation can cut lifelines. Hence are concerned with absolute rather than relative asymmetry. This is the case of free trade agreements (FTAs). As a result of such asymmetry, FTAs cover not only the reduction or elimination of tariffs and other non-tariff barriers on the trade of goods and services, but also broader elements that had become difficult to obtain in the WTO game such as investment rules, intellectual property rights and so on. Far from being the confused 'spaghetti bowl' described by some observers, FTAs are the manifestation of coherent geopolitical strategies on the part of the major trading countries.

Taking clear issue with a number of the assumptions about the GATT-era *belle époque* rule of law, this introductory chapter discusses the place of power asymmetries in current multilateral and bilateral trade regimes. Differences of national strength, capabilities and competence are what the study and practice of international relations is almost entirely about. But circumstances are not fixed. Since these change we need to see how the range of alternative strategies is available for developing countries affected but asymmetries in the trade system

---

2   The character of small and large number systems is a classic research area in both economics and international relations (Baumol 1952, Russett 1968, Waltz 1979).

3   Robert Zoellig, then United States Trade Representative, ushered in a binary distinction between can do and won't do countries. The first group was offered terms of competitive liberalisation for access to the US market.

and processes.[4] How can developing countries manage the terms of integration into the global economy? How do different sets of external pressures place constraints on national development strategies? What offsetting mechanisms have emerged? These questions are the centre of current challenges of the trade system with deep implications for global order and future development prospects.

Asymmetry is unavoidable. But its more destructive outcomes need not be

The underpinning of this chapter is the simple thought that asymmetry must not be viewed as static. Form and content suffer tortuous twists and remain in constant flux. In the first part we discuss the dynamics of trade negotiation processes in multilateral and bilateral fora to show to what extent they reflect, as well as reproduce, entrenched power asymmetries. These asymmetries are revealed in the unequal conditions affecting the participation and representation of countries' interests in trade negotiations; the prevalence of reciprocity over dispensations of special and differential treatment; the recurrent bias of the agenda-setting; and in the choice of trade fora.

The second section explores the opportunities and constraints available for developing country governments to offset the unequal power structure that characterise international trade negotiation processes. To do so it identifies some of the main elements which countries can seize on to increase bargaining power in a creative process that can affect the outcome of a process of permanent and constant negotiations. To this end, we have to revert to a micropolitical approach in order to examine the conditions of asymmetry, whereby the loss of power to do certain things is compensated by seeking power with kindred spirits, collective forces and alternative partners.[5] Victims act! Yet balancing cannot take place without mustering power and increased bargaining competence. Two broad strategies to confront power asymmetry are open confrontation and strategic influence. The chapter leaves aside defection, opt out strategies and open confrontation to concentrate on how countries act in alliances of convenience to address vulnerabilities and strategically influence the process in which they have chosen to persist.

---

4   In this chapter, developing countries are treated as a group that includes the sub-group of least developed countries (LDCs).

5   The difference between power *to* and power *with* is drawn from feminist frameworks of power. Power to refers to the capacity to take action. Power with refers to cooperation with others to solve problems and attain goals. It addresses capacity building, social networks and organisational strength. The underlying notion is that of 'I cannot, but we can' (Wong 2003).

Asymmetries in processes

Participation and representation

For a good 40 years after World War II, most developing countries did not perceive the GATT as a friendly or fruitful institution in which to promote their interests. Inward-oriented industrialisation and nationalist ideologies of development prevailed, turning trade relations into the crux of the North-South debate. Involvement in the GATT reflected these preferences: developing countries adopted a 'passive' or 'defensive' attitude, refraining from significantly engaging in the exchange of reciprocal concessions. Moreover, many developing countries were not members, and among those that were, many failed to maintain official representation in Geneva. The result was a situation in which developing countries had negligible obligations and liberalisation in sectors of export interest to them was disproportionately small (Tussie 1987).

The passage from the GATT to the WTO represented a major turning point in the participation and representation of developing countries. These evidenced a new willingness to take on new commitments, come out of the fringes and shed their mostly defensive pre-Uruguay Round position. Their strategic dilemma turned from expanding their rights to free themselves from prevailing rules to choosing an appropriate strategy of participation, focusing on what commitments to make and on how to micromanage a bloated trade agenda. The challenges of inclusion soon proved to be highly demanding. Developing countries learned that greater participation did not translate automatically into leverage, as they found it difficult to decisively influence the process of agenda setting and to shape the final outcome of negotiations.

As in most earlier rounds, decision-making in the Uruguay Round negotiations was 'pyramidal' in structure in the sense that the major trading partners (US, EU and Japan) had implicit, yet effective, veto power over the negotiation's overall outcome (Winham 1997). Formal equality in the WTO, in which every country has an equal vote, does not translate in a democratic decision-making process. Decisions over key issues of the agenda are decided exclusively by the few major industrial countries in the so-called Green Room process during and prior to the WTO Ministerial Conferences. The 'green room' is the name given to the traditional method used in the GATT/WTO to expedite consultations; it involves the Director General and a small group of members, numbering between 25 and 30 and including the major trading countries, both industrial and developing, as well as a number of other countries that are deemed to be representative. Once a narrowed down consensus is obtained, agreements are passed on to exclude governments for their approval or rejection, thus legitimating negative 'consent' (Helleiner 2002, Kumar 2007: 5, UNDP 2001: 13–14, 77–78, Smythe 2007).

The composition of the green room tended to vary by issue, but there is no objective basis for participation. This procedure worked when most developing countries were quiet bystanders. After the significant concessions made in the

Uruguay Round, developing countries felt entitled to be included in the green-room process, and on several occasions they submitted declarations stating that they would not adhere to any consensus reached without their effective participation. The subsequent ministerial meetings, especially Doha in 2001 and Hong Kong in 2005 were more inclusive and open to all members.

The democratic deficit has begun to be firmly resisted since the Cancun ministerial meeting in 2003 with the emergence of a number of issue-based coalitions. It may be too early to conclude that the influence gained by developing country coalitions is enough to remedy the undemocratic practices in the WTO. However, it certainly suggests that the leading position of industrial states in the international trade system is being contested by a group of emerging economies from the South. The broadening of participation and interest representation has reduced northern domination of the multilateral agenda and hence reduced the value of the new WTO to older established interests.

Constraints to participation and representation in trade negotiations are also derived from limited capacity of some state bureaucracies to follow complex negotiations with often limited financial resources. With the incorporation of the 'new issues' (services, intellectual property rights and investment measures) at the Uruguay Round, trade negotiations shifted the policy focus from border barriers – as it had been under the GATT – to domestic regulatory and legal systems. This introduced great complexity and technical sophistication to the negotiations, making knowledge a strategic and highly valuable asset. Poor countries with limited access to this kind of technical information became invariably disadvantaged in comparison to industrial countries with sufficient resources to produce information to assist negotiators. Countries with insufficient resources fell into a 'knowledge trap' (Ostry 2007: 28) which, in turn, further reinforced existing asymmetries in the trading system.

This limitation is even worse in cases of countries that do not have a Mission in Geneva where the WTO is headquartered, or others that are understaffed or unable to adequately follow the discussions and the negotiations (Tussie and Lengyel 2002). This invariably affects their capacity to participate effectively in the WTO system – to take advantage of their rights, defend their interests and even meet their obligations. In this regard, the Uruguay Round imbued the multilateral trading system with a structural asymmetry that served to disadvantage poor developing states (Ostry 2007).

Weak bureaucracies and limited resources is also an impediment for poor countries to use the WTO Dispute Settlement System (DSS). This mechanism was introduced to constrain power and so protect weak states from the bullying and arbitrariness of the strong. At least in principle, this creates incentives for developing countries to participate in the multilateral trade system. It also increases their bargaining power in multilateral negotiations, allowing them to obtain greater concessions from more powerful states than in bilateral negotiations (Davis 2006).

However, in practice developing countries are restricted in their use of the dispute settlement mechanism due to the high costs involved in taking retaliatory action against an erring country (UNDP 2001: 12). The 'juridification' of the trade process has made access to expensive legal services a necessity, which in most cases poor countries cannot afford. This creates an asymmetric situation, since when large countries 'breach the agreed rules at the expense of the small and ill-endowed, the cost of a legal challenge may exceed the financial capacities of the latter (or, in some cases, even the relevant trade losses)' (Helleiner 2002: 327).

In addition to financial limitations of developing countries to use the dispute settlement system, there are also political costs which can often act as effective deterrents. The mere threat of anti-dumping action, for instance, is enough to discourage small exporters without the wherewithal to launch a legal defence. Pressure used to deter countries from dissonant behaviour includes threats to withdraw food aid or market access benefits under the Generalised System of Preferences (GSP) or, as in the case of Bolivia and Ecuador, from the Andean Trade Promotion and Drug Eradication Act (ATPDEA).

Unequal conditions are even greater in bilateral or inter-regional trade processes than in multilateral processes. The lack of technical capacity has been a key factor in weakening the positions of governments in the negotiations of preferential FTAs with the US or the EU – particularly in relation to negotiations of intellectual property rights (Díaz 2008: 102).[6] From the US and EU perspective, the opportunity of obtaining a WTO-Plus regulatory setting for intellectual property rights, investments and services provision holds out obvious advantages to push special interests. In this regard, bilateral trade agreements are not even subject to a minimal degree of international consensus to smooth problems of governance and compliance.

Reciprocity vs. special and differential treatment

In international trade negotiations asymmetries are also evidenced in the predominance of the principles of reciprocity and the single undertaking at the expense of the use of the special and differential (S&D) treatment principle. The Most Favoured Nation (MFN) principle was originally introduced in the GATT in order to prevent strong countries from exercising undue power against smaller countries through trade discrimination. However, equal treatment among unequal partners constitutes a form of discrimination in itself, since this assumes that all countries have the same economic conditions to be able to participate and benefit from international trade. The principle of S&D was incorporated in the GATT in recognition that the multilateral trading system consists of countries at markedly different levels of development.

Broadly reflecting these concerns, S&D provisions are designed to accomplish two objectives: to enhance the market access conditions facing the beneficiary countries, and to exempt them from certain multilateral trade disciplines and thus give them some flexibility in the use of various trade and trade-related measures.

---

6   See also Chapter 6 (Garay et al.).

In operational terms, enhanced market access has been implemented through trade preferences offered by the industrial countries on an individual basis to specific countries. The right of the developing and least-developed countries to regulate access to their own markets is operationalised through substantial exemption from several GATT/WTO disciplines. The exemptions enable them to use quantitative import restrictions for both infant industry protection and balance of payment reasons; to establish preferential regional trading arrangements among themselves; and to benefit from tariff reductions achieved in the process of multilateral trade negotiations, in accordance with the most-favoured-nation (MFN) principle, but without reciprocity.[7]

After reaching a climax at the GATT Tokyo Round, S&D treatment became increasingly less important in multilateral trade negotiations to the point of being ultimately displaced by the demand for reciprocity in the course of Uruguay Round (Sai-wing 1998). The reason for this was the lack of interest among industrial powers to negotiate a system of trade rules with developing countries if they could not open new markets for their exports in the developing world. S&D represented an obstacle to their commercial ambitions of industrial countries. Industrial countries started to see the engagement through new lenses. The minimal size of markets in developing countries had previously been perceived as not being worth the effort of pressing for greater access. But as competition among the major trading players intensified, the opening and greater contestability of markets in developing countries became a more highly valued goal. The United States was firmly determined to extend the GATT into services and other new areas and was no longer willing to accept free-riding of developing countries on such issues as intellectual property.[8]

As these interests pressed on, the issue of economic asymmetries was addressed by granting developing countries longer periods to adjust to standard liberalisation commitments. Market convergence became the ultimate goal that could be reached at different times depending on the different characteristics of economies. In this regard, the Uruguay Round reduced S&D treatment for developing countries to extended transition periods (Oyejide 2002). The incorporation of the Single Undertaking – emerging out of the Uruguay Round – meant that all member countries were required to agree on, and abide by, an entire set of rules that were multilaterally negotiated within the WTO. More flexible arrangements used in GATT for joining and/or opting out of particular sub-agreements within the overall package were all but eliminated. Hoekman and Kostecki (2001) point out that most of the 97 S&D provisions in the agreements are nonbinding, 'best endeavor' commitments (392–93).This move showed the changed world view that would eventually dominate the WTO, in contrast to the somewhat more Keynesian approach in which S&D treatment was a legitimate

---

7   Part 4, Trade and Development, Article XXXVI.
8   See Chapters 6 (Garay et al.) and 7 (Pupphavesa et al.) on the Colombian and Thai cases, respectively.

and technically admissible instrument of 'embedded liberalism'.[9] All countries had to take 'normal' responsibilities and bargain as equals.

The restoration of the reciprocity rule in trade negotiations had profound implications for developing countries in their aspiration to reduce asymmetric conditions in the trade system. First, the application of the reciprocity rule in negotiations benefits the (stronger) less trade-dependent countries at the expense of the (weaker) more trade-dependent countries (Epifani and Vitaloni 2006). Secondly, it reduces the policy space of states in which keeping an active role of public institutions is key to advance growth and development policies. Thirdly, the emphasis on reciprocity has added a previously absent domestic dimension. With the need to offer reciprocal concessions, every international negotiation has necessarily turned into a parallel domestic negotiation whereby the gains of one sector abroad require another sector to adjust to heightened import competition.

Trade issues have acquired a salience in domestic politics that is without precedent in the postcolonial era. Single issue lobbies mean that the government must contemplate sacrificing one issue to gain in another in a bargain where economic and political calculus becomes mixed. To be sure, the raw nerve of domestic politics today is not the same as half a century ago. In the era of globalised markets, segments of production chains that used to function within national boundaries are now internationally integrated. The pace of international integration is, naturally, uneven, leading to tensions within sectors as different patterns of supply and investment emerge. Although the pattern may vary from sector to sector and from country to country, there is widespread awareness that residual protection or trade relief measures for one product add an additional cost to the next link in the production chain. The bid to have access to inputs at international prices in order to improve competitiveness coexists uneasily with the quest to retain domestic market shares.

As is discussed in more detail in the second part of the chapter, since the WTO Cancún Ministerial a group of developing countries have stepped up their demands for S&D treatment as a prerequisite for progress in the negotiation round as well as clarity and specificity of S&D (Charlton 2005: 4). In particular, a group of 12 developing countries[10] demanded a framework agreement on S&D that: makes S&D legally binding and enforceable before the Dispute Settlement Body; allows for an evaluation of the development dimension according to verifiable goals (such as the United Nations (UN) Millennium Development Goals); links transition periods to objective economic criteria (debt level, industrial development, Human Development Index, etc.) and social criteria (literacy level, life expectancy, etc.); incorporates cost estimates for financial and technical assistance; established

---

9   The concept of 'embedded liberalism ' refers to the social regulation of capitalism through Keynesian macroeconomic policies, full employment, public investment and the welfare state. The classic work is Ruggie (1982).

10   India, Dominican Republic, Cuba, Honduras, Indonesia, Kenya, Malaysia, Pakistan, Sri Lanka, Tanzania, Uganda and Zimbabwe.

that trade policy measures in developing countries must not be prohibited unless there is a clear proof of trade-distorting effects; and that the principle of 'Single Undertaking' is not automatically to be applied to developing countries (Fritz 2005: 36).

The Group of 33 subsequently worked hard to provide a higher degree of clarity and specificity, especially in relation to agricultural liberalisation. The most visible achievement in this regard has been the right to identify special agricultural products on which there would be no tariff reduction commitment and no new tariff rate quote commitments (Mably 2009).[11]

While S&D may have been 'a historic relic, surely it is essential to confront the issue of trade and development in analytic terms and aim for a new approach termed policy space (or whatever)' (Ostry 2007: 32–33). As coalitions of developing countries joined forces to make these claims more operational and these moves gained ascendancy in the WTO, the remains of S&D were wiped out in bilateral and interregional preferential agreements which led to 'one-sided reciprocity'.

In the agreements involving a northern and a southern party, the latter generally starts at a lower initial point and takes larger steps than the northern counterpart. This has been particularly clear even in the case studies in this volume that have not come to fruition (Bilal in Chapter 3, Botto and Bianculli in Chapter 4, Giacalone in Chapter 5, and Pupphavesa et al. in Chapter 7) and in the case of the Colombia-US FTA (Garay, De Lombaerde and Barberi in Chapter 6). However, there have been exceptions. Concessions are much more even in the EU-Chile agreement and in the EFTA-Mexico FTA. The reason for this relatively more level playing field in these cases was that the southern partner in both cases already had an encompassing and tight agreement with the US. In such cases the drive for the second agreement (the EU) is meant to reduce trade diversion.

Agenda-setting, issue selection and selective liberalisation

Asymmetries are most evident in the capacity of industrial countries to select issues and turn them into negotiable propositions. Knowledge governance represents a paradigmatic example. Since the inception of the Agreement on Trade-Related Aspects of Intellectual Property Rights (TRIPs), intellectual property has been harmonised and protected in almost every WTO Member State. The rationale for regulating intellectual property at the WTO was made to look plausible: only *trade-related* aspects of intellectual property would be regulated under the aegis of the WTO. Still, determining what is trade-related has proven to be a Pandora box (Maskus and Penubarti 1995).

Some authors even question whether intellectual property is a good that can be linked to market freedom, because, paradoxically, the very essence of intellectual property is a state-granted monopoly right that excludes competition albeit for a limited period of time. As Stiglitz points out:

---

11   This is the G-33 which is discussed in a subsequent section on coalitions.

> Intellectual property does not really belong in a trade agreement. Trade agreements are supposed to liberalise the movements of goods and services across borders. The TRIPs ... was concerned with *restricting* the movement of knowledge across borders (2006:16).

Crucially, regulating intellectual property at the WTO level has had a major impact, not only on external transfers to holders of patents, fiscal outlays to implement national patent regulations,[12] but also on important public policy sectors dealing with education, freedom of expression, cultural rights, access to medicines, food safety and so on and so forth.

Telling evidence is also found with regard to the selectivity of agricultural trade. Freer trade in a greater number of areas would have a beneficial impact not only on markets but also on rural livelihoods and export earnings. Cotton, for one, employs more than ten million people in West Africa. It plays an important role in alleviating poverty involving more than thirty countries. The US not only make access selective but also deploy subsidies that drive world prices down. Cotton subsidies in the US have damaged several developing and least developed countries, which find it next to impossible to penetrate the American market and compete with American cotton in third markets. In this regard, Burkina Faso, Mali, Chad and Benin launched the so-called Cotton Initiative at the WTO, calling for the subsidies to be eliminated and for compensation to be paid to damaged countries while the subsidies remain.

The more general point, however, is that developed countries are allowed to continue to spend large amounts on export subsidies, while developing countries shed tariff layer after tariff layer. One type of protection is a central concern while the other plagued by conceptual and procedural loopholes, not to mention implementation problems. The agreement on subsidies, for example, allows the use of subsidies that are most widespread in and available in rich countries, subsidies for research and development, fiscal transfers to backward areas, for the protection of the environment and for labour retraining, but deems other subsidies which may be necessary in developing country conditions as out of bounds. Perhaps the most controversial of these is the one related to export financing which is carried over to the WTO from a long standing agreement at the Organisation for Economic Cooperation and Development (OECD).

The OECD oversees an arrangement among its member countries that governs the conditions and rates under which export financing may be offered. The agreement sets minimum premium rates (also called exposure fees) for country and sovereign risks. The WTO list of prohibited export credit subsidies tracks the OECD arrangement; under the single undertaking package of the Uruguay Round these commitments were extended to all WTO members, which had not taken part of the OECD negotiation and, moreover, faced quite different credit markets – and

---

12 Lengyel (2005) has calculated that in the case of Argentina the costs of implementing TRIPs over the period 1996–2000 reached US $70 million.

hence interest rates for public financing. Within the WTO subsidies agreement, an illustrative list of export subsidies makes reference to the OECD arrangement, indicating that '…if in practice a Member applies the interest rates provisions … an export credit practice which is in conformity with those provisions shall not be considered an export subsidy prohibited by this Agreement.'

In other words, if a country complies with the interest rate provisions of the OECD arrangement, (even if there is a subsidy element) it is given a safe haven in terms of being 'WTO-proof'. This haven is available only to OECD participants. Suddenly 138 WTO members had obligations – item (k) – that had been agreed elsewhere. The WTO Secretariat, as a result, requested observer status at OECD arrangement meetings to gain a greater insight into the implications of what had been signed in the WTO, but individual countries still came under the loop (Palacios, 2003). The Brazilian Foreign Minister, Celso Lafer, stated at the Doha Ministerial Conference of 2001:

> It is easy to perceive that there is a large measure of special and differential treatment in favour of the developed countries. Such is the case, for instance, of the Agreement on Subsidies and Countervailing Duties which grants a special exemption to members of the OECD Consensus with regard to rules on export subsidies that other Members of the WTO must comply with.[13]

In short, the endogenous game was institutionalised, consolidated, and extended by the bargain struck during the Uruguay Round. The grievances of many developing countries with this system mounted. Sound levels went up several decibels. The Doha Round opened under new auspices, if only because considerable knowledge and experience had been gathered. The Ministerial Conference at Cancun in 2003 catalysed the emergence of at least four new coalitions – the G20, the G33, the Core Group on Singapore Issues, and the Cotton group – in addition to the activism of others that pre-dated the ministerial, including the ACP group, the LDC group, the Africa Group, the Small and Vulnerable Economies, and the Like Minded Group (LMG).

Forum selection – free trade agreements as the institutionalisation of asymmetries

The ritual of global negotiations provides a useful instrument in the global legitimation struggle because it can be carried out in universalistic terms and in the language of common interests. When this fails, the upper hand will seek adherence or acquiescence by other means and move elsewhere in an encircling manner, zigzagging, dividing, apportioning.

The deadlock of the Doha Round drove industrial countries to pursue the negotiation of bilateral and inter-regional integration projects with developing

---

13   10 November, 2001, Statement by Ambassador Celso Lafer, WT/MIN(01)/ST/12, www.wto.org.

countries.[14] Most of the divisive issues of the trade agenda which have faced stiff opposition from developing countries are now being negotiated – and implemented – through bilateral tracks. These issues include greater levels of intellectual property protection than what has already been agreed multilaterally under TRIPs, rules in investment, services, liberalisation of government procurement, as well as labour and environmental protection rules. They all spearhead an agenda of 'deep integration' considering they entail the obligation of countries to harmonise domestic legislation in line with unilateral set benchmarks. In this respect, preferential agreements have served to open up new markets for industrial economies, to lock-in market liberalisation reforms that have already taken place in developing countries, as well as to cement new levels of regulation, i.e. one-sided reciprocity.

The set-up of preferential agreements is more asymmetric than multilateral negotiations because smaller countries cannot compensate for their weaker capabilities through cooperation and alliance formation with other weak states. Accordingly, the outcomes of these negotiations have been considerably unbalanced, often in favour of the most competitive sectors in industrial countries, and in detriment of small producers and policy space in the developing world. By the same token they also pose strains on domestic governance. Negotiations are often conducted by the executive branches of government, in close contact with business, without participation of parliaments and civil society. Harmonisation of domestic legislation therefore often becomes a top-down process. The push towards global and/or international harmonisation is not followed with a push towards greater representation – mainly of those sectors and actors that will be the most affected by the distributive effects of the preferential agreements.

The investment rules contained in the recent preferential agreements also posed a challenge to democratic governance. The state-investor provisions contained in the investment protection chapters give rights to investors/corporations to take legal action against governments when they consider their interests have been affected by the adoption of new legislation that may modify the investors' return expectations. The North American Free Trade Agreement (NAFTA) Chapter 11 on investment rules and extended into a spate of many other preferential agreements, provides numerous examples of the limitations on democracy in cases where government had to compensate corporations financially in following the passing of legislation to protect public health or the environment.

Preferential agreements also introduce a greater reduction of policy space of developing countries. With the liberalisation of government procurements, states give away an important tool to favour the development of local industry and to generate growth and employment. Likewise, the prohibition of performance requirements on investment eliminates the possibility of nudging firms to perform socially or economically desirable goals, such as employment creation, establishment of local research and development, creation of value chains. The

---

14   See e.g. Heydon and Woolcock (2010).

liberalisation of services also represents the signing away of the role of states in the provision of basic public services that are key for development in societies with deep social asymmetries, such as education, health and others.

Bilateral, inter-regional and multilateral processes become inter-twined in a spiral of precedents. The agendas that are negotiated and implemented in preferential agreements become the floor from multilateral negotiations eventually begin in the WTO. In other words, preferential agreements are used to change the balance of power which is currently preventing the completion of the Doha Round due to the resistance of developing countries to accept issues of the agenda that undermine their development policy space. They are also more readily used for issue-linkage in areas such as military security or migration (see Garay, De Lombaerde and Barberi in this volume, Chapter 6).

This assertion still begs the question of why do developing countries resist commitments in the WTO which they gladly accept in free trade agreements with their northern counterparts (Shadlen 2008). Three reasons can account for this. The first is that the most reluctant countries are not the ones with major FTAs with northern countries. The second is that resistance in the WTO creates the space for FTAs of interest to exporters in the North for their markets. The third is that even in conditions of asymmetry where gains are divided there is ample room for relative gains.

So far we have identified some of the main challenges introduced by power asymmetries in trade negotiation processes. Such power asymmetries show that the majors have rights of tutelage; they can ensure the direction of policy and shape a number of outcomes in minor countries, driven by specific interest group pressures or broader political calculations to maximise their states' power.

Yet even within such institutional constraints, a rank of countries can enjoy certain degrees of freedom in setting parts of the agenda and influencing outcomes. These degrees of freedom depend on the prevalent epistemic consensus, but also on strategies that are born out of adaptation and learning, framing/re-framing the issue to fit into the dominant norm, and building supportive inter-state and transnational coalitions. A reflection on balancing behaviour is particularly relevant at a time when the rise of emerging economic powers such as India, China, Brazil and South Africa is creating new political opportunities to redefine existing global and regional structures and practices. The conditions under which the increased influence of these countries can effectively translate in the overcoming of power asymmetries in trade processes are addressed in the second part of the chapter.

Addressing vulnerabilities? The pursuit of sources of leverage

It is as well to concede one obvious truism, the problem of confronting massively disproportionate power in economic diplomacy. But a methodology that considers a situation asymmetrically offers a way not only to analyse situations, but to look at these as arenas for power contests. Such contests involve efforts by the historically weak or under-represented to coalesce in order to trim and reshape rules and reduce pressures to accept policies they wish to evade, delay or resist in order to reduce costs and change their fates.

In this part of the chapter we argue that the bargaining power of states in trade negotiations relies on at least four dimensions:

1. the relative size of the market in each country,
2. the type of intergovernmental coalition created as part of negotiation processes,
3. the alliances governments establish with business organisations and labour/social organisations in civil society, and
4. the particularities of domestic institutions.

These conditions represent sources of state power that affect the capacity of government to increase their bargaining power in trade negotiations (Drahos 2003). To see how these are used to improve conditions and sell proposals, we now turn.

Market power: size matters after all!

The size of domestic markets is an important factor affecting the degree of governments' bargaining power in trade negotiations. Market power is a relational concept. This means that the extent to which securing market access is a policy priority for a given country is related to the degree of dependence of that country's economy from its exports to other markets. It is often the case that this equation involves minor countries being more dependent on market access in major industrialised countries than it is in the inverse direction. In the global economy characterised by uneven levels of development and an increasingly transnationalised production structure, differences in market size act as powerful factors affecting the dynamics of trade integration processes.

In his seminal work on market size asymmetries, Albert Hirschman (1945) argues that when trade with a larger country accounts for a very large proportion of the total imports and exports of a smaller economy, the latter is increasingly vulnerable to coercion by the larger country. The implication of this point is that, rather than small countries being concerned about the potentially threatening effects of floods of imports from a larger country, countries ought to be more concerned when most of their own exports go to any one country. The argument is that if a large country A decides to stop exporting to a small country B, it will be relatively easy for B to find alternative sources for its imports. On the other hand, it will be relatively difficult for B to find alternative markets for its exports, 'all countries being ready to sell and none ready to buy' (Hirschman 1945: 32).

Governments can use market access as powerful bargaining chips in trade negotiations; either to persuade export dependent economies to offer greater concessions than they would otherwise be willing to offer, as well as to threaten them with the ending of existing market access preferences. The effectiveness and credibility of threats is reduced as with the size of a country's market.

The fear of losing market access is so great that some governments have gone a long way to ensure that their exports will safely reach the markets in industrialised countries. Shadlen (2008) has shed some light on the specific reasons that led the governments of Colombia, Peru, Chile and Central American countries to negotiate bilateral preferential agreements with the US in highly asymmetric conditions which resulted in the abandonment of policy space and key development tools.[15] These countries already export to the US under the GSP scheme. However, GSP schemes generate market access that is unstable since there is always the risk that changing political conditions in the US and lobbying pressures could threaten market access privileges, whose renewal has to be periodically reviewed. In the WTO, under the MFN principle a country that withdraws market access rights is liable to demands for compensation. This option is not available in GSP schemes. Shadlen then concludes that the incentive for embarking in such negotiation processes was the reduction of uncertainty and risk derived from the possibility of being excluded from the US market. In so doing, these governments tied their economies to a common set of rules that dissipated the risk of losing market access. This was nonetheless done at the expense of great economic costs and policy space (Shadlen 2008).

The growth of emerging Southern economies that has taken place in recent times is beginning to shift the balance of power in trade processes. The clearest example is China, but also India, Brazil and South Africa are in that rank. As market size begins to count, so does the bargaining power of these countries in trade negotiations. The potential for gaining greater influence is also tied to the progress in promoting more substantial trade relations between such emerging powers facing the fear of being swamped by the major countries. The IBSA initiative (India, Brazil and South Africa) to promote South-South cooperation and closer trade relations is a positive step in this regard. This leads to the much-needed diversification of export markets away from the traditional industrial countries with the resulting consequence of gaining greater autonomy.

Likewise, pooling of market size through South-South regional integration projects is also a way of gaining leverage in trade processes. This permits minor countries to unite forces by combining their small markets. Much southern regional activity grows out of the need for mitigating asymmetries and balancing crystallised inequalities between states; it is also concerned with retaining power in the region, filling spaces in which global structures are seen as encroaching or excessively constraining. In a number of sectors where producer interests sometimes compete with foreign business and often plays a crucial political role, governments may well respond to the globalisation wave in ways that attempt to preserve and nurture spaces for local players. The regional arena is used by governments, business and other actors to resist and shape markets, the model

---

15   See Chapter 6 (Garay et al.) in this volume.

emphasising the primacy of concerted state intervention, domestic politics and economic or social values such as distributive outcomes rather than global efficiency. Governments, deriving political legitimacy from their capacity to undertake traditional social responsibilities for the societies they govern, may be compelled to turn to regional collective action as an option to maintain levels of employment and policy instruments.

The proponents of this type of regionalism play a circular game of alternating pro and anti-liberalisation stances through regional structures and arrangements. A lesson stemming from Europe is that regional integration projects often need large member states with technocratically capable cadres in order to provide vision and leadership for the rest of the group. France and Germany played this role in the European Economic Community and its antecedents from the 1950s, and Singapore and Thailand seem to aspire to a similar partnering role in the Association of South East Asian Nations (ASEAN).

However, for regionalism to be conducive to the reduction of international power asymmetries it also needs to be able to address domestic and regional asymmetries. This requires that countries succeed in keeping policy space over key public instruments needed to adopt long-term development strategies at the national and regional level. It is not sufficient to integrate markets. Regional governance instruments are indispensable: macro-economic coordination, a common development strategy based on complementarity and integration of productive chains, regional public instruments to address internal asymmetries (smaller economies and/or sub-regions). A successful and sustainable project of regional integration based on a common development strategy will eventually reduce the unequal power conditions that currently affect countries with small markets.

Intergovernmental coalitions

The usual response to the problem of weak bargaining power is the strength-in-numbers argument. The formation of intergovernmental coalitions constitutes another source of bargaining power to contest asymmetries (Odell 2006). The incorporation of new members to the WTO in recent years has opened a political opportunity for developing countries to increase their leverage in negotiations by building coalitions around a series of common issues and agendas. Approximately 100 of the WTO's 144 members are developing countries. This presents a favourable situation for weaker states to build coalitions to reduce the power asymmetries in trade negotiations, make decision-making processes more equitable and transparent (Narlikar 2003, 2006, Kumar 2007: 5).

Developing country coalitions such as the LMG, the African Group and mainly the G-22, G-33 and G-90 have gained considerable repercussion in recent years. The resistance of the LMG and the African Group against the exclusionary decision-making procedures at the WTO led to the breakdown of the ministerial meeting of Seattle in December 1999. This set an important precedent for developing countries in signalling the relevance of forming new groupings as a means to promote their views on key issues collectively (Keet 2006: 14). Moreover, the pressures of the G-22, G-33 and G-90 led to the impasse at the Cancun meeting in 2003. This created a new precedent in the history of the WTO. They also succeeded in getting three of the four Singapore issues (investment, competition policy, and government procurement) dropped off the negotiating agenda of the Doha Round (Kumar 2007: 5). In the aftermath of the Cancun meeting, the G-33 stepped up its demands for special and differential treatment (S&D) as a prerequisite for progress in the Round, particularly the right to identify special products of interest to developing countries on which there would be no tariff reduction commitment and no new tariff rate quote commitments (Charlton 2005: 4, Mably 2009).

Other indications of the influence acquired by developing country government coalitions can be seen in relation to TRIPs and public health (Odell and Sell 2006), and to the Cotton Initiative led by the Cotton-4 supported by the African Group (Patel 2007: 7). The influence of these coalitions in trade discussions has changed the institutional dynamics of the WTO (Narlikar and Tussie 2004, Patel 2006).

Not all the developing country coalitions that have gained preponderance in recent times are new creatures, however. There has also been a revival of old coalitions such as the Non-Aligned Movement and the revitalisation of the G-77-Plus China group in the United Nations.

New coalitions differ from their older counterparts and predecessors. They adopt a more prominent and publicly visible role in negotiations, which often involves issuing public declarations, holding press conferences, engaging in media campaigns, creating logos and forms of branding. Another distinctive feature of new coalitions is their engagement with NGOs in the framing of negotiating positions and in the undertaking of public advocacy campaigns. The case of the campaign of developing countries allied with NGOs to frame the negotiations of intellectual property as a health issue in the Doha conference illustrates this point (Odell and Sell 2006).

Finally, there is also considerable cooperation between various coalitions which at times can overlap (Patel 2006: 7–9). The resulting openness to other coalitions rather than a us versus the rest antagonism, and logrolling that is not completely random but relatively more focused on a smaller set of issues (partly as a result of the research) makes the more recent coalitions considerably evolved, and certainly more evolved than the traditional ideology inspired third wordlist demands.

The particular form that is adopted by these coalitions depends largely on kinds of agendas for which they were created. Coalitions that are built in response to particular threats – which tend to dissipate over time – are formed by 'alliance-type' groups that come together for 'instrumental reasons'. Conversely, coalitions built for the negotiation of a variety of issue areas generally consist of 'bloc-type' groups of like-minded states. In this case, such coalitions rely on identity-related methods (Narlikar 2003) and often develop some kind of formal structure to facilitate sharing technical capacity, division of labour and the articulation and coordination of joint negotiating platforms.

Amongst these coalitions, the G-20 (in which the big countries such as Brazil, India, China, South Africa, Argentina) is particularly important, not only because it carries weight by its sheer market power but because it has significant development implications to smaller developing countries which remain at the margin of the negotiating process. However, the G-90 plays a key role with regards the transparency and democracy in the WTO, mainly by questioning participation conventions in the rule-making process, in particular the set of negotiation practices that continues to sideline them. Furthermore, the G-33 which represents over 40 developing countries in agricultural negotiations calls for an approach to tariff reduction that does not result in developing countries paying high prices and experiencing disruption in their rural economies. It proposes the recognition of 'special products' for special treatment (i.e. lower market access obligations). The argument is that, in the absence of deep pockets, tariffs are the only instruments available to protect their farmers.

Intergovernmental coalitions that rely on the production of knowledge to argue their case are better positioned to increase the bargaining power of developing countries in asymmetric multilateral trade negotiations. The reason for this is that formalised and shared knowledge can gradually change rules of engagement as they assist developing country governments with technical and analytical resources. This capacity is needed to deal with the dilemmas of the circular game between bilateral and multilateral negotiations that lives on as a system of escalators. Informality is a rich learning ground; it has the advantage of having low start-up costs, allowing greater flexibility in the negotiations, avoiding costly sanctions. By way of example, following the Cancun Ministerial, some members of the G-20 were compelled to drop out in response to pressures from the US. Colombia, Costa Rica, Ecuador, El Salvador, Guatemala, and Peru broke away from the group for some time but after concluding their bilateral negotiations with the US they returned to the fold and were accepted with no acrimony ready to charge on.

These flexible arrangements also serve as safety nets when regional agreements are watered down and even split as a result of the push of North-South agreements. This has been the case of the Andean Community of Nations, the Central American Common Market and ASEAN (see Garay, De Lombaerde and Barberi in Chapter 6, Giacalone in Chapter 5 and Pupphavesa et al. in Chapter 7 in this volume)

Alignment with networks of non-state actors

As was discussed in the first section, the new emphasis on reciprocity has added a previously absent domestic dimension, whereby the gains of one sector abroad require another sector to adjust to heightened import competition. The sensitivity of domestic actors to the distributional impact of trade concessions has tended to generate conflicts and resentments. Unleashing sufficient passion from below, civil society campaigns and new forms of organisation and resistance were triggered. These increasingly mobilised actors have created transnational networks and coalitions exercising voice and demanding participation. Moreover, some of these civil society actors have taken the next step of beginning to construct social movements in an attempt to articulate responses to the push of asymmetric negotiations.

The capacity of a government to seize the opportunity and to enrol with non-state actors can become an additional source of bargaining power in trade negotiations. Leaning on these campaigns, governments can manipulate value conflicts, trim proposals and react with counterproposals either through regional agreements or the looser coalitions in the WTO. Dealing with asymmetry becomes less of an exercise in helplessness. Instead, it becomes more of an exercise in negotiated accommodation where state and non-state actors interact and feed off each other in a process whereby values become shared, rules gradually codified, and all actors get to reinvent themselves. There is then a constant weaving of negotiations to build consensus at home by incorporating and/or co-opting some anti-globalisation movements.

In terms of alignments with transnational civil society networks, there is the well recorded case of the alliance crafted between developing countries and non-governmental organisations (NGOs) like Consumer Project on Technology, Médecins Sans Frontières and Oxfam has been a crucial aspect of the Declaration on TRIPs and Public Health that was agreed by ministers in Doha (Drahos and Mayne 2002, Odell and Sell 2006).

Another prevalent example is the informal alignment of the Venezuelan government with social movement coalitions in Latin America in the context of the negotiation of a Free Trade Area of the Americas (FTAA). This alignment centred on building regional opposition to the neo-liberal trade agenda contained in the FTAA project, as well as fostering the construction of alternative integration projects in line with the Bolivarian Alternative for the Americas (ALBA) initiative (Saguier 2007). The ALBA project and the Trade Treaty of the Peoples proposed by Bolivia to create a new model of cooperative development evidence recent shifts in the balance of forces regarding global trade processes (Keet 2006: 4) as well as the strategic importance of governments' alignments with organised civil society sectors.

Concessions of selective participation to some civil society actors, a common currency used by the United States in classic two level games to increase leverage in negotiations (Putnam 1988) are emulated by weaker governments in their challenging strategies. What emerges from these trends is an interesting relationship between the use of mobilisation and resistance in which it is not always clear how governments will adapt in response to claim-making and mobilising by civil society groups and balance the move with the risk adverse mindset of elites with popular disaffection.

Discursive/normative power

Negotiations are embedded in an intellectual landscape that directly affects course and outcome. Perhaps this is the least-discussed element and the one leading to the reproduction of intangible asymmetries. Ideas in trade relations have become so dominant that they are embedded in trade institutions and promulgated by those institutions. They can remain then largely unquestioned and taken for granted, playing a subtle background role in shaping and limiting public debate and the articulation of policy alternatives, thus de-politicising issues. As such ideas can exercise a non-coercive form of power wielded by dominant actors, often called soft power or cultural hegemony, concealing power relations that stratify the global system into a core of rule makers and a broad band of heterogeneous rule takers.

Ideas may also be used, however, to frame or re-frame an issue and influence the public discourse around it (Sell and Prakash 2004, Odell and Sell 2006). Used as tools ideas can contribute to the definition of interests, identification of policy problems and preferred solutions, especially in their capacity to posit causal relationships. They have also been seen to be useful in building the types of coalitions mentioned above. Norms, ideas about what is right or wrong behaviour, can legitimate action or challenge legitimacy. Ideas can also become weapons to undermine prevailing ideas and institutions particularly in periods of crisis or uncertainty. As contending players grow in strength and stature, relying on the creation of coalitions, they must at the same time invest in becoming technically empowered to challenge asymmetry through knowledge, research and value creation. Value creation and the crafting of operating principles all play a role in balancing asymmetry and claim-making.

Peter Haas's work (1992) on the role of international epistemic communities illustrates how the transnational collaboration of 'professionals' can shape policy preferences and are applied to problem solving.[16] The term of epistemic communities refers to a congregation sharing a world view (or episteme). It is an international network of professionals with recognised expertise and competence in a particular domain and an authoritative claim to policy-relevant knowledge within that domain or issue area. The professionals in an epistemic community have a shared set of normative and principled beliefs: common casual beliefs, which are derived from the analysis of practices leading or contributing to a central set of problems in their domain and which then serve as the basis for elucidating the multiple linkages between possible policy actions and desired outcomes. They also share notions of validity and a mutual policy enterprise.

Political networking with governing institutions lays the groundwork for a broader acceptance of the community's beliefs and ideas. Economic and political networking allows them to control the channels by which these innovations diffuse and to become the torchbearers of new ideas, setting standards for some policies and freezing out others as wrongheaded. Once achieved, that inner circle

---

16   See also Botto (2010) in the case of EU-MERCOSUR.

can be expanded to broader and broader international sets of governments and civil society networks until it is shared by enough to persuade the world that its policy aspirations are achievable.

Such constructions can matter, not simply because they can provide the substantive content of demands in a trade negotiation, but also because it can serve as an important legitimising device. This source of power in trade negotiations concerns the ability of governments to frame particular demands and agendas in terms of concepts or themes that can enhance the imperatives of one position over another avoiding or softening visibly ideological grounds.

Ideas, like interests, are not static. Uncertainty, crises and unforeseen or unintended consequences of past policies and actions can present opportunities for change, which is, learning. Ideas and interests may also be reshaped through interactions with other actors. In this context, policy networks and communities of knowledge can serve as a focal point to share analyses of the environment, the consequences of policies, and the legitimisation of change. The power politics of knowledge can influence first the conceptual change and then legitimise the implementation of an agenda that has evolved as a result of several other, often political, forces. The value of ideas and knowledge is that it can justify and explain demands of one group to other groups; and can help to disentangle the knowledge trap. Likewise, ideas and knowledge are also powerful insofar as they make it possible to envisage alternative scenarios and aspirations on which political visions can take form.

Conclusions

Where does our analysis lead by way of conclusion? We drew attention at the outset that trade negotiations on a reciprocal basis take place in conditions of severe asymmetric power relations with scarce if any chance of fair play. Put bluntly, such reciprocity is one sided. Many have argued that the renewed North-South imbalance embedded in the North-South agreements is a straightjacket that compels developing countries to follow standard neoliberal policies.

This depiction, applauded by some and assailed by others, understates the difficult dilemmas that countries face. It is undeniable that changes in the contemporary international political economy limit past options, and that today's developing countries are being deprived of opportunities to use many of the policy instruments that more developed countries used at similar levels of income. But this argument does not count the opportunity costs, the cost of being excluded and the domestic political frictions involved;[17] nor does it take into account that the

---

17   If there is an opportunity for an actor to achieve an export gain, an 'opportunity logic' may be invoked by the actor presented with the opportunity, often highly conditioning government action.

straightjacket is never watertight. This is not to say that some of the choices we might wish to make have not become more costly.

What continues to be a key concern for developing countries is how to control a trade process that they cannot control, but whose conditions for doing so in the current historical context are substantially better than those in the past. The trend is towards reduced policy discretion. The behaviour of dependent parties conforms to the preferences of those they depend on. This no doubt is the beginning of current wisdom. Yet the ultimate outcome remains one where a range of significant alternatives continues to exist. One also needs to know how, and how much, new options are made available to relieve strains and reduce vulnerabilities while the old options get caught in the web. This point is critical to our understanding of the dynamics inherent in asymmetric relations.

Asymmetrical trade negotiations are driven intensely by knowledge and ideas that were linked strategically to the interests of proponents. Policy failures at some point clear away lingerings of loyalty to these ideas while underlings continue to open new territories for policy and build new alliances for offsetting asymmetries and create room to manoeuvre. The overarching challenge for minor countries as asymmetric negotiations press on does not lie in making a compelling case that economic analysis and expectations of great benefits to come from asymmetric negotiations bear little fruit. Nor are moral and ideological cleavages sufficient to develop viable policies and negotiating positions. Negotiations require interest-based problem solving, hands-on research and alliance building oriented at transforming the trade agenda and governance processes.

The overarching challenge is the development of power on the basis of inequality; that is to make incremental changes in power positions building new alliances; to provide structure and principles to handle such changes and to allow for transitions that might otherwise prove unmanageable or too costly to face. This requires mustering of collective forces where coalitions cooperate with each other to mobilise for change, to solve problems and attain goals. While intergovernmental coalitions and regional agreements are mechanisms to strategically *influence* the process, civil society networks can also serve to *challenge* the process. They have all become significant symbolically as well as practically. Agenda setting, assessment, and the construction of counter-proposals involve continuous evaluations and filtering to suggest alternative modes of actions.

To belabour the point; victims act! Its possibilities rest on mustering sources of leverage increased bargaining competence, a vision, a map and operating principles. Herein lays the challenge of participating in the building of new ideas, practices and institutional arrangements for trade governance to overcome entrenched asymmetries for the goal of a more egalitarian regime. There is no doubt that the asymmetric power relation in the centre-periphery model still holds, but it is also the case that all inherited orthodoxies have been proven to be inadequate. This is why the issues of regional and global governance have become so prominent and are likely to loom even larger.

References

Baumol, W. 1952. *Welfare Economics and the Theory of the State*. London: Longmans, Green.

Botto, M.I. 2010. The Role of Epistemic Communities in the 'Makability' of MERCOSUR, in: *The EU and World Regionalism. The Makability of Regions in the 21st Century*, edited by De Lombaerde, P. and Schulz, M. IPENR Series, Farnham-Burlington: Ashgate, 171–85.

Charlton, A. 2005. *A Proposal for Special & Differential Treatment in the Doha Round*. June, Mimeo, Geneva.

Davis, C.L. 2006. Do WTO Rules Create a Level Playing Field?, in *Negotiating Trade – Developing Countries in the WTO and NAFTA*, edited by Odell, J.S. Cambridge, UK: Cambridge University Press, 219–56.

Díaz, A. 2008. *América Latina y el Caribe: La propiedad intelectual después de los tratados de libre comercio* Santiago: CEPAL [Online], 94. Available at: http://www.cepal.org/publicaciones/xml/4/32614/LCG2330-P.pdf.

Drahos, P. 2003. When the Weak Bargain with the Strong: Negotiations in the WTO. *International Negotiation*, 8(1), 79–109.

Drahos, P. and Mayne, R. (2002) *Global Intellectual Property Rights: Knowledge Access and Development*, Hampshire and New York: Palgrave Macmillan.

Epifani, P. and Vitaloni, J. 2006. GATT-think with Asymmetric Countries. *Review of International Economics*, 14(3), 427–44.

Fritz, T. 2005. Special and Differential Treatment for Developing Countries. *Global Issue Paper*, Heindrich Böll Foundation, (18), 2–46.

Haas, P. 1992. Introduction: Epistemic Communities and International Policy Coordination. *International Organization*, 46:1, 1–35.

Helleiner, G.K. 2002. Developing Countries in Global Economic Governance and Negotiation Processes, in *Governing Globalization, Issues and Institutions*, edited by D. Nayyar. Oxford: UNU-WIDER and Oxford University Press, 308–33.

Heydon, K. and Woolcock, S. 2010. *The Rise of Bilateralism. Comparing American, European and Asian Approaches to Preferential Trade Agreements*. Tokyo: UNU Press.

Hirschman, A. 1945. *National Power and the Structure of Foreign Trade*, 1980 expanded ed. Berkeley: University of California Press.

Hoekman, B. and Kostecki, M. 2001. *The Political Economy of the World Trading System: The WTO and Beyond*. Oxford: Oxford University Press, 2nd edition.

Keet, D. 2006. *South-South Strategic Alternatives to the Global Economic System and Power Regime*. Amsterdam: Transnational Institute. [Online]. Available at: www.tni.org.

Kumar, N. 2007. Building a Development-friendly World Trading System, *Bridges*, International Centre for Trade and Development (ICTSD), 11(5), 3–5.

Lengyel, M. 2005. *Implementación de los Acuerdos de la Ronda Uruguay*, LATN Brief. [Online], (27) Available at www.latn.org.ar.

Mably, P. 2009. Centralized Production: The Group of 33, in *The Politics of Trade: The Role of Research in Trade Policy and Negotiation*, edited by Tussie, D. Dordrecht, Leiden and Boston: Brill, RoL, IDRC.

Maskus, K.E. and Penubarti, M. 1995. How Trade-Related are Intellectual Property Rights? *Journal of International Economics*, 39, 227–48.

Narlikar, A. 2003. *International Trade and Developing Countries: Coalitions in the GATT and WTO*. London: Routledge.

Narlikar, A. 2006. *Bargaining over the Doha Development Agenda: Coalitions in the World Trade Organization*. Series LATN Papers, (34).

Narlikar, A. and Tussie, D. 2004. The G20 at the Cancún Ministerial: Developing Countries and their Evolving Coalitions in the WTO. *World Economy*, 24(7), 947–66.

Odell, J.S. 2006. Introduction, in *Negotiating Trade – Developing Countries in the WTO and NAFTA*, edited by Odell, J.S. Cambridge, UK: Cambridge University Press, pp. 1–40.

Odell, J.S. and Sell, S.K. 2006. Reframing the Issue: The WTO Coalition on Intellectual Property and Public Health, in *Negotiating Trade – Developing Countries in the WTO and NAFTA*, edited by Odell, J.S. 2001. Cambridge, UK: Cambridge University Press, pp. 85–114.

Ostry, S. 2007. Trade, Development and the Doha Development Agenda, in *The WTO after Hong Kong*, edited by Lee, D. and Wilkinson, R. London: Routledge, pp. 26–34.

OXFAM 2006. *Unequal Partners: How EU–ACP Economic Partnership Agreements (EPAs) could harm the development prospects of many of the world's poorest countries*. [Online]. Available at: http://www.oxfam.org/en/files/bn0609_unequal_partners_epas/download.

Oyejide, T.A. 2002. Special and Differential Treatment, in *Development, trade and the WTO: A Handbook*, edited by Hoekman, B., Mattoo, A., and English, P. Washington: The World Bank, 504–8.

Palacios, G. 2003. *Latinoamerica frente a la negociación internacional de subsidios*. Serie LATN Brief. [Online], (16), 1–4, Available at: www.latn.org.ar.

Patel, M. 2007. *New Faces in the Green Room: Developing Country Coalitions and Decision-Making in the WTO*. GEG Working Paper 2007/33, 1–37 [Online], Available at: www.globaleconomicgovernance.org].

Putnam, R. 1988, Diplomacy and Domestic Politics: The Logic of Two-Level Games, *International Organization*, 42(3), 427–60.

Ruggie, J.G. 1982. International Regimes, Transactions and Change: Embedded Liberalism in the Post-War Economic Order, in *International Regimes*, edited by Krasner, S.D. Ithaca, NY: Cornell University Press, 195–231.

Russett, B. (ed.) 1968. *Economic Theories of International Politics*. Chicago: Markham.

Saguier, M.I. 2007. The Hemispheric Social Alliance and the Free Trade Area of the Americas Process: The Challenges and Opportunities of Transnational Coalitions Against Neo-liberalism. *Globalizations*, 4(2), 251–65.

Sai-wing 1998. Multilateral Trade Negotiations and the Changing Prospects for Third World Development: Assessing from a Southern Perspective. *Journal of Economic Issues*, 32, June, 375–83.

Sell, S. and Prakash, A. 2004. Using Ideas Strategically. *International Studies Quarterly*, 48, 143–75.

Shadlen, K. 2008. Globalisation, Power and Integration: The Political Economy of Regional and Bilateral Trade Agreements in the Americas. *Journal of Development Studies*, 44(1), 1–20.

Smythe, E. 2006. Assessing the Doha Development Round, in *The WTO after Hong Kong*, edited by Lee, D. and Wilkinson, R. Chippenham, UK: Routledge, pp. 205–26.

Tussie, D. 1987. *The Less Developed Countries and the World Trading System: A Challenge to the GATT*. London and New York: Pinter.

Tussie, D. and Lengyel, M. 2001. Turning Participation into Influence, in *Development, Trade and the WTO: A Handbook*, edited by Bernard Hoekman, Aaditya Mattoo, and Philip English. Washington: The World Bank, pp. 485–92.

UNDP. 2001. *The Multilateral Trading System: A Development Perspective*. Report Prepared by the Third World Network for the UNDP. New York: United Nations Development Programme (UNDP).

Waltz, K. 1979. *Theory of International Politics*. Reading, Massachusetts: Addison-Wesley Publishing Company.

Wilkinson, R. 2007. Building Asymmetry: Concluding the Doha Development Agenda, in *The WTO after Hong Kong*, edited by Lee, D. and Wilkinson, R. Chippenham, UK: Routledge, pp. 248–61.

Winham, G.R. 1997. Explanation of Developing Country Behaviour in the GATT Uruguay Round Negotiation. *World Competition*, 21(3), 109–34.

Wong, K.-F. 2003. Empowerment as a Panacea for Poverty: Old Wine in New Bottles? *Progress in Development Studies*, 3(4), 307–22.

Chapter 2

The Scope for Asymmetry in the
World Trade Organisation (WTO)

Stephen Woolcock

Introduction

This chapter is about the scope for asymmetric provisions in North-South free
trade agreements under WTO. It looks in particular at the provisions governing
the exception from the most favoured nation obligations of Article I of the General
Agreement on Tariffs and Trade (GATT) under Article XXIV. Asymmetric
provisions favouring developing countries and especially least developed
countries can provide the flexibility these countries need to pursue trade policies
suited to their level of development. The general theme of this volume is however,
asymmetry in general, including asymmetry in the ability of WTO member states
to shape outcomes. Provisions in the WTO and power relationships between
WTO members are of course related. Developing countries have had much less
ability to shape outcomes and thus the WTO rules. This is likely to remain the
case, especially for the least developed countries. This is the case even though the
WTO, unlike other international organisations such as the International Monetary
Fund (IMF), is more 'democratic' in the sense that it is 'one member one vote'. In
practice individual developing countries have not had the kind of veto power that
this suggests.

At the time a large number of developing countries joined the GATT as they
gained independence, there was an asymmetry in the obligations that developing
countries had to meet. Part IV of the GATT provided that developing countries
did not have to adopt the same obligations as the developed economies, such as in
terms of tariff liberalisation. As the developed country GATT Contracting Parties
were obliged to conform to the Most Favoured Nation (MFN) obligations of Article
I this meant asymmetry in favour of developing countries, because the developed
countries extended their liberalisation to all GATT Contracting Parties including
the developing countries (DCs), while the DCs were not obliged to reduce tariffs
to the same extent. Part IV of the GATT therefore effectively established a two
tier membership. There was also the 'enabling clause' of the GATT that provided,
among other things, scope for developing countries to enter into preferential trade
agreements among themselves without being subject to the full disciplines of
Article XXIV of the GATT. The benefits of this two tier membership for developing
countries have long been a subject of discussion between those who adopt the

view that liberalisation is the best strategy for development and the proponents of import substitution or infant industry policies for economic development. It is not the aim of this chapter to discuss the normative aspects that shape this debate. Our concern is the more concrete question of the scope for asymmetry under the WTO.

Another general issue relating to the pros and cons of asymmetric provisions under the GATT/WTO such as part IV is the relationship between power and obligations. The case has been made that by opting for asymmetric obligations under Part IV, the developing countries were opting for second class membership of the GATT. Being less than fully paid up members of the club they were then not able to have much of a say in how the rules were drawn up. In other words there is a relationship between the level of obligations under the WTO and member states ability to shape the rules.

Influence in trade negotiations is largely shaped by the size of each economy. A WTO member's ability to shape outcomes in the WTO is of course a factor of its size. In the case of trade negotiations relative power is somewhat easier to measure than in international relations in general and the measure of economic power is the size of the domestic market that can be used as leverage in reciprocal market access negotiations. This is not to say that trade policy should only be about reciprocity, but it must be recognised that reciprocity was the established GATT practice and has for better or worse been carried over into the WTO. The principle of reciprocity dictates that a country's ability to get others to change policy or make concessions is a factor of the size of its domestic market and thus the concessions it can offer in terms of market access. This is of course relevant to the debate on asymmetric provisions for developing countries.

One must first differentiate between the least developed countries and other developing countries. According to the United Nations (UN) classifications there are 50 least developed countries that have very limited economic power by themselves and are often still dependent on a few commodity exports. For these the provision of asymmetric benefits under the WTO has been less controversial than for the larger emerging markets. The WTO provides for preferences such as under the Generalised System of Preferences (GSP) and other schemes for such countries. But these have been granted unilaterally by the more developed WTO members. While the WTO uses the UN classification for least developed countries, there are no agreed criteria for determining when a WTO member is a developing country. Indeed, the developing country status within the WTO is by self designation. As a consequence there has been a debate on graduation. In other words the developed members of the GATT/WTO have argued that as a country develops it should progressively assume the same responsibilities and obligations as other WTO members and not use the self designation practice as a means of avoiding such obligations. The debate has therefore been at which point or at what speed should the developing countries assume obligations equivalent to the developed countries? Today this issue is particularly sensitive for the large 'emerging markets' such as China and India, which are clearly developing countries if one compares their per capita income to that of the developed Organisation for

Economic Coordination and Development (OECD) economies, but which have become or are becoming major exporters of goods and services.

Changes in the nature of the GATT/WTO trading system

The nature of the GATT system up to the Uruguay Round could therefore be characterised as a two tier system in which the developed countries, initially led by the United States, but then subsequently by a group of OECD countries with the United States (US) and the European Union (EU) very prominent, largely determined the trade agenda and shaped policy outcomes, while developing countries made use of Part IV to limit their obligations but also had little say in the nature of the GATT rules. The Uruguay Round of the GATT and developments in the international trading system during the 1990s have changed this.

First, the Uruguay Round did away with Part IV of the GATT and replaced it with the Single Undertaking. Thus all WTO members were obliged to comply with the WTO rules, even if developing countries were still granted special and differential treatment in other forms, such as longer periods to implement WTO provisions or rather unspecific commitments to provide technical assistance from the developed WTO members. At the same time there has been a shift in the relative power relationships in the international trading system. Neither the United States nor the former Quad (US, EU, Japan and Canada), can still shape agendas and outcomes by themselves. At the same time it is important to remember that there can be no agreement in the WTO without the support of the US and the EU. The emergence of China and the increased economic leverage of India and to a lesser degree other leading developing countries such as Brazil and South Africa has produced a more heterogeneous power structure within the WTO. The adoption of the Single Undertaking has also raised expectations on the part of other smaller developing country members and least developed countries that they will have a greater say in the outcome of trade negotiations, now that they are full members of the club.

Just how much the previous asymmetric power relationship between developed and developing countries within the WTO has been redressed depends on a number of factors. As noted above, there has only been a real increase in relative market power in the case of the larger emerging markets in Asia such as China and India. While Brazil, South Africa and a number of other Latin American and African WTO members have sought greater influence in the WTO, their ability to wield much power has been constrained by relative economic weakness. The least developed members of the WTO have not seen much change in their ability to shape outcomes, at least not as individual members. This does not of course rule out the creation of coalitions among developing and least developed countries that may enhance their influence.

It is also worth differentiating between traditional market access issues and rule-making in the WTO. The large emerging markets have influence in the former because other WTO members, not least the developed economies, want access to their growing domestic markets. This gives them some real market leverage in negotiations on tariffs or access to services markets. When it comes to rulemaking however, the OECD countries still tend to dominate. This is because they have more developed domestic or regional rules governing trade-related topics, such as technical barriers to trade, government procurement or intellectual property rights, and because developing country members of the WTO have shown no interest in such topics and have indeed often gone out of their way to avoid any engagement in a discussion of how such rules could be shaped to match the interests of developing countries.

Another important shift in the nature of the international trading system since the late 1990s and early 2000s has been the steady growth of bilateral free trade agreements.[1] The international trading system has never been a purely multilateral system. There have always been strong elements of bilateralism and regionalism in trade relations both before and after the GATT was created in 1948. Even in tariffs, where the MFN obligation of Article I helped ensure a largely multilateral system, there were elements of bilateralism. For example, tariff reductions were negotiated with principle suppliers first and then multilateralised through the MFN clause. This was done to simplify the process of negotiating tariff reductions before general tariff formulae were introduced. But it had the effect of creating asymmetric bargaining relations between the major protagonists, i.e. the US and smaller GATT Contracting Parties. In the area of trade rules or trade-related topics there has never really been a very pronounced multilateral order. Issues such as technical barriers to trade, government procurement, services, investment and intellectual property rights were developed within the plurilateral OECD and then transferred into the multilateral system of the GATT/WTO, sometimes still in the form of plurilateral agreements or qualified MFN agreements that therefore constituted another element of the two-tier membership of the GATT.

With difficulties making progress in the WTO there has clearly been a shift towards a much greater use of bilateralism since the beginning of the 2000s. In contrast to the 1960s or 1980s when most preferential agreements were at the regional level, the focus since 2000 has been on bilateral agreements. Indeed, the growth of bilateralism may well be challenging some regional arrangements. For example the strength and cohesion of the Association of South East Asian Nations (ASEAN) is challenged by the increase in bilateral agreements concluded between individual ASEAN members and third countries. Even long-established regional organisations such as the European Free Trade Association (EFTA) are under threat. A bilateral agreement between Switzerland and the US, which was contemplated in 2007–2008, would have questioned the utility of what remains of EFTA. The EU alone remains free from the corrosive effects of bilateral agreements on its internal cohesion. The EU has sought to promote regional integration through region-to-region trade agreements, but this policy has not produced much success thus

---

1   See, for example, Heydon and Woolcock (2009).

far. The EU-MERCOSUR negotiations have made no progress and even the EU has concluded bilateral interim Economic Partnership Agreements (IEPAs) with individual African Caribbean Pacific Group (ACP) states because of its concern with the 2008 deadline for the end of the WTO waiver for ACP preferences under Cotonou. Such bilateral IEPAs represent at least a complication if not a setback for ACP regional initiatives in West Africa for example.

The growth of bilateralism can be seen as the reestablishment of the asymmetric power of the major developed countries. At a time when they are losing an ability to shape the WTO because of the growth of emerging markets and increased engagement of all developing country members of the organisation, bilateral trade negotiations will always help maximise the asymmetry of the US or EU vis-à-vis developing countries. In other words the negotiation of bilateral trade agreements may be seen as a means of selfish hegemons maximising their relative gains vis-à-vis smaller states. An alternative more benign view of bilateralism is that it has come about because of the difficulties making progress in the WTO with 154 more or less active members and that bilateralism does not exclude the possibility of concluding balanced agreements that meet the needs of all parties. Such balanced agreements would take account of the interests of the smaller parties including the development interests of smaller WTO members. In other words bilateralism could still include asymmetric commitments favouring the developing parties just as the GATT did in the past and the WTO does to a lesser degree today.

Whether bilateral agreements can serve the interests of the southern, developing country partners depends on what scope there is under WTO rules for such asymmetric obligations. The next section will discuss this, with particular reference to Article XXIV of GATT 1994. This is followed by a discussion of what scope there is for asymmetry in other WTO agreements. In each case there is also a brief assessment of the degree to which existing bilateral agreements have used what scope exists.

The scope for asymmetry under Article XXIV of the GATT

Scope for asymmetry under the WTO flows from de jure provisions that specify specific exceptions for developing countries and the de facto scope for flexibility due to the existing interpretation of WTO provisions. In the debate on asymmetry developing countries have stressed the need for formal legally secure exemptions in the belief that de facto flexibility is always at risk from challenges under WTO dispute settlement. This fear is not without foundation since a number of cases have been brought against North-South preferential agreements by – in some cases – developing countries excluded from the agreement. For example, a number of Central American developing countries, along with the United States, brought the case against the preferences for ACP banana exporters under the Lome Agreement that led the EU to seek more reciprocal, North-South preferential agreements that are more easily defended under Article XXIV of the GATT.

There are two key provisions in the GATT at the centre of the debate. These are Article XXIV of the GATT and the enabling clause. The General Agreement on Trade in Services (GATS) is also important because it governs services, which constitute a growing share of North-South trade. But GATS has been subject to less debate on asymmetry because Article V contains an explicit reference to 'flexibility' for developing countries.[2] The enabling clause of 1979 provides for considerable flexibility when it comes to a preferential agreement between two developing countries. In such cases the obligations of Article XXIV do not apply. But the enabling clause can only be applied to preferential agreements between developing country members of the WTO, it is not applicable when at least one of the parties to a preferential agreement is a developed country. So on the question of what scope for asymmetry there is one must look at Article XXIV of the GATT and in particular the how the various paragraphs are interpreted especially requirements concerning (i) notification of agreements, (ii) the coverage of 'substantially all trade' (SAT), and (iii) the implementation of agreements within a reasonable period of time.

Notification

Under Article XXIV 7(a) preferential agreements are required to be notified to the WTO. For many years this provision was poorly applied. At the end of the Uruguay Round the Understanding on the interpretation of Article XXIV of the GATT (paragraph 7–11) sought to tighten up the procedures for monitoring preferential agreements. Such agreements then had to be considered by the Committee on Regional Trade Agreements (CRTA) that was established as part of the Uruguay Round agreements. Since 1996 neither the notification nor the CRTA have worked very effectively. There was therefore an effort to strengthen WTO scrutiny of preferential agreements, starting as is often the case for the WTO with improved transparency. Discussions under the Doha Development Agenda (DDA) led to the adoption at the Hong Kong WTO Ministerial of the target of agreeing on enhanced transparency provisions for preferential agreements.

The transparency mechanism for regional trade agreements was subsequently agreed in June 2006 and formally adopted by the WTO General Council in December 2006.[3] These new arrangements provide for the WTO Secretariat to prepare a factual presentation on each agreement notified to the WTO. Initially the WTO Secretariat worked on the backlog of Free Trade Agreements (FTAs) already notified, but in future this will be the standard procedure for new agreements.

---

2 Art V 3(a) of the GATS states 'where developing countries are parties to an agreement [a preferential agreement between any members of the WTO], flexibility shall be provided for regarding the conditions ... particularly with reference to [Art 1 (b) on substantially all trade] .. in accordance with the level of development of the countries concerned, both overall and in individual sectors and sub-sectors'.

3 See WTO/WT/L/67 Transparency Mechanism for Regional Trade Agreements.

The production of the factual presentations requires a good deal of information from the parties to the agreement. Technical assistance is offered for developing countries in providing this information, but some Least Developed Countries (LDCs) in particular may not have the capacity to provide the information. There is therefore an issue of flexibility in terms of what sort of information will be required from LDCs in particular. In North-South agreements involving LDCs there should be asymmetry in the sense that the northern developed party might be asked to provide most of the information required by the WTO Secretariat.

The factual presentations by the WTO Secretariat are then passed to the CRTA in the case of agreements notified under Article XXIV and the Trade and Development Committee in the case of South-South agreements under the enabling clause. The aim is to improve transparency and thus facilitate peer review of preferential agreements.

Substantially all trade

The limited effectiveness of WTO scrutiny of FTAs in the CRTA has also been due to the absence of agreed criteria for the implementation of Article XXIV. A central question here is what is meant by substantially all trade (SAT) in Article XXIV 8 (a). The idea of requiring preferential agreements to cover substantially all trade dates from the days of the League of Nations and thus predates much of customs union theory. The motivation behind it was that preferential agreements should be serious about liberalisation and not just liberalise those sectors that can withstand competition.[4] SAT covers duties as well as what are called 'other regulatory restrictions of commerce' (ORRCs). There was and remains no agreement among WTO members on what constitutes SAT or ORRCs for that matter. Some WTO members such as the EU argue that SAT should mean 90 per cent others such as Australia have suggested 95 per cent and still others, including the African Union, 80 per cent or less.

A further complication is that different metrics produce different results and there is no agreement on which is best. Both quantitative and qualitative measures are possible and there are also different possible quantitative measures. One measure is tariff lines, so that 90 or 95 per cent of tariff lines could be defined as constituting SAT. The disadvantages with tariff line measures are that it is possible to exclude sensitive sectors and it does not reflect the volume of trade. In other words it would be possible to exclude a few sectors that account for an important share of trade. For developing countries this could be good or bad. Good in the sense that DCs could exclude sectors that account for a disproportionate share of tariff revenue, bad in the sense that developed country exporters can exclude a large percentage of trade by excluding a few tariff lines. If these happen to be

---

4   Viner's contribution in 1950 on customs union theory was to identify that preferential agreements can result in trade creation as well as trade diversion. This then formed the basis of much of the subsequent work on the economic effects of tariff preferences.

the sectors in which developing country exports are concentrated SAT provides no defence for DCs. An alternative quantitative measure is the volume of trade. With this measure 90 or 95 per cent of total trade by volume should be subject to zero tariffs. The disadvantage here is that the measure relates to current trade only, not potential trade. So such a measure of SAT would take no account of the potential trade growth in new products as a result of the removal of tariffs between preferential partners.

Qualitative criteria include, for example, the requirement that no major sector should be excluded from coverage (liberalisation). With such a measure it would for example, not be possible to exclude agriculture. Further complications come from questions such as whether and if so how tariff rate quotas should to measured.[5] In order to get around these difficulties it has been proposed that any measure of SAT should include a combination of tariff lines and trade volume as well as qualitative measures.[6]

As North-South agreements have to be notified under Article XXIV the question is what scope is there for flexibility under Article XXIV. There are no explicit special and differential treatment provisions in Article XXIV. Developing countries have therefore argued for the introduction of such explicit provisions. The definition of SAT is one of the issues that has been discussed in the DDA negotiation on rules, but (to date) with no agreement. In these discussions developing countries have sought explicit special and differential treatment so that developing countries would not be obliged to liberalise high levels of trade. Although some WTO Members, such as the EU and Australia, have included reference to the possibility of such a provision, it has been argued that exceptions should only be discussed once agreement on what should constitute SAT has been reached. This reduces the likelihood of any agreement on special and differential treatment because the SAT issue has been so difficult to resolve.

Existing practice does provide some scope for asymmetry. For example, the EU has stated that it is ready to accept asymmetric commitments on tariff liberalisation with developing countries. This would take the form of the EU committing to higher levels than its developing country partners, so that an aggregate level of SAT of more than 90 per cent could be achieved. The case of the Trade Development and Cooperation Agreement between the EU and South Africa is held up as an example of this practice. In this the EU agreed to liberalise 98 per cent of trade and South Africa 82 per cent so that the aggregate coverage came out at 90 per cent of bilateral trade. Flexibility of this form can work both

---

5   A Tariff Rate Quota (TRQ) is a device according to which a only specific quota (number or tonnage) of goods can be imported at zero tariff or at a tariff below the MFN tariff. Once this quota has been filled any further imports would attract a higher tariff. TRQs are often used to provide protection for seasonal goods or crops.

6   The Appellate Body in its ruling in the Turkey – textile case, which addressed a number of issues relating to Art XXIV and the FTAs in general, suggested that both quantitative and qualitative measures of measurement are suitable.

ways however. The EU has been more flexible in its North-South negotiations and allowed its developing country partners to commit to levels of tariff reductions around the 80 per cent mark. But flexibility also means the EU exempts some of its most sensitive sectors, which it can still do even with high percentage figures for tariff line coverage. The USA has sought higher levels of commitment in its FTAs and therefore offered less flexibility and asymmetry, but this 'gold standard' for FTAs means the US has committed to nearly 100 per cent tariff liberalisation. Nevertheless with no specific criteria in Article XXIV there remains scope for asymmetric arrangements to be negotiated.

From a developing country point of view, de facto flexibility to negotiate asymmetric liberalisation under Article XXIV is seen as inadequate because it provides no legal security. In other words third parties could challenge such agreements either in the CRTA or in WTO dispute settlement procedures. As on other issues relating to North-South trade, the reluctance of the developed WTO members to agree exceptions for developing countries has at least in part to do with the lack of differentiation between developing countries. The EU or US is likely to be more ready to accept special and differential treatment for least developed countries, but as both negotiate bilateral FTAs with large emerging markets, they are unwilling to concede Special and Differential treatment (S&D) in the WTO negotiations.

Transition periods

Another area of discussion on Article XXIV concerns transition periods. Article XXIV states that substantially all trade should be liberalised within a 'reasonable period of time.' This was interpreted in paragraph 3 of the 1995 Understanding as normally meaning ten years. The Understanding also states that transition periods 'should exceed 10 years only in exceptional cases' and that any transition period longer than 10 years should be 'explained to the WTO Council on Goods.' Developing countries have called for a specific reference to special and differential treatment for developing countries here also. For example the African Union position calls for a twenty year transition period for developing countries on the grounds that they will need longer to adjust to increased competition than developed economies.

As for SAT the practice in terms of transition periods has been to provide some asymmetry. For example, the EU-Association Agreement with Tunisia (the first of the EuroMed agreements) grants Tunisia a 12 year transition. The later EU-Egypt provides for 15 years and the Canada – Chile FTA grants Chile 18.5 years to implement the liberalisation schedules. The US has also agreed to such long transition periods, but here the flexibility works both ways. In other words the US also has longer transition periods. In other words the US has dealt with protectionist sectors at home not by excluding them from liberalisation, as is more likely to have been the case in the EU, but by offering longer transition periods.

Again there is an issue of legal security. There is no guarantee that such transition periods will not be challenged as being inconsistent with Article XXIV. In the discussions on the interpretation of Article XXIV there have been some proposals to tighten up on transition periods. Australia has, for example, argued that 70 per cent of liberalisation should take place on entry into force of the FTA. In other words liberalisation should be front loaded. Many developing country partners in North-South agreements would wish to back-load their liberalisation.

Other restrictive regulations of commerce (ORRC)

Article XXIV includes 'ORRCs'. In other words ORRCs have to be removed according to the SAT and transition criteria. This is another area of uncertainty in the interpretation of Article XXIV. It seems fairly clear that quantitative restrictions are included in the definition of ORRCs, so that any quotas, for example, would also have to be liberalised. But it is not clear whether the ORRC term includes such measures as technical barriers to trade, sanitary and phytosanitary measures, or anti-dumping. At issue here is whether the adoption of common standards or mutual recognition in a North-South bilateral FTA could be seen as adding a new barrier to trade and thus infringing the provision in Article XXIV that FTAs should not lead to an increase in trade restrictions vis-à-vis third countries. Or whether the adoption of a common standard or mutual recognition facilitates trade for third countries. This would, for example, occur when different national standards are replaced with a common standard through the application of mutual recognition. Either way a third country exporting to a preferential area would only need to comply with one standard rather than two or more, or would only need to have its products certified as complying with the requirements of one party to an FTA under mutual recognition within that FTA. Given the lack of progress agreeing on substantive issues such as the definition of SAT, it is unlikely that there will be progress any time soon on what is included in ORRCs.

Scope for asymmetry for non-tariff provisions in North-South agreements

This section looks at some non-tariff barriers because more and more North-South FTAs now include specific provisions on a range of non-tariff barriers. This is followed by a discussion of some of the trade-related topics that now also form part of North-South FTAs.[7]

---

7   For a further discussion on the incorporation of these 'new' issues in bilateral and regional agreements, see for example, Woolcock (2006).

Technical barriers to trade (TBT) and sanitary and phytosanitary (SPS) measures

Whilst tariffs remain important for many developing countries, especially least developed countries, TBT and SPS measures have grown in importance as tariffs are reduced or eliminated. For developing countries that still rely heavily on the export of agricultural products, SPS measures can constitute a major barrier to market access in the northern markets by hampering efforts to move up the value chain and export higher value added products.

A preferential agreement implies WTO-Plus provisions, in other words provisions that go beyond existing multilateral provisions. In the case of technical barriers to trade and sanitary and phytosanitary measures the WTO rules are generally based on national treatment, in other words the treatment of foreign goods the same as nationally produced goods when it comes to health or food safety regulations. The WTO agreement on TBTs does however also encourage the use of international standards and mutual recognition. Even with mutual recognition the regulating authority in the importing country accepts the certification by testing bodies in the exporting country that products meet the required standards of the importing country. The WTO provisions on SPS are essentially science-based. There is scope for the use of precaution under Article 5 of the SPS Agreement, which means that temporary bans on the sale of imported products can be introduced in the absence of any scientific proof that the product is unsafe. But the stress here is on temporary bans and there is a requirement that scientific evidence is gathered to assess the degree of risk.

The issue in North-South FTAs is whether the generally higher standards required by northern developed countries facilitate or restrict trade and what scope there is for asymmetry in this area of trade policy? There is very limited evidence on the impact of provisions on standards in preferential agreements. What research has been done seems to suggest that the introduction of standards facilitates trade. But there is also some evidence that northern SPS measures in particular have restricted DC exports.

The WTO rules require non-discrimination in the shape of national treatment with regard to any technical regulation, standard or conformance assessment. But this does not prevent the more developed WTO members from introducing high standards. Indeed, the trend in recent years has been towards consumer pressure for higher standards in the wake of various failures in the science-based regulatory regimes of developed countries, such as for example, the case of BSE or mad-cow disease in the EU. Non-discrimination thus could be said to work against the interests of developing country exporters who would normally be expected to find it harder to meet high standards. Developing countries are particularly disadvantaged in that it is often difficult for their producers to adjust their processing methods to meet frequent changes in safety standards.

The scope under the WTO for asymmetric provisions favouring developing countries in the TBT/SPS field takes the form of technical assistance and special and differential treatment. Both the WTO TBT and SPS Agreements provide for technical assistance for developing country members in Articles 11 and 9 respectively, but there is no specified level of assistance. Generally speaking the EU has provided more funds for technical assistance, $29 million for DCs in the field of TBT against $9.6 million from Japan and $3.4 million from the US between 2001 and 2005. There is also assistance provided through the bilateral arrangements. For example, most EU FTAs include special committees on TBT and SPS measures that both promote the exchange of expertise and knowledge as well as seek to resolve difficulties for market access caused by technical regulations.

In terms of special and differential treatment, rules on TBTs and SPS generally require notification of new regulations. As noted above this is a particularly important issue for developing country exporters which may find it harder to adapt to new standards. The WTO TBT provisions in Article 2.12 of the TBT Agreement state that there should be 'a reasonable period of time between publication and entry into force' of any new regulation to allow suppliers 'and particularly those in developing countries to adapt' to the new regulations. Article 10 (2) of the SPS Agreement is slightly more specific in that it provides for a 'longer time frame for developing country exporters to adapt' their products to new regulations. So there is scope for asymmetry for DC exporters, but unlike the case of tariffs there does not appear to be much use made of such asymmetry by developed country regulators.

Developing countries also face increased costs in terms of implementing the rules of the TBT and SPS Agreements. Of particular importance are for example, the requirements to have central points of information on standards and technical regulations. For DC exporters these help to provide the transparency they need to access developed country markets. For DC authorities these can represent a considerable cost. There is however, scope for asymmetry in the TBT and SPS Agreements of the WTO in Article 12.8 and 10.3 respectively to exempt DCs for a time-limited period from the obligations of all or part of the agreements.

The WTO does therefore provide scope for asymmetry in the field of TBT and SPS. In terms of the provisions on TBT/SPS in bilateral North-South agreements, the main asymmetric provisions in favour of DCs appear to be in the shape of technical assistance. In some cases this has been rather limited. There is no evidence that developed countries have shown any willingness to see exemptions from health and safety rules for products from developing countries.

Commercial instruments

Commercial instruments such as safeguards and anti-dumping duties can have effects on developing country exports and imports. Scope for flexibility in the use of safeguards can work against DC exporting interests when this is used by developed WTO members to restrict imports from developing countries. On the other hand flexibility that provides scope for a wide interpretation of provisions on safeguards and/or anti-dumping may be used by developing countries to address injury caused by rapid increases in imports. In this context asymmetry would take the form of provisions that allow developing countries more flexibility to use commercial instruments than developed countries.

Broadly speaking the WTO provides a good deal of scope for asymmetry in that the rules on safeguards, anti-dumping and countervailing duties leave scope for discretion in how they are implemented. In terms of safeguards there is special and differential treatment of developing countries in that safeguard actions shall not be taken against a DC if its exports account for less than 3 per cent of imports. However, the cumulative imports from developing countries in this category should not exceed 9 per cent of imports. If they do the developed WTO member applying the safeguard can act against DC exports.

As importers, developing countries can also apply a safeguard for a longer period. Under the Agreement on Safeguards in the Uruguay Round developed country members can apply a safeguard for a maximum period of four years and cannot re-impose a safeguard action for a period equivalent to the period the initial safeguard action was in force. In other words if a safeguard is applied for the maximum period of four years a similar safeguard cannot be applied on the same products for another four years. For developing countries it is possible to impose a safeguard for a period of six years and to re-impose the safeguard within a shorter period.

The scope for such asymmetry provided by the WTO has not always been taken up in North-South agreements. If anything there is a trend towards a tightening of the rules in FTAs, such as a reduction in the number of years that a safeguard measure can be maintained. For example, the FTA negotiated between the US and Peru provides for safeguard actions for up to two years only and the US – Morocco three years only. On the other hand, FTA partners may be excluded from safeguard actions, as in the case of the North American Free Trade Agreement (NAFTA), if their imports do not account for a large share of trade or contribute importantly to the injury caused to the industry of the importing country. In the case of NAFTA this means that exports from Mexico, for example, may be excluded from a safeguard action provided they are not one of the top five exporters of the product concerned.

On the import side the EU (and EFTA) have included an element of asymmetry in safeguard provisions in their agreements with Mediterranean partners. Thus the North African partners can re-impose import duties to support an infant industry or an industry undergoing adaptation, especially if this has social implications (i.e. results in increased unemployment in concentrated locations).

On anti-dumping there is a rather weak provision for developing countries in Article 15 of the Agreement on anti-dumping in the Uruguay Round. This appears to avoid use of special and *differential* treatment, and refers to the need for developed countries to have 'regard for the special situation of developing countries' and to consider the possibilities of constructive remedies available under the agreement on anti-dumping before imposing anti-dumping duties on developing country exports. It is not specified what these constructive remedies might be, but they could include use of the *de minimis* provision in Article 5 (8) of the Agreement on Anti-dumping which suggests that imports from a country that account for less than 3 per cent of all imports should not be considered in anti-dumping procedures, provided that the cumulative total of countries in this category does not exceed 7 per cent.

Most North-South FTAs simply apply the anti-dumping provisions of the WTO, so do not offer any additional asymmetry in terms of a formal text. The only exceptions to this are those rare North-South bilaterals that provide for the replacement of anti-dumping measured by the application of competition policy. The Canada-Chile FTA is one such agreement.

Services and investment

The GATS Agreement includes an explicit provision on flexibility for developing countries in Article V 3 (a). This states that 'flexibility shall be provided for developing countries participating in 'economic integration.' Article V of the GATS sets out the conditions for preferential agreements in services and is similar to that of Article XXIV of the GATT. GATS Article V. 1 (a) includes a provision that any services agreement should have 'substantial sectoral coverage.' A footnote sets out the criteria for assessing what is substantial, which must include a consideration of the sectors covered, the volume of trade and the modes of supply (i.e. cross border, establishment in the target market, consumption in the market of the supplier or service provision through the movement of people). It is also stated that no mode of supply should be a priori excluded. This means for example, that mode 4, the provision of a service through the movement of personnel providing the service, cannot be excluded. So Article V 3 provides an exemption from the requirement to include substantial sector coverage for developing countries. This would seem to provide more scope for asymmetry than is the case under Article XXIV.

Like Article XXIV of the GATT there is a requirement to complete the preferential liberalisation within a 'reasonable timeframe'. The expectation must be that this will be interpreted along similar lines to Article XXIV (i.e. 10 years).[8]

With scope for flexibility under Article V the question then arises how this has been used in North-South bilateral agreements? As for tariffs, measures of coverage of services are rather inexact. If one takes the number of sectors for which commitments have been made under FTAs and compares this to the number of sectors for which commitments have been made under the GATS, then most FTAs including North-South FTAs are GATS-Plus. This is not surprising considering that the GATS commitments were negotiated nearly twenty years ago. But some bilaterals are also GATS-Plus in that they go beyond the parties' offers in the services negotiations of the DDA. The northern partners in FTAs take a different

---

8   Preferential agreements in services are to be notified to the Committee on Trade in Services, so it will be this committee of the WTO that will have an input into the interpretation of the Article.

approach to coverage. The United States has used negative listing for service sector coverage. This means that only those sectors, or sub-sectors, listed are excluded from coverage. This has also been adopted by Mexico and other NAFTA parties in the bilaterals they have negotiated with third countries. Generally speaking, negative listing is seen to be liberal in character, but the USA still excludes regulatory restrictions on services trade at the state level. The European Union uses positive listing to determine coverage of services in its North-South bilateral or region-to-region agreements. This is generally assumed to be less liberal as only those sectors listed are included, but facilitates flexibility in that developing country governments do not need to liberalise unless they explicitly agree to do so. Other northern partners such as Japan use hybrid listing systems.

Whether positive or negative listing is used to determine coverage there remains scope for flexibility in the GATS, which is why the developing countries favoured a separate regime for services. When it comes to asymmetry, there are indications that northern trading partners are willing to accept asymmetry in the coverage of the numbers of sectors. For example, in the EU-CARIFORUM Economic Partnership Agreement the CARIFORUM states made commitments for between 60 and 75 per cent of service sectors, while the EU made commitments for 90 per cent. A full assessment of the degree of asymmetry would however, require a detailed analysis of the schedules. The northern partners tend to favour large and important sectors such as telecommunications and financial services, while southern partners favour sectors in which mode 4 are prevalent, because with lower costs these are the sectors in which the developing countries have a comparative advantage.

The GATS agreement covers investment in services in that market access via mode 3 (establishment) is essentially about investment. There is no general investment provision under the GATT 1994 for industrial investment, such as foreign direct investment in manufacturing. As such there is considerable scope within the WTO for asymmetry. The only area in which there are binding obligations under the WTO concerns performance requirements under the Trade Related Investment Measures (TRIMs) agreement of the Uruguay Round. This is by-and-large a liberal interpretation of existing GATT Articles as they relate to the ability of countries to impose performance requirements in foreign investors. Developing countries often use performance requirements, such as local content obligations, to ensure that foreign investment contributes to value added in the local economy. The TRIMs agreement effectively bans a number of performance requirements that have been interpreted as inconsistent with Article III (national treatment) provisions of the GATT (e.g. local content rules) and Article XI quantitative restrictions (e.g. trade balancing).

The scope for asymmetry with regard to investment in goods has been used differently in different North-South bilaterals. The US approach has been to expect all developing country partners to accept the comprehensive investment rules of NAFTA, which has been the de facto model for investment as well as other topics in US negotiations. This provides little scope for asymmetry. The EU has very limited investment provisions in its bilateral or association agreements for a number of reasons that have as much to do with the lack of European Community competence for foreign direct investment as they have to do with a desire to give developing country partners policy space. With little by way of commitments there is not really much scope for asymmetry.

Intellectual property

The Trade Related Intellectual Property rights (TRIPs) agreement of the Uruguay Round has been the subject of considerable debate with regard to the flexibility it offers for developing countries to pursue national policies aimed at dealing with, for example, national public health emergencies, such as HIV-Aids, through the compulsory licensing of pharmaceutical products. The Doha Declaration of 2001 on TRIPs and the provision of essential medicines sought to clarify the scope for such action under the TRIPs and went some way towards easing the constraints of the agreement. The Doha Declaration therefore provides flexibility that can be used in bilateral North-South bilaterals on this topic.

Broadly speaking what has happened in the bilaterals has been a TRIPs-Plus tightening of the rules. This is the case across the board for bilateral agreements negotiated by the US. For example, copyright protection is typically extended to 70 years in US FTAs compared to 50 years in the TRIPs and trademark protection extended to 10 years from 7 in the TRIPs. There are also TRIPs-Plus provisions in US FTAs that effectively extend patent life if this has been limited or shortened due to delays in registration or authorisation of a patent. The US FTAs also have TRIPs-Plus provisions on enforcement, such as tighter wording on enforcement procedures than are offered in the TRIPs. For its part the EU broadly sticks to TRIPs provisions in the North-South FTAs it has negotiated, except in the area of Geographic Indicators (GI), where it is seeking to use bilaterals as a means of pressing its pro-GI agenda.

Government procurement

One of the trade-related or Singapore issues that is finding its way into North-South bilateral agreements is government procurement. There are no multilateral rules governing government procurement, because these have been resisted by developing and some developed countries. But there is the plurilateral Government Procurement Agreement (GPA) of 1994 negotiated as part of the Uruguay Round. Any provisions on procurement in bilateral North-South FTAs will therefore be negotiated against the background of the GPA. Article V of the GPA provides for special and differential treatment for developing countries. This takes the form of general provisions under which developed country participants in the GPA will take account of developing country interests in areas such as balance of payments or the desire to establish or develop domestic industries in sectors that supply public contracts. In addition to these general provisions there are also specific provisions that allow for less coverage and exemptions for developing countries. These must however, be negotiated. If asymmetric provisions have to be negotiated this raises some doubt about the ability of the developing country to achieve asymmetric outcomes to its advantage given the asymmetric power relationship in favour of the developed country. There are also provisions on technical assistance including help for developing country exporters to supply developed country procurement markets.

North-South agreements increasingly include provisions on government procurement. Again there tends to be a difference between the US agreements and those negotiated by the EU and Japan. In all cases the framework provisions of the GPA have been applied. In other words the transparency requirements in the bilateral North-South agreements are essentially the same as the GPA model. When it comes to 'liberalisation' commitments in the bilateral FTAs (i.e. commitments on national treatment in the awarding of contracts), these are negotiated as in the GPA. Indeed, one reason the developing countries have not signed on to the GPA is that 'liberalisation' commitments are negotiated bilaterally under it, thus maximising the asymmetric power of the developed parties. In the case of the US, coverage appears to be closely driven by reciprocity. In the case of the EU there has been some asymmetry. For example, the EU-CARIFORUM agreement of 2008 provides asymmetric access to the EU procurement market in that the EU commits to coverage equivalent to its commitments under the GPA, while CARIFORUM states are not required to make any commitments to provide national treatment/ liberalisation, at least not yet. Japan has not pressed procurement in its FTAs and those negotiated with Asian neighbours have no provision at all on procurement.

Conclusions

The existing WTO rules governing North-South FTAs do not provide for specific exemptions for the developing country signatories in all cases. Article XXIV is perhaps the clearest case of there being no special provision for developing countries. While there is de facto scope for flexibility on sector coverage of Article XXIV, this does not provide for legal security for developing countries and the degree of asymmetry offered by the northern partner in a bilateral agreement will depend on the northern partner. The EU has shown more flexibility, but this has also been used to benefit certain sensitive sectors in the EU. In the case of transition periods there is also a degree of flexibility to grant developing countries longer periods to liberalise, but the US has also used the de facto flexibility available to retain longer periods for its sensitive sectors.

When it comes to services trade there is explicit reference to flexibility for developing countries in the GATS agreement, so most of the comment on services has been to the effect that the GATS provides more scope for asymmetry, which is correct. But aside from the legal security question the degree of asymmetry will still, of course, depend on how much the northern partner in any bilateral is willing to accept.

In the case of non-tariff barriers WTO TBT and SPS rules are based on national treatment which offers little by way of special exemptions for developing country products. There is also no evidence that developed countries are willing to accept lower standards of safety or food quality from developing country suppliers. The developing country interest may be best served by promoting the use of agreed international standards over national standards of the developed countries. There is scope under the WTO agreements for providing developing country suppliers with longer periods to comply with TBT or SPS regulations and this has for the most part been carried over into bilateral agreements.

In government procurement the absence of multilateral rules means there is scope for asymmetry and the plurilateral GPA provides for explicit special and differential treatment. This has to be negotiated however, so does not ease the problem of asymmetry in economic power between the developed and developing country signatories to any agreement.

References

Heydon, K. and Woolcock, S. 2009. *The rise of bilateralism: comparing American, European and Asian approaches to Preferential Trade Agreements*. Tokyo: UNU Press.

Viner, J. 1950. *The customs union issue*. New York: Carnegie Endowment for International Peace.

Woolcock, S. (ed.) 2006. *Trade and investment rulemaking: the role of regional and bilateral agreements*. Tokyo: UNU Press.

Chapter 3

Asymmetric Trade Negotiations for Development: What Does the Experience from the ACP-EU Economic Partnership Agreements Tell Us?

Sanoussi Bilal

Asymmetry is at the core of the relationship between the European Union (EU) and the group of African, Caribbean and Pacific (ACP) countries. All former colonies of European countries, the ACP group of countries has enjoyed a privileged, and yet unbalanced, relationship with Europe since the independence years.[1] Over time, the EU has developed a comprehensive partnership with the ACP, based on significant development assistance, a preferential trade regime and an enhanced political dimension, based on the principle of equal partnership. The decision to initiate negotiations on ambitious free trade agreements (FTAs), officially referred to as economic partnership agreements (EPAs), has been the biggest challenge so far on the relation between the ACP and the EU. Aimed primarily at fostering development, they have become however a major source of continued tension between the partners. Asymmetry seems also to characterise all dimensions of these negotiations; asymmetry in terms of economic development, trade patterns and dependence, agenda, interest, capacity, experience, power, but asymmetry also in terms of (liberalisation) commitments and engagements.

The aim of this chapter is to review the EPA negotiations process to assess the various dimensions of this asymmetric relationship and identify some lessons and perspectives on the EPA process. The discussion is structured as follows. Section 1 provides a brief historical context to the relationship between the EU and the ACP countries and its trade dimension. This background is important to understand the shift to EPAs proposed under the Cotonou Agreement, as outlined in Section 2, which also highlights some key features of EPA negotiations process. Section 3 then sketches some of the rationale and factors to engage in EPAs and the diverging interests between the EU and the ACP, but also among ACP countries and various stakeholders. These differences between the parties prevented most ACP regions or countries, to the exception of the Caribbean, to conclude a comprehensive EPA as initially envisaged. The tense and at times acrimonious negotiations culminated

---

1   For a historical account of the ACP-EU relations, see Frisch (2008).

in 2007, as described in Section 4. While some countries managed to conclude interim, or 'stepping-stones', agreements with the EU, the temporary outcome of the negotiations, summarised in Section 5, has generated deep and persistent dissatisfaction among the parties, discussed in Section 6. By the end of 2010, the EPA negotiations were still ongoing at a slow pace, while the attention of most policy-makers, both in the EU and the ACP, seemed to be shifting away from the EPA process. The lack of political leadership and vision, in the face of adversity, is perhaps the most striking element of this highly asymmetric relationship between the EU and the ACP countries, whose long-standing partnership has been based on seemingly innovative development and equality principles, as reflected upon in the concluding Section 7.

A historical and contextual perspective

European cooperation with the ACP dates back to the Treaty of Rome that established the European Economic Community (EEC) in 1957. In the Treaty, the signatories expressed solidarity with the colonies and overseas countries and territories and committed themselves to contribute to their prosperity. The first formal association of ACP and EEC countries took shape through the so-called Yaoundé I (1963–69) and Yaoundé II (1969–75) agreements. At the time, the lion's share of the resources went to French-speaking Africa, mainly aiming to build infrastructure in the wake of decolonisation.

EEC membership by the United Kingdom in 1973 led to the signing of the wider Lomé Convention between 46 ACP countries and then nine EEC member states (1975–80) and the effective creation of the ACP group. The first Lomé Convention was very much a child of its time. It reflected the relative geopolitical power of ACP countries in the context of the Cold War, the oil crisis and the prevailing ideological debate on a 'new international economic order'. From 1975 to 2000, four successive Lomé Conventions (1975, 1979, 1984 and 1989 – for ten years) governed the development and trade ACP-EU relations. They represented the world's largest financial and political framework for North-South cooperation. Under this development framework, the EU has granted non-reciprocal trade preferences for ACP exports to its market. Most ACP products were allowed to enter duty free on the European market, with the exception of some 'sensitive' agricultural products covered by the Common Agricultural Policy (CAP) of the EU. Four commodity protocols, annexed to the Lomé Convention, provided free access for a specified quantity of exports from a selected group of traditional ACP providers of bananas, rum, sugar and beef.

Despite receiving preferences for more than 25 years, ACP exports have, in general, performed poorly. The share of ACP exports to the EU market fell by more than a half under Lomé, from 8 per cent in 1975 to 2.8 per cent in 2000, as illustrated in Figure 3.1 (up to 4.5 per cent in 2009). This is not to say preferences did not work, contrary to common claims, notably by the European Commission

(EC). They have! Indeed, Lomé preferences have boosted ACP exports by an estimated 30 per cent (see Persson and Wilhelmsson 2006). However, judging from the composition of aggregate ACP exports, trade preferences have in general failed to promote diversification, which are still mainly concentrated on few natural resources and primary commodities (see Figure 3.2), with only 3 products (petroleum, diamonds and cocoa) accounting for about half of ACP exports to the EU.

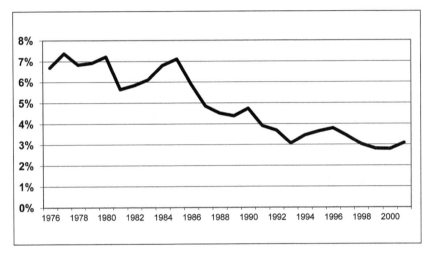

Figure 3.1 Share of ACP exports in the EU market

Source: DG Trade.

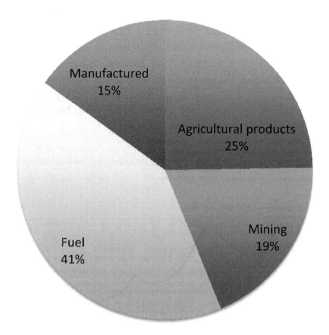

Figure 3.2 ACP exports to the EU by sector (2009)
Source: ITC Trade Map.

Besides the disappointing results of the Lomé Conventions, pressures increased on the ACP-EU trade relations to be more consistent with the rules of the multilateral trading system, since the establishment of the World Trade Organisation (WTO) in 1995. The problem with the Lomé trade arrangements was not that the EU offered non-reciprocal trade preferences *per se*, but that it discriminated in an arbitrary way between ACP and non-ACP countries of similar levels of development. WTO rules, under the Enabling Clause, allow developing countries to be exempted from the principle of non-discrimination,[2] provided that the preferences are based on transparent and objective criteria related to development considerations. Following mounting pressures at the GATT (General Agreement on Tariffs and Trade)/WTO, including as a result of the 'bananas dispute', the EU did obtain a waiver from other WTO members for the period of Lomé IV bis (1995–2000), temporarily exempting the ACP-EU trade regime from complying with the most-favoured nation (MFN) principle.[3]

---

2   Also referred to as the Most-Favoured Nation (MFN) principle, Article I of the General Agreement on Tariffs and Trade (GATT).

3   With the creation of the WTO in 1995 and its new enforceable mechanism for dispute settlement, the need for compliance with GATT/WTO rules became more prominent.

As a consequence, facing pressures from WTO members and in view of the disappointing effects of trade preferences, the EU clearly indicated, right from the start of the post-Lomé negotiations, that it was not willing to seek further WTO waivers to defend its trade regime with the ACP. As one of the main proponents of the multilateral trading system, it argued that it had to fully comply with the principles of the WTO, and therefore needed new WTO-compatible trading arrangements with the ACP. These development and WTO-compatibility considerations were the key arguments put forward by the European Commission to propose Economic Partnership Agreements.

The ACP initially took a defensive position to maintain and improve the non-reciprocal trade preferences, arguing that preferences were a necessary but insufficient condition for development. They also stressed the need for more EU support to address the supply-side constraints of the ACP economies, so as to enable them to take advantage of the preferential trade regime. But the EU insisted on the merits on economic reforms based on a more liberal trade and economic regime, which the EPAs would support.

The EPA negotiations framework

The legal framework

The Cotonou Partnership Agreement, signed in June 2000, contains the basic principles guiding the relations between the EU and the 77 ACP countries for the following 20 years (see ECDPM 2002, Laporte 2007). The EU and ACP parties agreed to redefine the ACP-EU trade regime in order to make it compatible with WTO rules and with the main aim of promoting growth, sustainable development and poverty alleviation, as well as helping the ACP countries integrate into the world economy.

The concept of EPAs comes down to WTO compatible and reciprocal FTAs between the EU and (preferably) sets of ACP regional groupings. EPAs would aim to go beyond 'traditional' free trade agreements, solely covering trade in merchandise goods. Instead, EPAs would include trade in agriculture and fishery products, trade in services, as well as rules on investment. In addition, cooperation is foreseen in a number of trade-related (regulatory) areas such as competition, intellectual property rights, standardisation and certification, sanitary and phytosanitary measures (SPS), trade and the environment, trade and labour standards, consumer policy and food security.

The Cotonou Agreement foresaw that the negotiations on EPAs should start in September 2002, and be concluded by the end of 2007, so as to enter into force no later than 1 January 2008. The intention of the parties was to provide ample time for the ACP to prepare for the negotiations (during the period 2000–2002) and to conduct the negotiations at a reasonable pace, taking into account the capacity constraints of the ACP countries and regions (during the period 2002–2007). A formal review was even planned in 2006 'to ensure that no further time is needed for preparations or negotiations' (Cotonou Agreement (2000), Article 37.4).

The parties agree that this 'preparatory period shall also be used for capacity-building in the public and private sectors of ACP countries, including measures to enhance competitiveness, for strengthening of regional organisations and for support to regional trade integration initiatives, where appropriate with assistance to budgetary adjustment and fiscal reform, as well as for infrastructure upgrading and development, and for investment promotion' (Cotonou Agreement (2000), Article 37.2).

Lomé-type of unilateral preferences for ACP exports was extended during this transition period. In the framework of the Fourth WTO Ministerial Conference in Doha in November 2001, a waiver was granted for the current ACP-EU trade regime to be maintained until the end of 2007, on the basis of a clear commitment that the period was necessary to negotiate new WTO-compatible trading arrangements, the EPAs.

The Cotonou Agreement of 2000[4] therefore did not encompass a full-fledged trade regime, but contains the basic principles and objectives of the new economic and trade cooperation between the ACP and EU. The explicit aim of the arrangement is to 'foster the smooth and gradual integration of the ACP States into the world economy, *with due regard for their political choices and development priorities*, thereby promoting their sustainable development and contributing to poverty eradication' and to enable 'the ACP States to play a full part in international trade' (Article 34.1 and 2, *emphasis added*). The EPAs were thus designed first and foremost as instruments of development, in line with the development strategies chosen by the ACP.

Asymmetry and special and differential treatment, taking into account the respective levels of development of the ACP countries and regions are enshrined in the EPA approach as repeatedly stated in the Cotonou Agreement, *inter alia*:

• "Economic and trade cooperation shall be implemented in full conformity with the provisions of the WTO, including *special and differential treatment, taking account of the Parties' mutual interests and their respective levels of development.*" (Article 34.4, emphasis added);
• "Economic and trade cooperation shall *take account of the different needs and levels of development of the ACP countries and regions*. In this context, the Parties reaffirm their attachment to *ensuring special and differential treatment for all ACP countries* and to maintaining *special treatment*

---

4   The Cotonou Agreement covers a period of 20 years, from 2000 until 2020, and is subject to formal revision every five years. The 2005 revision did not really affect the economic and trade cooperation chapter, but the 2010 did, to reflect the evolution in the EPA process. References to the Cotonou Agreement in this chapter refer to the initial version in 2000.

for ACP LDCs and to taking *due account of the vulnerability of small, landlocked and island countries.*" (Article 35.3, emphasis added)

- "Negotiations shall take account of *the level of development* and the *socio-economic impact* of trade measures on ACP countries, and their *capacity to adapt and adjust their economies* to the liberalisation process. Negotiations will therefore be as *flexible* as possible in establishing the duration of a sufficient transitional period, the final product coverage, taking into account sensitive sectors, and the *degree of asymmetry in terms of timetable for tariff dismantlement,* while remaining in conformity with WTO rules then prevailing." (Article 37.7, emphasis added); a flexibility to be jointly defended at the WTO (Article 37.8).

The ACP even managed to successfully push for a provision in the Cotonou Agreement that foresee that for those countries that do not feel in a position to negotiate EPAs, alternative possibilities will be considered in 2004, 'in order to provide these countries with a new framework for trade which is equivalent to their existing situation and in conformity with WTO rules' (Art. 37.6). Those alternative options have actually boiled down to the EU Generalised System of Preferences (GSP). As for the Least Developed Countries (LDCs), since March 2001 they could benefit from duty-free and quota-free access to the EU market through 'Everything-But-Arms' (EBA), an EU unilateral initiative within the GSP.

These EPAs, as development-oriented FTAs, were also to build on and strengthen regional integration processes in the ACP (e.g. Articles 35.2 and 37.5). Negotiations were thus conducted at the regional level between self-determined regional groupings of ACP countries and the EU. Besides trade in goods and agricultural products, EPAs were aimed at enhancing cooperation in all areas relevant to trade (Article 36.1). It was thus agreed they would also cover services, possibly beyond commitments under the General Agreement on Trade in Services (GATS). For some ACP countries, this could also be of key importance because services constitute an increasingly significant sector of their economies, and present a possible engine for further economic growth in the future. EPAs would address tariff, non-tariff and technical barriers to trade. Moreover, a whole range of trade-related matters would be covered under EPAs. Among them, issues such as competition policy, investment, SPS measures, trade facilitation, standards and certification, protection of intellectual property rights, anti-dumping and anti-subsidy measures, customs procedures, rules of origin, public procurement, trade and environment, trade and labour standards and health and safety regulations (Articles 45–54).

The negotiations structure

Initially, the EPA negotiations process was structured around only two phases. At the insistence of the ACP Group, the European Commission accepted a first phase of the negotiations, which started on 27 September 2002, between the European

Commission (EC) and the ACP Group as a whole. The second phase of substantive negotiations would be conducted at regional level.

The objectives of this first phase were to define the format, structure and principles for the negotiations for all ACP countries. The EC would have preferred to engage directly with ACP regions, so as to move ahead with the content of the negotiations. A couple of ACP regions, notably in West Africa and to a lesser extent Central Africa were also keen on starting bilateral negotiations.[5] But not all regional groupings were clearly identified yet for the negotiations.[6] More importantly, many ACP countries believed that adopting a unified approach would strengthen their bargaining position. They were also trying to 'buy time' to build their own negotiating capacity before engaging with the EU. This latter argument probably weighed heavily in the decision of the EU to accept an initial all-ACP round. The European Commission did not try in any case to engage in substantive discussion, let alone negotiations, with the ACP at this stage. As for the ACP Group, they made a serious attempt to present and defend a united front based on strong development concerns. But internal tensions, between the ACP Secretariat and the ACP group of ambassadors in Brussels, soon emerged. The ACP Secretariat was eager to play a central role in the conduct of this first phase, and was therefore reluctant to reach out to potential allies, political or technical, to strengthen the position of the ACP Group. Instead, it tried to lead the process alone, which quickly turned out to be rather ineffective, mainly due to its lack of capacity and somewhat weak political credibility. As for the ACP ambassadors, too many were looking to raise their profile as key negotiators, while lacking the technical expertise and political vision to do so. More surprisingly, ACP regional groupings, which were destined to be the pillars of the EPA negotiations, were partly sidelined during this first all-ACP phase. This certainly greatly contributed to undermine the credibility and thus partly the legitimacy of the first phase of all-ACP 'negotiations', which never really constituted real negotiations. Regions were quietly waiting for their time to play a lead role, when not expressively calling for an earlier start of the regional negotiations, as in the case of West and Central Africa.[7]

The difficulties of this first phase illustrate the problems of the ACP to speak with one voice. The ACP Group had no experience in formal trade negotiations, let alone any capacity to do so. They also illustrate the lack of trust of many ACP with the EU, and yet the need by some to show good will towards the European Commission, in the hope to benefit from greater sympathy and perhaps a better

---

5   They did have informal bilateral talks with the then European Trade Commissioner Pascal Lamy, to the dismay and sometimes anger of other ACP members.

6   This is notably the case for the overlapping regional configurations of the Common Market for Eastern and Southern Africa (COMESA) and the Southern African Development Community (SADC), which initially considered forming a joint negotiating grouping.

7   In an ironic twist of history, these two regions are probably in Africa the furthest away from reaching a regional agreement on EPA with the EU, as far as one can tell at the end of 2010.

treatment from the EU. These problems have marred the whole negotiations process until now.

The second phase of regional negotiations has started from October 2003, between the EU and the six self-determined ACP negotiating groupings (see Annex 3.1):

- Central Africa, with the Communauté Economique et Monétaire de l'Afrique Centrale (CEMAC), since 3 October 2003;
- West Africa, with the Economic Community of West African States (ECOWAS), which includes the francophone West African Economic and Monetary Union (WAEMU/UEMOA), since 6 October 2003;
- Eastern and Southern Africa (ESA), since 7 February 2004;
- The Caribbean, with the Caribbean Forum of ACP States (CARIFORUM), which comprises the Caribbean Community (CARICOM) and the Dominican Republic, since 16 April 2004;
- Southern Africa, with some countries of the Southern African Development Community (SADC), which includes the Southern Africa Customs Union (SACU), since 8 July 2004; and
- Pacific ACP States (PACP), since 10 September 2004.

This configuration has been rather stable during the negotiations, though with some modifications. South Africa, which is already part of a free trade agreement with the EU, the Trade, Development and Cooperation Agreement (TDCA), negotiated during the late 1990s and implemented since 2000,[8] asked to join the SADC EPA negotiations in 2006, and was accepted by the EU in this setting one year later, in February 2007. The Democratic Republic of Congo (DRC) has been very passive for most of the negotiations, and there was some confusion at a time as to whether it would remain in the ESA configuration or would join the Central Africa EPA grouping, which it ultimately did in 2007. Finally, countries of the East African Community decided, in the summer of 2007, to come together to present their own common liberalisation schedule, though they have kept close ties with the ESA grouping.

Initial EPA negotiations at the regional level focused on the framework for an EPA, technical barriers to trade and SPS measures, and the regional integration process of the ACP regions concerned. This latter issue is rather surprising in the context of formal trade negotiations. The rationale was for the EU to better understand the regional integration dynamics so as to anchor the EPA in the regional context and ambitions. The EPA negotiations did therefore help the ACP countries to better focus on their own regional integration process. But these talks on regional integration did not constitute any form of negotiation of course.

---

8 For a discussion on the asymmetry of the TDCA negotiations of South Africa with the EU, and potential lessons for the ACP-EU EPA negotiations, see Bilal and Laporte (2004).

Another important cornerstone of the EPA negotiation process has been the development dimension of the EPAs. A discussed in Sections 3 and 6, the EU envisaged EPAs as tools for development in their own right. While the EU has always recognised the need for accompanying support measures to facilitate adjustments required by the EPA and accompanying reforms, it has until the end of 2006 contended that development cooperation was not part of the EPA negotiations. This should be covered by the development cooperation pillar of the Cotonou Agreement, under the European Development Fund (EDF), which the EU claimed was significantly increased for that purpose. Instead, the EU put in place Regional Preparatory Task Forces (RPTF) to facilitate the discussion on aid needs and allocations, in parallel, but not formally connected to, the EPA negotiations.

The ACP, for their part, have always insisted on the need for *additional* provision of aid by the EU, to help them face the additional costs that EPA implementation would generate. This, they argue, should be an integral and key part of the EPA negotiations, which would indeed condition their capacity to commit to an EPA and determine the level of ambition pursued within this EPA.

The EU has always rejected their claim, which has a consequence became a major issue of disagreement and even resentment between many ACP countries and the EU. The European Commission did finally accept though, but at the end of 2006 only, the need to explicitly acknowledge the call for additional development assistance in the text of the EPA. The development cooperation chapter included in various EPAs thus mention the EU collective responsibility to look for additional funding to accompany the EPA implementation and reform process. But it falls short of any binding commitment on the EU, let alone in terms of financial commitments. All provisions are couched in a best endeavour language.

Serious negotiations on market opening and specific liberalisation schedule commitments, a key element for any FTA, did not start before the end of 2006, and in most cases 2007. This is very late in a five-year process due to be concluded by the end of 2007. In March 2007, the then EU Trade Commissioner Peter Mandelson publicly set the criteria for reciprocal trade liberalisation. The EU would liberalise all its trade, provided duty-free quota-free market access under an EPA, but would require the ACP to liberalise at least 80 per cent of their imports from the EU over a maximum period of 15 years.

It is also in the first half of 2007 that the formal EPA Review foreseen by Article 37(4) of the Cotonou Agreement was finally concluded. Internal reviews conducted by the various ACP regions all highlighted the major capacity constraints faced by EPA negotiators and the major challenges they had to face (including insufficient technical preparedness and political leadership).[9] In contrast, the formal joint EU–ACP Review concluded, in May 2007, that in spite of some difficulties, the EPA process was well on track and just needed to speed up to be concluded by the agreed deadline at the end of 2007 (see Council of the European Union 2007b).

---

9 For an overview, see ECDPM (2007).

After an intense and at times acrimonious few months of negotiations, 2007 ended with most ACP countries failing, or unwilling, to conclude an agreement with the EU (see Section 4 for a discussion). Only the Caribbean region concluded an EPA as initially foreseen, whereas only some 20 other ACP countries concluded interim agreements, i.e. goods-only FTAs, mainly to preserve their preferential access to the EU market (see Section 5). As of 1 January 2008, the unilateral preferences under the Cotonou Agreement have ceased to exist. ACP countries have thus been trading with the EU under one of the following regimes: an (interim) EPA, EBA, the standard GSP or the TDCA for South Africa.

Since 2008, negotiations have continued at a slow pace (see Section 6). By early 2011, none of the African or Pacific ACP countries had concluded a final EPA with the EU.

The EPA agenda: diverging interests

The main rationale given for EPAs are threefold: a focus on using the agreements as 'tools for development', an emphasis within the agreements on enhancing regional integration through agreements that are negotiated at the regional level, and a trade regime that is securely compliant with WTO rules. The central feature of the agreements is a shift from a non-reciprocal trading regime – under which ACP countries could export duty-free to the EU while maintaining their own tariffs on EU imports – to one based on reciprocal liberalisation in trade in goods, albeit with flexibilities allowing the ACP side to liberalise over a certain period of time and to retain tariffs on a certain proportion of goods, in line with WTO rules. In addition to customs duties, the agreements also cover a number of other commitments governing trade in goods, relating *inter alia* to the removal of import charges, elimination of export taxes, safeguard measures, non-tariff barriers and general exceptions, as well as to rules of origin and development assistance. Trade in services and a number of trade-related issues could also be covered in a final EPA.

While there is a formal consensus between the ACP and the EU on the basic rationale for an EPA, the incentives and scope of ambitions vary depending on the actors.

It can be argued that the EPA project, proposed by the European Commission in 1996 (European Commission 1996), was the result of an ambitious vision. ACP countries would be given the chance to stamp out poverty by reforming their economies and institutions, and adjusting their infrastructure and production capacities. Moreover, the creation of bigger markets and regional cooperation would allow the ACP to benefit from the size of the new arrangement. By establishing an all-encompassing economic partnership, the EU could effectively stimulate, support and anchor regional integration, reform and the restructuring processes in the ACP. Indeed, the EU believes that, in complement to regionalism among developing countries, regional integration between developed and developing countries and regions can be extremely beneficial. The EU therefore promotes both North-South agreements, and building on Southern regional integration, what it calls South-South-North FTA (European Commission 2002). EPAs are such ambitious South-South-North agreements that could thus act as a catalyst for development.

But far from embracing this vision, many ACP actors and civil society actors have vividly contested it over the years. More pragmatic considerations – such as making the ACP-EU preferential trade regime compatible with WTO rules while at the same time maintaining EU interests have been advanced to explain the EPA agenda. There is wide spectrum of positions that have been expressed on the EPA agenda.

At one extreme stand the 'EPA enthusiasts', led in a rather lonely way by the European Commission (and few Caribbean EPA negotiators). It is by their sheer scope and depth of ambition that EPAs can effectively contribute to address some of the systemic impediments to economic development in ACP countries. In particular, EPAs can foster the creation of a business-friendly environment that, with the appropriate regulatory framework, can in turn lead to sustainable development in the ACP. EPAs, by their regional coverage, by encompassing a broad agenda for extensive trade liberalisation, including goods and services, by addressing nominal as well as technical barriers to trade, and most importantly, by tackling behind-the-border issues such as investment and competition rules, public procurement, intellectual property rights and trade facilitation issues, are believed to be effective instruments to stimulate endogenous growth in Africa. Combined with strong commitments on social, labour and environmental rules and accompanied by appropriate levels of development cooperation, as repeatedly pledged by the EU, EPAs could effectively stimulate sustainable development. EPAs could also play a critical role by providing a credible international guarantee against future backlashes and policy reversals that would erode the prospects for sustainable domestic growth. Or at least so goes the argument.

The direct consequence for the negotiation process is that regional final and comprehensive EPAs should be concluded as soon as possible with the remaining African and Pacific ACP regions concerned. The global financial and economic crises, combined with previous food and energy crises, though having their origin outside the developing counties, have further stressed the need for ACP countries and regions to embark in reforms that would enhanced their sustainable and equitable development; a reform dynamics which could be stimulated, or at least strengthened, by the conclusion and timely implementation of comprehensive EPAs. These arguments explain why the European Commission has been so persistent over the years, and in spite of serious setbacks, in its efforts to conclude EPAs: (1) at the regional level; (2) liberalising most of the trade over a reasonable period of time; (3) comprehensive in their scope, with significant commitments in services and on trade-related issues; (4) in a timely manner, avoiding delays in finalising negotiations, signing and ratifying and implementing the agreements;

and (5) accompanied by appropriate measures, including regional Aid for Trade (AfT) packages.

At the other end of the policy spectrum stand the 'EPA fearful' or 'EPA sceptics' (ICCO 2008, Oxfam 2008, South Centre 2010, Weller and Ulmer 2008). They tend to view EPAs as another attempt by developed countries, in this case Europe, to impose an obsolete model of development based on too rigid neo-classical recipes that ignore key lessons from both the historical development of rich nations (Reinert 2007) and recent experiences in supporting developing countries, notably through the Washington consensus which many consider as obsolete (Rodrik 2007, Serra and Stiglitz 2008).[10] In a nutshell, some critics claim that EPAs, with their liberal agenda forced upon Africa would exacerbate, rather than alleviate poverty and hinder sustainable development. While serving EU economic, and in particular business, interest, the new trade policy and regulatory framework embodied in the EPA would ultimately undermine the African ACP countries ability to pursue their own development strategy, including through regional integration, at a pace and level of ambitions that match their objectives and capacities, not the diktat of the EU agenda. In particular, they argue that opening up local markets to international competition from EU products would significantly contribute to put domestic production under pressure, as it would not be able to compete against EU production. Increased access to the EU market would also prove of little value if productive capacity and domestic infrastructure are not significantly enhanced. In addition, the removal of custom duties from EU imports would reduce fiscal revenues and thus exacerbate problems of tightened budgetary and debt management. This, combined with liberal regulatory commitments under the EPA, would in turn reduce the capacity of ACP governments to pro-actively intervene in their domestic economies, through appropriate industrial policy measures, targeted domestic subsidies and export taxes, as well as specific social programmes. More broadly, the EPA sceptics fear that EPAs would unduly limit the policy space required by ACP countries and regions to pursue their own development strategies while at the same time further exposing them to predatory behaviour from Europe interests and international shocks, such as the current financial, economic, food or energy crises (Reid Smith 2009). Such concerns were echoed by the United Nations Commission, which highlighted the risks that liberalisation and de-regulation in some trade agreements may pose for the economic prosperity of the developing countries concerned (United Nations 2009).[11] Last, but not least,

---

10   At the last G-20 Summit, the UK Prime Minister himself, Gordon Brown, claimed that the 'old Washington consensus is over' (see for instance Painter 2009).

11   Similarly, in a recent report on the Caribbean experience, the World Bank, while recognising that 'Trade liberalization under the EPA may have significant economic and social gains for the Caribbean region', notably in services, warned that 'trade liberalization in the Caribbean is being implemented in a fragile macroeconomic and structural environment. Trade liberalization (and more specifically the EPA process) should pay more attention to these constraints, which go beyond trade issues per se and cover a large

EPAs have been accused of undermining regional integration processes instead of strengthening them. Several reasons have been advanced,[12] including that EPAs:

- put undue pressures on the weak institutional capacity of most regional organisations;
- create tensions among regional members who may have divergent interests and have no experience in negotiating collectively as a regional grouping an agreement with a major trading partner;
- do not respect the pace and scope and own agenda of some regional integration processes;
- unduly constrain the regional configuration of ACP integration processes;
- split regions along diverging positions on the EPA.

Most ACP countries have shared many of these fears. However, some governments, in particular in the Caribbean (and its regional team of negotiators in the Caribbean Regional Negotiation Machinery), as well as in some African countries (such as Mauritius), have shared the grand design of an EPA as a tool to foster or accompany domestic reforms. In fact, irrespective of the many critics, it has been widely acknowledge, in the ACP like in the EU, that for the EPA vision of development to succeed, ACP countries and regions must be willing to embark on an ambitious reform agenda for development. EPAs alone cannot transform ACP economies, but could encourage and accompany the changes. Not surprisingly, reformers' governments have been more positive about the opportunities of an EPA that more static or conservative ones. However, many ACP countries have claimed that their reforms agenda for development has not been supported by the EPA process, as pushed by the EU, but on the contrary could be seriously derailed by it.

As a result, most ACP countries have engaged in EPA negotiations with reluctance. The prime objective has been to maintain their preferential market access to the EU while making minimal commitments in terms of opening markets or regulatory reforms (including on the so-called trade-related issues). EPAs are generally not perceived as an opportunity, but as destiny, 'the price which must be paid to continue to export to Europe' – the main trading partner for many ACP countries (see Figure 3.3). The EU is also the ACP main provider of development assistance. The prospect of getting additional aid, though arguably illusionary in practice, has been a string factor for ACP countries to engage in and for few of them conclude EPA negotiations. Worse, the fear of falling out of the EU's favours, and thus receive less aid in future, has been and remain a strong factor for many ACP countries engagement in the EPA process. This has been the case for many

---

range of issues, such as macroeconomic imbalances, small economic size, infrastructure deficiencies, and economic vulnerability of the Caribbean.' (World Bank – OAS 2009: ix)

12   For a discussion on EPAs and regional integration, see for instance Bilal and Braun-Munzinger (2008), Commission for Africa (2005), Faivre-Dupaigre (2007), Keet (2010) and Ukaoha (2009), among others.

ACP LDCs, which already benefit from duty-free and quota-free market access to the EU under the EBA. In terms of trade preferences, the EPA is of little benefit to them, with the exception of rules of origin, which are more favourable for some products under the EPA than the EBA.[13] For most ACP LDCs, negotiations on an EPA with the EU have not been triggered by trade considerations or more ambitious reform agenda, but by the imperative of keeping a good relationship with the EU.

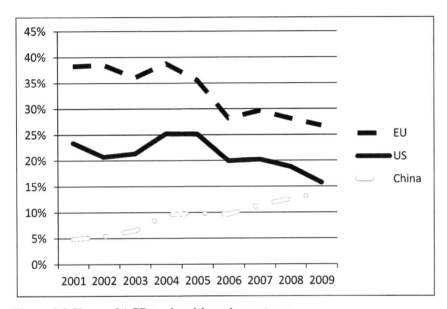

Figure 3.3 Share of ACP trade with main partners

Source: ITC Trade Map

A tense process

The challenges of the highly asymmetric negotiation process between the ACP and the EU led to crystallised tensions in 2006 and in particular in 2007, as the deadline for an agreement came in sight. By October-November 2007, however, none of the African regions and the Pacific were in a position to conclude a full EPA. The ACP therefore asked for an alternative to EPAs that would safeguard market access from 2008 onwards. Proposals ranged from an extension of the Cotonou preferences (through a formal request for a prolongation of the WTO waiver) to the granting of GSP+ preferences to all ACP countries (see Bartels 2007; Bilal 2007; Bilal and Rampa 2006; Bouët, Laborde and Mevel 2007; Sharman 2005;

---

13   For a discussion and further references, see Bilal (2008).

and Stevens 2007). The European Commission however refused such approaches and stressed that failure to reach agreement by the end of the year would not spur the EU to engage in an alternative strategy. The EU insisted instead on abiding by the letter of the WTO rules and on not seeking any further derogation (see ICTSD/ECDPM 2007). As indicated before, the only alternative trade regimes available for those ACP countries not signing an EPA has thus been EBA for LDCs and the standard GSP for others. For non-LDC ACP countries the GSP offers less favourable conditions, notably as it does not cover key products such as sugar and bananas. Market access has not been such a pivotal issue for LDCs as under the EBA initiative LDCs benefit from duty-free and quota-free access to the EU, although the regime has more stringent rules of origin than those provided under the Cotonou preferences (see ODI 2007).

As it became clear that EPAs would not be concluded by the target date of 31 December 2007, the European Commission issued a communication on 23 October 2007, in which it proposed to conclude WTO-compatible interim agreements (that cover trade in goods as a minimum requirement) to safeguard preferential market access for non-LDC countries from 1 January 2008 and allow for more time to negotiate on outstanding issues. These interim agreements could be signed at regional, sub-regional or national level.

The interim agreements proposed by the European Commission, focused on an FTA on goods, provided a legal alternative to the conclusion by the end of 2007 of comprehensive EPAs, as originally envisaged. However, this proposal maintained the pressure on ACP non-LDCs to conclude an FTA compatible with GATT Article XXIV by the end of 2007 if they did not want to face new protection measures by the EU.

These market access considerations are key to understanding why some ACP countries have initialled an interim agreement with the EU, while others have not. In Africa, all non-LDCs have concluded such deals, with the exception of oil rich countries (Congo, Gabon and Nigeria) and South Africa, which already has an FTA with the EU, the TDCA. Their concerns related mainly to preserving preferences for a limited number of commodities, notably bananas (e.g. Cameroon, Côte d'Ivoire), sugar (e.g. Mauritius, Swaziland), beef (e.g. Namibia), and fisheries (e.g. Seychelles, Mauritius). With regard to LDCs, those that have initialled an interim agreement have done so in the context of a regional agreement, as in the case of EAC (East African Community), and/or because they had some specific concerns related to less favourable rules of origin for certain products under EBA, as in the case of the small islands in the Indian Ocean Commission for fisheries, or Lesotho with clothing and textiles.

Although the interim agreements offered ACP countries an opportunity to temporarily safeguard market access, the European Commission has been accused of pushing ACP countries into signing what are *de facto* simply FTAs. Some have interpreted this as the EU showing its real face after years of empty rhetoric, while others considered this interim approach merely as a face-saving exercise that allows the EU to avoid re-imposing tariffs on ACP countries, thereby buying time to negotiate full EPAs without pressure from the WTO.

The EU defends its approach and interpreted the signing of several interim agreements in late 2007 as significant progress. According to its argument the interim deals are stepping stones towards comprehensive regional EPAs. The European Commission criticised the 'myths and fictions' that surrounded the EPA debate (European Commission 2008), which according to the then Trade Commissioner Peter Mandelson has been 'subjected to an aggressive NGO (non-governmental organisation) campaign' (quoted in Cronin (2007)). He further criticised NGOs for 'show[ing] no respect for the many ACP negotiators and reform-minded ministers who have worked hard with the EU to build agreements that do reflect development needs' (Cronin 2007).

The lack of progress in EPA negotiations since 2008, while most NGOs have shifted their attention away from EPAs, is a sign however that African and Pacific ACP countries are the ones reluctant to embrace the EPA agenda, irrespective of NGO campaigns. The European Commission has since recognised the lack of enthusiasm from many of its ACP partners (European Commission 2010). However, the assessment by the Directorate General (DG) Trade of the European Commission is that the Commission has failed to explain the merits of an EPA and thus loss the communication battle against anti-EPA campaigners. Apparently, the European Commission, and DG Trade in particular, does not seem able to admit that the EPA framework may not be suitable for many African and Pacific countries or regions. Several EU member states have now come to question the EPA policy pursued for the last eight years. But they do so behind closed doors, and keep supporting in public the European Commission's approach.

The harsh approach by the European Commission and the tense process during the run up to the end of 2007 deadline was real and certainly soured relations between the EU and the ACP.

Although the European Commission denies having exerted any pressure, there are plenty of ACP accounts to the contrary. The ACP Council of Ministers December 2007 'deplore[d] the enormous pressure that has been brought to bear on the ACP States by the European Commission to initial the interim trade arrangements, contrary to the spirit of the ACP-EU partnership' (ACP Council of Ministers 2007), in a process characterised by the ACP Secretary General Sir John Kaputin as 'fraught with panic, confusion and disagreements'.[14] Many ACP Heads of State and Ministers have publicly expressed their disquiet over these EPA negotiations.[15] Similarly, the Assembly of the African Union expressed its 'concern that the

---

14   See interview with ACP Secretary General Sir John Kaputin in Trade Negotiations Insights (2008).

15   The Ministerial Committee of ECOWAS on 17 December 2007 similarly 'deplored the pressure being exerted by the European Commission', whereas Guyana President Bharrat Jagdeo accused the EU of 'bully[ing] the countries into meeting the deadlines' (Stabroek news 2008).

process leading to the conclusion of Interim Economic Partnership Agreements did not build on what was negotiated earlier and in particular that political and economic pressures are being exerted by the European Commission on African countries to initial Interim Economic Partnership Agreements' (Assembly of the African Union 2008).

The then European Trade Commissioner Peter Mandelson, in particular, has been perceived not only as a 'hard line' negotiator but also as being disrespectful to ACP negotiators and NGO representatives. Then European Development Commissioner Louis Michel was also accused of putting European interests at the expense of development. Being asked about South Africa's reluctance to agree on a most-favoured nation (MFN) clause (see Section 5), he was quoted as saying: 'Evidently, it is a question of national sovereignty. But it's also a question of sovereignty for Europe. The European Commission and our member states provide 56 per cent of all development assistance in the world. It is difficult to say that Europe should let our partner countries treat our economic adversaries better than us. *We are generous but not naïve.*'[16]

In addition to these general perceptions, concrete cases running counter to the partnership principle have been reported by observers and negotiators throughout the regions. In the Pacific region, reportedly, about ten countries were ready to sign late 2007, but by then end of November only two countries that are highly dependent on a few commodities exports to Europe, namely Fiji and PNG (Papua New Guinea), were left. A meeting with the European Commission mid-October 2007 was described as 'a humiliation' by Pacific officials, who reportedly felt 'insulted and disgusted'. According to reports, Mandelson threatened to walk out unless ministers were prepared to negotiate on the outstanding issues, so that they 'gave in on virtually every issue' (see Primack 2007).

According to observers in the CEMAC region, during the ministerial conference with the EU at the end of October, the European Commission threatened to suspend or 'delay' programming of regional EDF envelopes and raise tariffs to GSP level. In order to bypass differences within the region the European Commission further proposed to the Central African negotiation party to limit the CEMAC negotiation team to a handful of willing experts (see Ulmer 2007). Even in the Caribbean region, which was praised by the Commission as exemplary for its commitment and progress, tensions were exacerbated. In what has been described as 'as a particularly brutal meeting' late December, the European Commission threatened to impose GSP tariffs if the Caribbean could not improve its market access offer (see Jessop 2007). The European Commission has further been accused of trying to play regions and countries off against each other. Reportedly, EC negotiators have in some cases claimed progress on certain contentious areas (agreement on certain provisions) in one region, to convince another to agree to the same. According to several actors this negotiation stance illustrated the Commission's attempts to secure an EPA signature at any price.

---

16   Emphasis added; see IPS News (2008).

The appointment of Catherine Ashton as European Commissioner for Trade in October 2008, succeeding Peter Mandelson, certainly contributed to reduce tensions between the EU and the ACP. Her conciliatory approach has been welcomed by ACP policy-makers. However, it has not led to any concrete change in the EU stance on EPAs. Under her watch, negotiations towards a final EPA did not progress much. Several DG Trade officials privately characterise her tenure as a loss of time, with no clear political leadership to conduct the EPA negotiations. The new Trade Commissioner Karel De Gucht has not managed to achieve much further progress in 2010. He has initially adopted a wait-and-see attitude for several months. More recently, he seems to be leaning towards a continuation of the long-standing EU approach on EPAs, and has so far failed to provide any new impetus or direction in the negotiations.

The EPA negotiations have also strained relations at the regional level. Since 2007, the European Commission has switched from a regional to a double approach with negotiations at both national and regional levels. Regional market access offers were foreseen, but when it became apparent in the second half of 2007 that it would not be possible to reach an agreement, as a fallback position, the European Commission started conducting bilateral negotiations in parallel with single countries and sub-regions (see for instance Makhan 2009, and Watson 2007). In West Africa, the European Commission reportedly sent regional drafts to ECOWAS and the WAEMU/UEMOA, as well as national drafts to Ghana and Côte d'Ivoire. In Central Africa the European Commission changed its tactics and negotiated a bilateral interim agreement with Cameroon, without involving CEMAC.

According to the European Commission this was the only WTO-compatible way of securing market access, one of the major concerns of most ACP countries. The European Commission repeatedly highlighted its commitment to negotiate comprehensive full regional EPAs and defended the interim agreements as stepping-stones towards full regional agreements specifically drafted to provide a basis for negotiations towards full regional EPAs to continue. Yet, by adopting the double approach, the European Commission by-passed the formal regional negotiation structures and was therefore accused of actively weakening regional solidarity. The fragmentation of countries has led to tensions within the regions and put non-LDCs in an extremely difficult situation. They had to make the difficult choice of either concluding an agreement individually, thus disrupting regional integration, a politically costly option, or align with the region and fall back to GSP, an economically costly option.[17] However, some countries were also more inclined to favour national interests over those of the region, as they did not

---

17   This dilemma has been especially striking for Cameroun in Central Africa, and Cote d'Ivoire and Ghana in West Africa. Not surprisingly, none of these countries has yet the intension to implement their interim EPA, hoping instead to negotiate a final EPA at the regional level with the EU (see also Section 5).

see the need to find a regional compromise on their exclusion baskets. This is the case notably of many ESA signatories, which are not yet sufficiently integrated.

The EPA process clearly exposed the weak regional cohesion in most EPA regions in which national interests still prevail over regional integration agendas.

Conducting interim agreements bilaterally provided the opportunity to also safeguard market access in those regions were regional solutions were not possible in the remaining time. The bilateral approach adopted by the EC and some ACP counterparts, however, is clearly at odds with one of the key objectives of the EPAs, which is to build on and reinforce regional integration.

Negotiations in 2008 have aimed at reconciling the actual EPA process with its initial objective of fostering regional integration in the ACP. Despite interim agreements having been concluded on a bilateral basis in several cases, in 2008 negotiations have been taking place at regional level again in all groups. However, different starting situations and interests among members of African and Pacific negotiating regions remain. The signature and implementation of interim EPAs have proved difficult, and at times controversial (see Section 5). As a result, EPA negotiations are still ongoing in 2011.

The ACP countries have their share of responsibility as well in the tortuous EPA process. Many left contentious or difficult issues until the end of the formal negotiations period in 2007. The EU cannot be held accountable for the fact that some market access offers were prepared in a rush and under great pressure, as the countries and regions knew about the 2007 deadline for years. The ESA region reportedly met in mid-October 2007 in Madagascar in an attempt to create a unified regional market access offer. As more countries submitted their national lists of sensitive products it became apparent that it would be impossible to reach a unified position, given that the regional list of sensitive products covered over 90 per cent of trade with the EU (see Watson 2007). With time running out, no common position could be reached. But the issues of market access could have been addressed earlier.

In the end, it seems that those countries and regions, which have shown strong commitment to the EPA process and were better prepared, will be more likely to benefit from the agreements.

A deadline can often be regarded as a stimulus for the parties to move ahead and may have helped to put trade higher on the agenda of policy-makers. But both parties certainly started too late to negotiate on substantive issues while spending the initial years discussing systemic questions without being able to reach agreement. The push given by the looming deadline may thus have helped to propel both parties to the negotiating table and to focus on the major issues (notably market access, a core issue in any FTA). The current absence of new binding deadline in the EPA process may explain why so little progress has been achieved in the negotiations since 2008. However, the 2007 events also demonstrated that too much pressure in an asymmetric relationship like that between the EU and the ACP, can lead to a lot of suspicion and a lack of ownership of the final result and is certainly not conducive to a harmonious relationship. The EU therefore may have succeeded in getting some countries to conclude and then sign an (interim) EPA through pressure and the threat of imposing tariffs under the GSP. However, many ACP stakeholders have been left with the perception that the agreements have been externally imposed. As a consequence, there is a loss of domestic ownership and some African and Pacific governments seem since to have been be less willing to bring forward the process and related reforms.

In addition, the tense EPA negotiations process, with its 2007 'climax', has contributed to leave many with the perception that commercial and political interests, in both the EU and ACP countries, too often prevail over development concerns. It seems that largely pragmatic concerns with regard to preserving market access ultimately overshadow the outcome of the negotiations.

Main substantive outcomes

Out of the 77 ACP countries, only 37 have concluded some type of agreement and by the beginning of 2011, only 25 have confirmed their commitment by signing an agreement with the EU. Only the 15 CARICOM countries have agreed a comprehensive EPA, and this at a regional grouping, as initially envisaged, which they have all signed and are in the process of ratifying. The implementation process has barely started though. In parallel, negotiations towards final EPAs in Africa and the Pacific have been progressing only very slowly, when they have not been stalled.

Of the 41 ACP countries that have not initialled or signed an (interim) EPA, ten were non-LDCs and 31 were LDCs. As a result of the perceived stringent commitments that they were asked to make under the interim EPAs, these LDCs opted to continue to trade with the EU under the EBA, where they enjoyed duty free quota free market access, despite stricter rules of origin compared to those under the Lomé and Cotonou unilateral preferences and those obtained by interim EPA beneficiaries. This has been a major cause of concern as it has been felt that they were made worse off than under the previous Cotonou Agreement. The non-LDCs that did not initial an EPA shifted under the GSP scheme, which provides for unilateral preferential market access for all developing countries to the EU in a selected number of products. Although the GSP+ Scheme, which provides more preferences to support 'vulnerable' countries, is in principle open to all the ACP non-LDCs, none of them are currently eligible to it, given its strict conditionalities linked to the signature, ratification and implementation of human rights, core labour law and good governance conventions. Nigeria and Gabon have applied for GSP+ preferences but their requests were not granted since they have not ratified some of the Conventions under the Scheme (see ICTSD 2009). In all (interim) EPAs, the EU has granted duty-free quota-free market access for all ACP products under the EU Market Access Regulation 1528 related to EPAs, with a transitional period for rice and sugar as from 1 January 2008 (Council of the European

Union 2007c).[18] With regards to development, IEPAs contain provisions, aimed at assisting signatory countries in building capacity and in supporting countries in implementing the agreements. However, the agreements contain no binding financial commitments from the EU to provide additional resources that would help signatories meet the transitional costs linked to a fall in fiscal revenue as a result of liberalisation or to address supply side constraints.

Table 3.1 presents a synthetic overview of the scheme under which each ACP country trades with the EU as of the end of 2010, with some basic characteristics. In particular, the EPA negotiations have led to the following outcomes in the current seven EPA regional groupings.[19]

The CARIFORUM EPA covers *inter alia*, trade in goods, investment and trade in services, competition policy, transparency in government procurement, intellectual property right, fisheries and development. In addition to free market access for goods and improved rules of origin, the CARIFORUM region obtained a range of new market access concessions from the EU on investment and services (see Sauvé and Ward 2009, and Francis and Ullrich 2008). In terms of sectoral coverage, the EU has taken commitments in services on more than 90 per cent of the sectors (ranging from business services – including professional services, communications, construction, distribution, financial, transport, tourism and recreational services). In the field of investment (covering non-services products), the EU has opened almost all sectors for CARIFORUM states, with only targeted exclusions and limitations, often applicable only to its new member states. The coverage of goods liberalised by CARIFORUM countries amounts to 61.1 per cent of CARIFORUM imports from the EU in value over ten years, 82.7 per cent over 15 years (84.7 per cent of tariff lines) and 86.9 per cent over 25 years (90.2 per cent of tariff lines). Liberalisation started in 2011, after a three-year moratorium.[20] The first Joint CARIFORUM-EU EPA Council of Ministers was held at the margin of the EU-LAC (Latin America Caribbean) summit of Madrid in May 2010. This first meeting took important procedural steps to ensure the effective implementation

---

18   Council Regulation (EC) No. 1528/2007 of 20 December 2007 applying the arrangements for products originating in certain states which are part of the African, Caribbean and Pacific (ACP) Group of States provided for in agreements establishing, or leading to the establishment of, Economic Partnership Agreements (Council of the European Union 2007c).

19   For an analytical overview of the content of African ACP IEPAs, see notably Bilal and Stevens (2009), and World Bank (2009); for the Caribbean and Pacific regions, see Stevens, Kennan and Meyn (2009). For a series of articles on the outcomes of the 2007 EPA negotiations, see also ECDPM and ICTSD (2007). More relevant reports and studies are available at www.acp-eu-trade.org/library.

20   The main exclusions for sensitive products include: agricultural products (poultry and other meat, dairy products, certain fruits and vegetables), fishery products, food preparations (sauces, ice cream, syrup), beverages, ethanol, rum, vegetable oils, chemicals (paints/varnishes, perfumes, make up/cosmetics, soaps, shoe polish, glass/metal polishes, candles, disinfectants), furniture and parts, apparel (cotton pullovers/jerseys/cardigans).

of the EPA, including adopting rules of procedure for establishing the framework of the conduct of mechanisms established under the EPA. They also agreed on rules of procedure for the Joint CARIFORUM-EU Council, the CARIFORUM-EU Trade and Development Committee, special committees set up under the EPA, dispute settlement and code of conduct for arbitrators and mediators under the EPA. A CARIFORUM 'High Representative' was designated to the European Commission until December 2011.

The ESA region is a very diverse and heterogeneous group, which did not manage to maintain a fully cohesive approach, though it still offers a useful umbrella for EPA coordination. At the end of 2007, six ESA states initialled an interim EPA with the EU, but in August 2009, only four countries (Madagascar, Mauritius, Seychelles and Zimbabwe) signed the interim EPA, as Comoros and Zambia did not. By the end of 2010, only the Seychelles had ratified the Agreement. Those that have initialled the interim EPA have all submitted individual market access offers, with different liberalisation schedules and exclusion lists, although all offers were based on the Common External Tariff of the Common Market for Eastern and Southern Africa (COMESA), which had yet to be finalised. After a five-year preparatory period, tariffs will be dismantled over a period of ten years. While all countries are fully committed to conclude the final EPA, the region emphasised the need for appropriate sequencing between strengthening regional integration and completing negotiations among the countries of the region on key issues such as services and investment, before engaging on binding commitments with the EU. Although much progress has been achieved so far on the framework for an agreement on services (namely vis-à-vis a legal text), progress has been relatively slow regarding the market access component. On the proposal of the EU to have ambitious commitments on trade related issues, such as investment and Government Procurement, the region has so far argued that it was ready to have an agreement covering cooperation and strengthening capacity but was not ready to negotiate market access in these areas at this stage. On the issue of development, ESA has proposed a Development Matrix to the EU. Negotiations are ongoing on the need to prioritise the various projects included in the matrix.

The EAC countries left the ESA group to conclude an interim EPA with the EU in November 2007, according to which EAC will liberalise 82.6 per cent of imports from the EU by value over the next 25 years (including 80 per cent over the first 15 years), after a six-year moratorium. EAC decided to exclude products such as agricultural products, wines and spirits, chemicals, plastics, wood based paper, textiles and clothing, footwear, ceramic products, glassware, articles of base metal and vehicles. Despite pressure from the EU and several set dates for a ceremony, the EAC countries have not yet signed the agreement. Part of the challenge in concluding negotiations towards a final EPA relates to the lack of consensus on several contentious issues contained in the interim EPA (see below), in particular on important issues of export taxes, the much debated MFN clause, the flexibility for future tariff modifications that could arise as a result of the implementation of regional integration programmes and the development matrix. Some progress has however been achieved on the article relating to dispute settlement and the standstill clause. On other outstanding issues towards the final EPA, such as trade in services, investment, SPS measures, TBT, Customs and trade facilitation, there have been varying degrees of progress by the end of 2010.

In Central Africa, only Cameroon agreed, after intense pressure from the EU, to an interim EPA in December 2007, to prevent trade disruption for its main exports, namely aluminium, cocoa, bananas and other agricultural products, after the expiry of the WTO waiver. Cameroon made the minimal liberalisation commitment required by the EU: 80 per cent of its imports from the EU over 15 years, so as to exclude a number of agricultural and non-agricultural processed goods, mainly to ensure the protection of certain sensitive agricultural markets and industries but also to maintain fiscal revenues.[21] Although Cameroon signed the interim EPA on 15 January 2009, it has made a request to the EU to delay implementation, including its tariff dismantlement as set out in its IEPA until conclusion of a regional EPA agreement in order to not disrupt the customs union of CEMAC. The EU has yet to formally respond to this request. Further negotiations towards a final regional EPA have been at a standstill since. The region wants to negotiate a 60 per cent tariff liberalisation on goods only within a transition period of 20 years (including a five-year preparatory period before liberalisation begins) and to exclude all EU subsidised products from trade liberalisation and to strengthen safeguard measures and the use of export taxes on certain products to counter the negative effects of tariff dismantlement. While preparatory work is ongoing, formal real negotiations are due to restart only in 2011, after several postponements. It is clear however that the region has little interest, not to mention capacity, to conclude soon a regional EPA with the EU.

In West Africa, out of 16 countries (15 ECOWAS countries and Mauritania), only Côte d'Ivoire and Ghana agreed to an individual interim EPA with the EU in December 2007, to prevent disruption to their exports to the EU, in particular on cocoa, bananas and other agricultural products. Cote d'Ivoire signed the interim EPA in November 2008, but has unilaterally postponed its implementation, due to start in 2009, whereas Ghana had yet to sign its interim EPA by the end of 2010. Over the next 15 years, Cote d'Ivoire will liberalise 81 per cent of imports, while Ghana will liberalise 80 per cent of imports from the EU. Côte d'Ivoire and Ghana excluded a number of agricultural goods and non-agricultural processed goods from liberalisation, mainly to ensure the protection of certain sensitive agricultural markets and industries but also to maintain fiscal revenues. The exclusion lists of Côte d'Ivoire and Ghana are not identical as they reflect the respective situation in each country, although both Ghana and Côte d'Ivoire have excluded chicken and other meats, tomatoes, onions, sugar, tobacco, beer, and worn clothes. Côte d'Ivoire has also excluded cement, malt, gasoline and cars, while Ghana has

---

21   These include most types of meat, wines and spirits, malt, milk products, flour, certain vegetables, wood and wood products, used clothes and textiles, paints, and used tyres.

excluded wheat, frozen fish and industrial plastics. Some progress has been made in the negotiations towards the final EPA on trade in goods only and development, with rendezvous clauses aimed at expanding to 'remaining topics'. The region tabled a regional market access offer in March 2010, suggesting the possibility of opening up to a maximum of 70 per cent of their market (in terms of tariff lines and value of trade) over a period of 25 years after a five-year preparatory period, falling short of EU expectations. Little progress has been made up to 2011 regarding the inclusion of the MFN clause, rules of origin and the inclusion of a non-execution clause, as well as the critical question for the West Africa of the Community levy, which finances regional institutions. Regarding development, the West Africa region has prepared an EPA development programme (EPADP) to address development needs arising from an EPA, which would be included in the final EPA as an annex. The EPADP was initially estimated by West Africa at 9.5 billion euros over the next five years (see ECDPM 2010). On 10 May 2010, in the form of a Council Conclusion, the EU Ministers of development outlined their expected support to the EPADP. Besides reiterating commitments on AfT and aid effectiveness, the EU estimated that 'funds available for EPADP-related activities from all of its financing instruments over the next five years amount to at least 6.5 billion euros', while 'total aid for trade to West Africa from all donors can be projected to exceed 12 billion US dollars in the same period'. While the region welcomed EU's response, they however felt that the financial commitments would be insufficient to meet the needs of the EPADP.

The SADC region consists of 15 members, seven of which (Angola, Botswana, Lesotho, Mozambique, Namibia, Swaziland and South Africa[22]) are negotiating an EPA with the EU; but by the end of 2007, only five countries concluded an interim EPA (Botswana, Lesotho, Mozambique, Namibia and Swaziland), while only four countries did sign it in June 2009, Namibia abstaining to do so. South Africa did not join the agreement because of a series of disagreements on some of the key provisions of the text. Angola, a large oil producer, did not join the agreement either, showing little interest in an EPA. Botswana, Lesotho, Namibia and Swaziland will liberalise 86 per cent of EU imports over the next ten years. Mozambique will liberalise 81 per cent of imports excluding mainly goods in the agricultural, textile and processed agricultural sectors.

A key issue in the region is the integrity of the SACU[23] and the coherence of tariffs towards the EU among SACU members. The conclusion of interim EPAs has threatened the SACU integration process and mere existence. As a result from this very specific current state of affairs, and in order to safeguard regional integration processes, implementation of the IEPA has not started in the region. Much progress has been achieved in 2010 in the context of the regional

---

22   South Africa is currently trading with EU under the Trade, Development and Cooperation Agreement (TDCA) negotiated bilaterally between the parties in 1999.

23   According to Art. 31 of SACU Agreement, all SACU members have to negotiate and conclude trade agreements as a group.

negotiations with the EU towards a final EPA, to align Annex III of the SADC interim EPA with the market offer of the South Africa TDCA with the EU. But differences with the EU remained regarding the opportunity to cover services, as well as a number of other contentious issues, in spite of the progress achieved notably at the Swakopmund meeting in March 2009.

Finally, in the Pacific ACP (PACP) group, which accounts for only 0.06 per cent of trade with the EU, only the two major Pacific countries, PNG and Fiji, agreed on an interim EPA with the EU in November 2007, signed on 30 July 2009. By doing so, they have benefited, since 2008, from a landmark, new preferential rule of origin for the export of processed fish and marine products to the European market.[24] PNG will liberalise 88% of EU imports from the date of application of the agreement and excluded products from the most sensitive economic sectors (e.g. meat, fish, vegetables, furniture) and luxury products (jewellery). Fiji will liberalise 87 per cent of EU imports over 15 years and excluded products from the most sensitive economic sectors and those important for revenue purposes such as meat, fish, fruits and vegetables, alcohol, tubes and iron. In 2009, Niue, Samoa, Cook Islands and Micronesia presented market access offers to the EU for trade in goods based on liberalising between 70–75 per cent of their trade and with transition periods up to 25 years. The EU claimed that this was not yet acceptable and requested for further work on the offers. Such work has been ongoing since. Some progress has been made on a number of issues including food security, cooperation in agriculture, infant industry protection, export taxes, SPS and TBT provisions. On trade in services, the region maintained its refusal to negotiate liberalisation commitments before completing negotiations on services liberalisation at a regional level (i.e. within the *Pacific* Island Countries Trade Agreement (PICTA)) and to prevent any negative precedents in relation to ongoing trade negotiations with their main trading partners, Australia and New Zealand. Services would thus remain covered by a rendezvous clause.

---

24   In effect, fish, regardless of their origin, are deemed to originate from these Pacific ACP countries as long as they are transformed from being fresh or frozen into a pre-cooked, packaged and canned product in Fiji or PNG, which can then be exported to the EU free of duties and quotas.

Table 3.1 Overview of ACP trade regimes status with the EU (as of December 2010)

Regional Grouping	Members[1]	Trade Regime[2]	Liberalisation commitment[3]	Signature	Notification to WTO
ESA EPA	*Comoros*	IEPA	81%		
	Djibouti	EBA			
	Eritrea	EBA			
	Ethiopia	EBA			
	Madagascar	IEPA	81%	29/08/09	
	Malawi	EBA			
	Mauritius	IEPA	96%	29/08/09	
	Seychelles	IEPA	98%	29/08/09	
	Sudan	EBA			
	Zambia	IEPA	80%		
	Zimbabwe	IEPA	80%	29/08/09	
EAC EPA	*Burundi*	IEPA	82%		
	Kenya	IEPA	82%		
	Rwanda	IEPA	82%		
	Tanzania	IEPA	82%		
	Uganda	IEPA	82%		
SADC EPA	*Angola*	EBA			
	Botswana	IEPA	86%	04/06/09	
	Lesotho	IEPA	86%	04/06/09	
	Mozambique	IEPA	81%	15/06/09	
	Namibia	IEPA	86%	04/06/09	
	South Africa	TDCA	86%	11/10/99	02/11/2000
	Swaziland	IEPA	86%		
CEMAC EPA	Cameroon	IEPA	80%	15/01/09	24/09/09
	Chad	EBA			
	Cent. African Rep.	EBA			
	Congo	Standard GSP			
	DR Congo	EBA			
	Eq. Guinea	EBA			
	Gabon	Standard GSP			
	S. Tomé/Principe	EBA			

Table 3.1 Continued

Regional Grouping	Members[1]	Trade Regime[2]	Liberalisation commitment[3]	Signature	Notification to WTO
ECOWAS EPA	*Benin*	EBA			
	Burkina Faso	EBA			
	Cape Verde[4]	EBA			
	Côte d'Ivoire	IEPA	81%	26/11/08	11/12/08
	Gambia	EBA			
	Ghana	IEPA	80%		
	Guinea Bissau	EBA			
	Liberia	EBA			
	Mali	EBA			
	Mauritania	EBA			
	Niger	EBA			
	Nigeria	Standard GSP			
	Senegal	EBA			
	Sierra Leone	EBA			
	Togo	EBA			
PACP EPA	Cook Islands	Standard GSP			
	Fed. Micronesia	Standard GSP			
	Fiji	IEPA	87%	11/12/09	
	Kiribati	EBA			
	Marshall Islands	Standard GSP			
	Nauru	Standard GSP			
	Niue	Standard GSP			
	Palau	Standard GSP			
	Papua New Guinea	IEPA	88%	30/07/09	
	Samoa	EBA			
	Soloman Islands	EBA			
	Tonga	Standard GSP			
	Tuvalu	EBA			
	Vanuatu	EBA			

Regional Grouping	Members[1]	Trade Regime[2]	Liberalisation commitment[3]	Signature	Notification to WTO
CARIFORUM EPA	Antigua/Barbuda	EPA	87%	15/10/08	16/10/08
	Bahamas	EPA	87%	15/10/08	16/10/08
	Barbados	EPA	87%	15/10/08	16/10/08
	Belize	EPA	87%	15/10/08	16/10/08
	Dominica	EPA	87%	15/10/08	16/10/08
	Dominican Rep.	EPA	87%	15/10/08	16/10/08
	Grenada	EPA	87%	15/10/08	16/10/08
	Guyana	EPA	87%	21/10/08	16/10/08
	Haiti	EPA	87%	11/12/09	
	Jamaica	EPA	87%	15/10/08	16/10/08
	St Kitts/Nevis	EPA	87%	15/10/08	16/10/08
	St Lucia	EPA	87%	15/10/08	16/10/08
	St Vincent/Grenadines	EPA	87%	15/10/08	16/10/08
	Suriname	EPA	87%	15/10/08	16/10/08
	Trinidad/Tobago	EPA	87%	15/10/08	16/10/08

Notes

[1] Countries in italics are classified as LDCs.

[2] EPA: economic partnership agreement; IEPA: interim; EPA; EBA: Everything-But-Arms; GSP: generalised system of preferences; TDCA: Trade, Development and Cooperation Agreement.

[3] Estimates of goods trade liberalisation in EPA/IEPAs as reported by the European Commission (in percentage of value of imports from EU); for independent estimates, see Bilal and Stevens (2009) for Africa and Stevens et al. (2009) for the Caribbean and Pacific countries.

[4] Cape Verde has been classified as non-LDC since January 2008 but is able to export to the EU under the EBA initiative for a transitional period of three years.

Main substantive concerns in the ongoing negotiations

Three major categories of issues have remained of key concern to African (and Pacific) countries in the continuation of the EPA process since 2008: the regional dimension, the development dimension, and a number of critical provisions contained in the interim EPAs and deemed as contentious.

The 'regional dimension' has remained one of the main concerns throughout the EPA negotiations. Out the 20 African countries that have concluded interim or 'stepping stone' agreements, which cover only trade in goods, only the five from

EAC have done so on a regional basis. Arguably the most important unsettled issue in the negotiations towards a final EPA remains the linkage, in practical terms, between EPAs and regional integration. Ever since the start of negotiations in 2002, a great deal of emphasis has been put on ensuring that the EPAs ultimately served to enhance efforts at breaking down barriers to intra-regional trade and furthering integration (see Section 2 and 3). The benefits to be gained from the agreements as a catalyst of regional integration are still cited regularly as one of the main reasons for concluding EPAs. Since has been reiterated on numerous occasions by the EU Council:

> The Council reiterates that EPAs should primarily build upon, foster and support ACP regional integration processes, including the development of regional agricultural markets based on an adequate market regulatory framework, while promoting the development objectives and strategies of the individual countries of the regions and recognising the existing political and economic realities and existing regional integration processes, thus providing flexibility. The Council encourages ACP States to carry out the necessary reforms at the regional level so as to improve the basis for successful EPAs. (Council of the European Union 2007a)

For many reasons, however, the practical effect of EPAs on regional integration has so far been mixed. One of the biggest hurdles in the African context has been the problem of 'overlapping membership' of countries within multiple regional groupings, which meant that the regional EPAs configurations does not necessarily coincide with the various regional integration processes. Besides, while the EPAs should aim at strengthening regional integration, they have often been resented as an attempt by the EU, through the EPA agenda, to drive the integration dynamics at a pace and in a direction not necessarily shared by the regional members. At the same time, regional cohesiveness suffers with the existence of a viable alternative trade regime for LDCs with EBA, whereas neighbouring non-LDCs are faced with the less attractive GSP. Differences in domestic priorities for economic reforms, as well as long-standing intra-regional tensions – for example between some dominant players and some smaller, more vulnerable ones – have also played an important role in some regions, highlighting that decisions to forge closer economic ties are seldom a matter of economics alone, but have important political elements as well.

Another fundamental concern for Africa and the ACP in general has been the development dimension of the EPAs, or at times the perceived lack of it. The commitment to development-oriented EPAs, agreed upon by all the parties to the Cotonou Agreement, has been reiterated in numerous occasions by the key EU institutions – European Commission, European Parliament and the EU Council and its member states – as illustrated in Box 3.1.

Box 3.1 The EU stance on the development support to EPAs

The EU Council "recognizes that regional integration as well as EPAs may entail adjustments and reforms in ACP economies and policies. In order to help ACP regions, countries and local communities, including small producers, reap all their benefits, EU development assistance will accompany these processes."[1]

Following the EU approach to aid for trade, the Council has stressed the need for a coordinated response from the EU to needs identified by the ACP, "in accordance with the principles of aid effectiveness, complementarity, division of labour and local ownership" as articulated in the Paris Declaration on Aid Effectiveness and in the Code of Conduct on Complementarity and Division of Labour in Development Policy.[2] This is important notably to ensure "increased predictability in the planning and delivery of AfT contributions" and in view of "the need of avoiding gaps in the geographical coverage of AfT". The Council further stressed that coordination and predictability "are essential for reaching the agreed level of ACP share in the collective increase of Trade Related Assistance (TRA) and for further stepping up efforts on the wider AfT agenda (productive capacity building, trade-related infrastructure, trade adjustment)", and thus "encourages the Commission and the Member States to continue working together to this purpose".

The European Parliament has also been particularly active in setting out its view of these challenges, notably by noting that "the adjustment costs resulting from the EPAs will have a significant impact on the development of ACP countries, which, whilst difficult to predict, will consist of direct impact through the loss of customs duties and the costs of regulatory reform and enforcement to comply with the wide range of regulations stipulated in the EPA, and indirect impact through the costs necessary for adaptation or social support in the areas of employment, skills enhancement, production, export diversification and reform of public financial management. [...]. The development impact of EPAs will result from their effects on:

— the reduction of net customs revenues and its effect on the budgets of the ACP States,
— the improvement of the supply of ACP countries' economies and provision of customers with imported EU products,
— growing exports to the EU from ACP countries through improved Rules of Origin, which would lead to economic growth, more employment, and increased state revenue which could be used to fund social measures,
— regional integration in the ACP regions, which has the capacity to improve the framework for economic development and would therefore contribute to economic growth,
— the successful use of financing for Aid for Trade in connection with the EPAs,
— the implementation of reform measures in the ACP countries, in particular as regards public finance management, collection of customs duties and establishment of a new tax revenue system."[3]

This section of the European Parliament resolution was also restated verbatim in a resolution of the ACP-EU Joint Parliamentary Assembly when they met in Prague in April 2009.[4]

Notes
[1] Conclusions of the 2870th External Relations Council meeting – Conclusions of the Council on Economic Partnership Agreements (EPAs), May 2008; [2] See GAERC Conclusions of 27 May 2008 and 10 November 2008; [3] European Parliament resolution on the development impact of Economic Partnership Agreements (EPAs), (2008/2170(INI)), 5 February 2009. www.europarl.europa.eu/sides/getDoc.do?type=TA&reference=P6-TA-2009-0051&language=EN; [4] Resolution of the ACP-EU Joint Parliamentary Assembly on EPAs and their impact on ACP States, Prague (Czech Republic) from 6 to 9 April 2009 http://www.europarl.europa.eu/intcoop/acp/60_17/pdf/re_epas_en.pdf.

This development dimension can be articulated along three distinct but closely-linked axes:

- EPA commitments to liberalise trade and establish clear rules for the promotion of a better business environment, taking into account the exclusions and transition periods available to ACP countries for tariff liberalisation and for implementation of other parts of the agreement, and flexibilities in areas such as safeguards and infant industry protection;
- the accompanying policies and reforms to institutions and structures that are necessary to take advantage of the new trading opportunities, and
- the provision of appropriate development support to cover adjustment costs, carry out reforms and implement the agreement.

Within this framework, the Parties have also recognised the clear need for the provision of development assistance to build capacity, and implement the EPA and accompanying reforms. The EU has committed to provide EPA-related development assistance as part of the AfT initiative, through the European Development Fund and other EU institutions and member states sources. However, African parties have called for larger and more comprehensive explicit binding commitments from the EU in the framework of the EPA.

Finally, a number of 'contentious' issues were identified in the interim EPAs concluded by many African states. In 2008, the AU Ministers of Trade and Finance identified a non-exhaustive list of those issues deemed 'contentious' that caused serious concerns in most African regions.[25] The EU has been implicitly accused of forcing upon ACP countries some provisions, which ultimately had to be accepted without much negotiation in order to reach an agreement by the deadline of the end of 2007. While the degree of 'contentiousness' varies across the different regions and among the different countries within the same region, all the regions have unanimously expressed the need to review those clauses to provide more flexibility in the context of the final EPAs, notably in order to take into account their special development needs.[26] These critical issues include, amongst others, concerns about market access, including definition of 'substantially all trade' and transitional periods for tariff liberalisation, quantitative restrictions, export taxes, the standstill clause, regional levies, bilateral safeguards, agricultural safeguards and food security, the treatment of Infant Industry, the most-favoured nation clause, the non-execution clause, the definition of parties and rules of origin.

Initially, most of the contentious and critical issues were considered to be questions that could be resolved at the technical level. Indeed, most countries and regions requested additional flexibility from the EU to take into account their

---

25   See African Union (2008). Concerns over the substance of the EPA process have been expressed in many other occasions, including the Elements for an ACP Position at the Joint Ministerial Trade Committee, 21 October 2010, and African Union (2010).

26   See Lui and Bilal (2009), and South Centre (2010).

special and differential needs, and in particular those of LDCs. In some cases (for instance in the case of the infant industry clause, standstill clause or the treatment of quantitative restrictions), technical solutions were found and agreed in some regions. In other cases however, although technical solutions could also be feasible, negotiations have been much more complex and intensive due to the fact that those issues were politically sensitive and therefore resulted in little advancement.

The debate on the contentious issues often appeared to be very technical. Yet, the absence of progress on many of these issues suggests that technical negotiators have failed, and that the discussion should, and most probably has somewhat shifted away from technical towards broader political considerations. Nevertheless, some technical compromise can be identified for several of these issues, suggesting that the asymmetrical nature of the negotiations rests less on technical matters than political stances. Some of the key issues are the following.

On *market access*, the EU has interpreted rules of WTO as requiring the ACP regions to liberalise at least 80 per cent of their trade with the EU over a period of 15 years, given that, in return, the EU grants them duty- and quota-free market access. Many African countries, and in particular LDCs, have contested this interpretation and asked for greater flexibility. ACP and EU officials have argued over the last ten years about the correct interpretation of the Article XXIV of the GATT 1994, for which no pertinent jurisprudence exists. The objective should not to arbitrarily interpret the WTO rule, but to consider what level of market opening is both politically acceptable and defensible at the WTO. According to many WTO insiders, in the current context, any free trade agreement that would cover 70 per cent or more of trade over a 15–20 years period is most likely to pass this WTO test – even more so if one the parties is an LDC or vulnerable economy, as in many African regions. The unwillingness of the EU to compromise shows more a political will to impose its views than a pragmatic approach to find a technical compromise to some African and Pacific concerns.

The inclusion of a *most-favoured nation* clause – whereby preferences granted to major third parties would be extended to the other parties of an EPA – has also been passionately debated. While this is not required or proscribed by the WTO, it is one of the most politically sensitive issues at stake. From the Africa (and Pacific) side, it is not acceptable as a matter of principle. African policy makers consider it an unacceptable constraint on their future trade agreements with third parties. The EU, however, views it as a matter of 'fairness' given their generous concessions under the EPA. A technical compromise would consist in explicitly narrowing the scope of application of the clause and relaxing the trigger mechanisms (in terms of joint decision-making process and thresholds) for its application. The MFN clause in the CARIFORUM EPA or the Pacific States interim EPA could be considered: signatories have committed to implement the MFN provision only after consultation, therefore removing any automatic and potentially arbitrary application of the more favourable treatment. The balance of obligations and benefits between a third-country FTA and the EPA could also be considered. Another option would be to increase the threshold (in terms of share of world trade) of what constitutes a major trading partner, so as to exclude more countries from the potential application of the MFN clause. However, whether an EPA will include an MFN clause is ultimately a political choice. But even if it does, some options to address concerns over future agreements with major third parties might be politically acceptable.

Another major stumbling block to the negotiations concerns the treatment of *export taxes*. The main concern of some Africans is the need to preserve sufficient policy space to industrialise their economies, a position that is challenged by the EU. This is a somewhat grey area at the WTO. However, strictly speaking, WTO rules do not expressly require countries to prohibit the use of export taxes. Therefore, there is no obligation to have a clause on export restrictions in the EPA; if there is one, a simple reference to WTO rules could suffice. Even with a binding provision on export taxes, countries could preserve some flexibility by excluding a list of products from the application of the clause. The introduction of temporary measures under specific circumstances could also be provided for, for instance in case of specific revenue needs, or to protect an infant industry, ensure food security, protect the environment or where a country can justify industrial development needs.

The *treatment of infant industries* has been another major cause of concern. As it currently stands in interim EPAs, it is covered under a general bilateral safeguard and therefore requires lengthy procedures before any measure could be applied to protect infant industry. However, technical remedies have been found, for instance by having a stand-alone provision with less cumbersome conditions of application.

Many African countries have proposed the inclusion of an *agricultural safeguards and food security* clause in the EPA given the importance of agriculture in many countries. However, the EU has argued that agriculture was sufficiently covered in the general bilateral safeguards. The EU has also forcefully rejected any proposal to address the question of agricultural subsidies through the use of agricultural safeguard measures on the argument that these issues were being discussed at the WTO and therefore should not be part of bilateral negotiations. While the issue of agricultural subsidies is not likely to be resolved in the context of the EPA, technical solutions could be found on treatment of agricultural products, in the light of the FTA between EU and South Korea.

The question of having a *standstill clause* that prevents a country from modifying its tariff schedules is another cause of concern. It is particularly challenging in the context of regional integration, where countries are in the process of adjusting their national tariffs to the regional common external tariffs. Possible technical solutions exist. It could apply only to the products subject to liberalisation and countries would not raise duties above their MFN applied rates. Parties could also jointly agree to allow countries to align their market access offers to their common external tariffs when the region moves toward a customs union. In addition, in exceptional circumstances (to be jointly agreed), such as to meet some special development needs or in case of serious economic difficulties, the country or region could temporarily suspend the application of the schedule.

Interim EPAs have a provision to remove existing *quantitative restrictions* and to prevent the introduction of new such measures. Again, in most cases, technical solutions have been found by making sure that the article is in line with Article XI of GATT 1994, which provides for the possibility to use quantitative restrictions in exceptional circumstances, in particular for the prevention of relief of critical food shortage.

On *services*, many of these fault lines are only just beginning to emerge and the regions – both between and within – will need to determine how best to reflect their own services-related development aspirations in the envisaged texts and commitments.

The way out of the current deadlock is a question of political will. The point here is that technical solutions can be found on many of the remaining issues, if only policy makers on both sides are bold enough to seize them. The question is whether the EU is willing to show some flexibility, and whether African and Pacific negotiators are committed enough to the EPA process to identify possible compromise and collectively defend them.

Perspectives on the EPA process

The EPA process has been most challenging for the ACP, exposing many of their vulnerabilities and the unbalanced relationship they have fostered with the EU. One problem the ACP countries have faced – typical for developing countries in general - is that they have had to conduct ambitious negotiations while their preparation has been underway, putting the ACP under considerable time and capacity pressure. Moreover, they have been required to negotiate as a group, at the regional level, which has been a new experience for many and has required most challenging regional coordination. Diverging interests, between many ACP countries and the EU, but also among ACP countries, has also proved a major hurdle, for collective action and consensus building and compromise. Finally, their negotiating partner is the EU (represented by the European Commission), which possesses a most sophisticated institutional framework, extensive resources and capacity, as well as significant experience in conducting such negotiations, for which it has *de facto* mainly set the agenda (see Bilal, Laporte and Szepesi 2007). Although the EU has provided asymmetric treatment favourable to the ACP (for instance in terms of market access and speed of liberalisation), the impact of an EPA is marginal on the EU while most significant for many ACP countries. Such is the unbalance of power between the EU and the ACP.

Protracted negotiations since 2002 have led to a general EPA fatigue, which is shared by all parties. It is quite apparent that the political attention and economic focus are shifting away from the EPA negotiations. The EU trade attention has turned to Asia and Latin America and to the strengthening of its neighbourhood policy. As for many ACP countries and regions, the EPA process has in many cases tarnished the EU's reputation as a friendly partner. Meanwhile, emerging powers such as China, Brazil and India have become attractive alternative new partners (see Figure 3.3). Such countries are often perceived as offering greater development prospects, with fewer conditions attached.

In a paradoxical way, EPAs, which should have strengthened and anchored the ACP-EU economic relationship, seem to have had the opposite effect. Many African and Pacific countries have resented the EU's insistence on domestic reforms and ambitious commitments in comprehensive economic and trade agreements. They want to maintain their policy space to determine for and by themselves the levels of ambition and commitment at which they will pursue their own development objectives. In spite of the EU's rhetoric, they also resent the EU's lack of flexibility in responding to some of their specific concerns on a range of issues, which are deemed contentious. Last but not least, the EU's tendency to lecture the ACP on how to pursue development with an EPA has more often been a source of irritation than inspiration. It is true that the ACP Group and the EU have jointly set out some development objectives in the context of the ACP-EU Cotonou Partnership Agreement, for which the EPA process is a key component. Nevertheless, it is ultimately up to the ACP countries and regions to determine how these objectives can best be achieved, in accordance to their own strategies for development and reform.

It is important to stress that many ACP countries have also implicitly revelled in the delayed EPA negotiations process. Since the end of the Cotonou unilateral preferences as of 2008, many ACP have 'settled' into the status quo.

All of the countries that have concluded an interim EPA have benefited from a duty-free quota-free market access to the EU under the EU Market Access Regulation 1528 of 2007 related to EPAs. Though the Regulation 1528 requires not only the countries to conclude, but also to sign, ratify and implement their (interim) EPA 'within a reasonable period of time' there seem to have been no negative consequences for any interim EPA country so far. This situation is therefore rather convenient for many ACP countries, which do not feel compelled to speedily adopt or implement the interim EPA. Besides, those ACP countries that have not been in a position so far to conclude an interim EPA have not really experienced any significant negative trade or economic effects for falling back on the EBA regime for LDCs or the standard GSP for the non-LDCs.

These ACP situations may partly explain why EPAs negotiations have lost momentum. Moreover, those African and Pacific countries or regions that would have no serious intention to conclude or implement an EPA may not have an interest in revealing their true positions and further extending the negotiation process, so as to postpone any fallout with the EU.

However, the EU has the means to flex its muscles to speed up the conclusion of final EPAs. The European Commission has shown in the past that it would not hesitate to do so it judges necessary, as in 2007. Setting firm deadlines for the removal of EPA preferences to those countries or regions that do not comply with their commitment to sign, ratify and implement EPAs that have been concluded could be a decisive move. It could also force some countries or regions to accept terms of the agreement reflecting EU preferences rather than their own. However, the imposition of too-tight deadlines with little flexibility from the EU could seriously disrupt regional integration processes if a particular region is split on how to move forward. It could also have detrimental effects on development if a deadline forces some countries or regions to endorse an EPA agenda that does not match their domestic development strategies. Effective implementation might also become illusionary. And it would surely also (further) sour relations with the EU, with long lasting negative consequences.

If the EPA process can still be rescued and asymmetry in power and economic relations explicitly be accounted for, a new impetus, based on a different political momentum, must be provided.

First, the ambitions of the EPAs must match the degree of commitment and strategic priorities of the countries and regions concerned. For most regions, this means a narrower agenda, focusing first on market access in goods and the development dimension, leaving aside services and a whole set of trade-related issues for future negotiations, and this in spite of the relevance of these issues for economic development. The EU accepted this principle for West Africa in June 2009, and it should extend the same flexibility to all other interested parties.

Second, parties that are still seriously committed to concluding an EPA must seek politically acceptable solutions to those 'contentious issues' that remain major stumbling blocks to the timely conclusion of the negotiations. This will require concessions from all parties. It will also require a differentiated approach, as not all countries or regions share the same concerns. Interestingly, in most regions possible compromise solutions have been identified on many of the issues deemed contentious in 2008. But in a bizarre twist, neither the ACP nor the EU seems too keen to capitalise on those solutions. That such compromises have been identified, however, shows that the negotiations are not as intractable as some have claimed.

Third, while it is a shared overall objective that EPAs should promote development, it is clear that the parties have different perceptions of the development merits of some of the specific EPA provisions. A positive way forward would be to acknowledge these differences, and ultimately to respect the ACP parties' assessments of their own development strategies.

Finally, countries need to seek politically acceptable solutions to those 'contentious issues' that remain major stumbling blocks to the timely conclusion of the negotiations. This will require concessions from all parties. It will also require a differentiated approach, as not all countries or regions share the same concerns. Interestingly, in many regions possible compromise solutions have been identified on many of the issues deemed contentious in 2008. Others could also to capitalise on those solutions.

While a coherent approach on EPAs would be desirable, at least among member countries of the same region and if possible at the continental level on a selected number of key issues, it is important to recognise the diversity of situations and interests across Africa. Various options can be followed in different regions or countries, based on the driving strategic objectives and specific development needs of each region or country.

Recognising that some African countries may not yet be ready or willing to conclude an EPA would be an important step, first for the African and Pacific countries or regions concerned, but also for the EU. Indeed, for the African (and Pacific) call on greater flexibility from the EU to be credible, including towards the EU negotiator in chief, EU Trade Commissioner Karel De Gucht, the countries not interested in concluded an EPA in the near future should better say so explicitly. The fact is that there is a persistent feeling in some European quarters that the quest for greater flexibility by some is only a tactical move to forever delay the conclusion of an agreement, and that whatever the extent of flexibility provided by the EU, some African countries are simply not interested in concluding any agreement with the EU, at least at this stage. So why should the EU try to accommodate their concerns in the first place? Right or wrong, this has become a prevailing perception among some key EU actors. This is at the detriment of more genuine concerns repeatedly expressed by Africa and Pacific; and thus at ultimately at the detriment of development objectives. A credible approach by Africa would thus be to explicitly acknowledge that some countries are not interested, or in a position, to conclude an EPA with the EU in the near future. A stable solution, in line with their development priorities, must be found with the EU for these countries. As for others, the articulation of a common African position, with concrete proposals on key specific EPA concerns, could pave the way to a successful agreement with the EU, which would reflect their fundamental development ambitions.

It still remains to be seen whether more EPAs will be concluded, and whether EPAs will ultimately foster or rather hamper development. To best promote the interests of ACP countries and regions, strong political leadership is required. Such leadership at the highest level with a clear strategic vision for development has, however, too often been lacking in the ACP. EPAs driven by the European Commission strong will power can be no substitute. A more humble attitude of the EU, as well as a better understanding of and respect for the various development dynamics in the ACP countries and regions would be more appropriate. But this would also require a new political leadership from the EU, one with a longer-term vision than the EPA mantra.

The EPAs have been presented as advanced and far-reaching instruments for binding trade and development. A failure to deliver on these development promises would be a serious setback to the EU trade and development agenda, including in the context of the Doha Round.

At the same time, it is important to acknowledge the political repercussions that EPAs have on the broader relations between the EU and the ACP, notably Africa. The EPA process is too serious of a matter to be left to trade people alone. A more strategic vision towards the ACP/Africa – EU relationship is required.

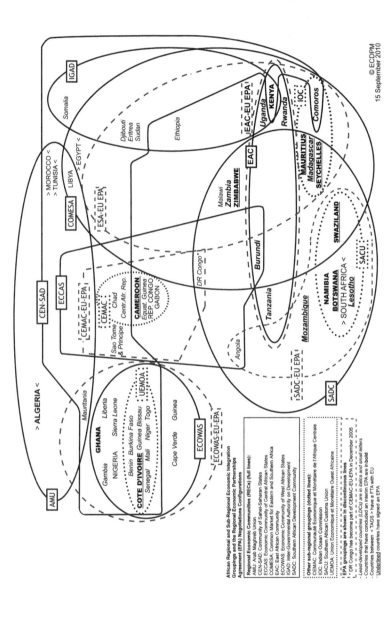

African Regional and Sub-Regional Economic Integration
Groupings and the Regional Economic Partnerships
Agreement (EPA) Negotiations Configurations

Regional Economic Communities (RECs) (full lines):
AMU: Arab Maghreb Union
CEN-SAD: Community of Sahel-Saharan States
ECCAS: Economic Community of Central African States
COMESA: Common Market for Eastern and Southern Africa
EAC: East African Community
ECOWAS: Economic Community of West African States
IGAD: Inter-Governmental Authority on Development
SADC: Southern African Development Community

Other sub-regional groupings (dotted lines):
CEMAC: Communauté Economique et Monétaire de l'Afrique Centrale
IOC: Indian Ocean Commission
SACU: Southern African Customs Union
UEMOA: Union Economique et Monétaire Ouest Africaine

EPA groupings are shown in discontinuous lines:
¹ DR Congo has become part of CEMAC-EU-EPA in December 2005
- Least-developed countries (LDCs) are in italics and small letters
- Countries that have concluded an interim EPA are in **bold**
- Countries between < TAGS > have a FTA with EU
- Underlined countries have signed an EPA

© ECDPM
15 September 2010

Annex 3.1 African regional economic integration groupings and EPA negotiations

84 Asymmetric Trade Negotiations

References

ACP Council of Ministers 2007. *Declaration of the ACP Council of Ministers at its 86th Session expressing serious concerns on the status of the negotiations of the Economic Partnerships Agreements*, ACP/25/013/07. Available at: www.acp.int/en/com/86/ACP2501307_declaration_e.pdf [accessed: 13 December 2007].

African Union 2008. *Addis Ababa Declaration on EPA Negotiations*. Available at: www.acp-eu-trade.org/library/files/AU-Ministers-of-Trade-and-Finance_EN_030408_AU_Addis-Ababa-Declaration-on-EPA-Negotiations.pdf.

African Union 2010. *Kigali Declaration on the Economic Partnership Agreement Negotiations, by the AU Conference of Ministers of Trade 6th Ordinary Session*, 29 October – 2 November 2010, Kigali (Rwanda). Available at: www.acp-eu-trade.org/library/library_detail.php?library_detail_id=5479&doc_language=Both.

Assembly of the African Union 2008. Declaration on Economic Partnership Agreements (EPAs), DOC. EX.CL/394 (XII), Assembly of the African Union Tenth Ordinary Session, 31 January - 2 February 2008.

Bartels, L. 2007. *The EU's GSP+ arrangement as an alternative to the EPA process*. Available at: www.acp-eu-trade.org/library/files/Bartels_EN_121107_GSP+-as-an-alternative.pdf.

Bilal, S. 2007. *Concluding EPAs: Legal and institutional issues*, ECDPM Policy Management Report 12. Available at: www.ecdpm.org/pmr12.

Bilal, S. 2008. ACP-EU negotiations on Economic Partnership Agreements (EPAs) and EBA: A dual relationship, in *European Union Trade Politics and Development: Everything but Arms unraveled*, edited by G. Faber and J. Orbie. Oxford: Routledge, 203–20.

Bilal, S. and Braun-Munzinger, C. 2008. *EPA negotiations and regional integration in Africa: Building or stumbling blocs*, Paper prepared for the 3rd trapca Annual Conference 'Strengthening and Deepening Economic Integration In Developing Countries: Current Situation, Challenges and Way Forward', 13–14 November 2008, Arusha (Tanzania). Available at: www.ecdpm.org/Web_ECDPM/Web/Content/Download.nsf/0/1E716849203844ABC12574FF005657AD/$FILE/Bilal 20-11-08 EPA negotiations and RI in Africa_final.pdf.

Bilal, S. and Laporte, G. 2004. *How Did David Prepare to Talk to Goliath? South Africa's experience of trade negotiations with the EU*, ECDPM Discussion Paper No. 53 [Online: European Centre for Development Policy Management]. Available at: www.ecdpm.org/dp53.

Bilal, S., Laporte, G. and Szepesi, S. 2007. Talking Trade: Practical Insights on the Capacity to Conduct Trade Negotiations, in *Navigating New Waters: A reader on ACP-EU trade*, edited by S. Bilal and R. Grynberg. London: Commonwealth Secretariat. Available at: www.ecdpm.org/Web_ECDPM/Web/Content/Download.nsf/0/63443CC148CD4731C125718F003FCAF5/$FILE/EPAs-CB_for_Negotiations-ECDPM_0506.pdf.

Bilal, S. and Rampa, F. 2006. *Alternative (to) EPAs: Possible scenarios for future ACP trade relations with the EU*, ECDPM Policy Management Report No. 11 [Online: European Centre for Development Policy Management]. Available at: www.ecdpm.org/pmr11.

Bilal, S. and Stevens, C. (eds) 2009. *The Interim Economic Partnership Agreements between the EU and African States: Contents, challenges and prospects*, ECDPM Policy Management Report No. 17 with ODI [Online: European Centre for Development Policy Management]. Available at: www.ecdpm.org/pmr17.

Bouët, A., Laborde, D. and Mevel, S. 2007. *Searching for an Alternative to Economic Partnership Agreements*, IFPRI Research Brief No.10. [Online: International Food Policy Research Institute]. Available at: www.ifpri.org/pubs/ib/rb10.pdf.

Commission for Africa 2005. *Our Common Interest*, Report of the Commission for Africa. Available at: www.commissionforafrica.info/2005-report.

Council of the European Union 2007a. *Conclusions of the Council and the Representatives of the Governments of the Member States meeting within the Council on Economic Partnership Agreements (EPAs)*, 15 May 2007.

Council of the European Union 2007b. *Conclusions of the ACP-EC Council of Ministers, meeting in Brussels on 25 May 2007*. Available at: www.consilium.europa.eu/ueDocs/cms_Data/docs/pressData/en/er/94328.pdf.

Council of the European Union 2007c. *Council Regulation (EC) No. 1528/2007*, 20 December 2007. Official Journal of the European Union, L348, 31.12.2007. Available at: http://eur-lex.europa.eu/LexUriServ/LexUriServ.do?uri=OJ:L:2007:348:0001:0154:EN:PDF.

Cronin, D. 2007. *Trade: EPAs Signed "Under Duress", Says South Africa.* IPS, 21 December 2007. Available at: http://ipsnews.net/news.asp?idnews=40567.

ECDPM 2002. *Cotonou Infokit* [Online: European Centre for Development Policy Management]. Available at: www.ecdpm.org/infokit.

ECDPM 2007. *Overview of Article 37(4) Reviews of the EPA Negotiations*, ECDPM Discussion Paper No. 81[Online: European Centre for Development Policy Management]. Available at: www.ecdpm.org/dp81.

ECDPM 2010. *The EU Commitment to Deliver Aid for Trade in West Africa and Support the EPA Development Programme (PAPED)*, ECDPM Discussion Paper No. 96 [Online: European Centre for Development Policy Management]. Available at: www.ecdpm.org/dp96.

European Commission 1996. *Green Paper on Relations between the European Union and the ACP Countries on the Eve of the 21st Century: Challenges and Options for a New Partnership*, COM(96)570, November. Brussels: European Commission. Available at: http://eur-lex.europa.eu/LexUriServ/LexUriServ.do?uri=COM:1996:0570:FIN:EN:PDF.

European Commission 2002. *Trade and Development: Assisting Developing Countries to Benefit from Trade*, Communication from the Commission to the Council and the European Parliament, COM(2002) 513 final, 18 September.

        Available at: http://europa.eu/legislation_summaries/external_trade/r12525_
        en.htm.
European Commission 2007. *Economic Partnership Agreements: Means and
        Objectives*. Available at: www.delnga.ec.europa.eu/epas/tradoc_115007.pdf.
European Commission 2008. *Six common misconceptions about Economic
        Partnership Agreements (EPAs)*, 11 January 2008. Available at: http://trade.
        ec.europa.eu/doclib/docs/2008/january/tradoc_137484.pdf.
European Commission 2010. *EPA Reflection Paper*, October 2010.
Faivre-Dupaigre, B. 2007. Will the regions emerge from the EPA negotiations
        stronger or weaker? *Grain de sel*, 39. Available at: www.inter-reseaux.org/
        IMG/pdf/15partie3_dupaigre.pdf.
Francis, A. and Ullrich, H. 2008. *Cariforum EPA and beyond: Analysis of
        the CARIFORUM-EU EPA*, GTZ (Deutsche Gesellschaft für Technische
        Zusammenarbeit) Working Paper. Available at: www.gtz.de/en/dokumente/en-
        epa-cariforum-and-beyond-cariforum-services-2008.pdf.
Frisch, D. 2008. *The European Union's development policy: A personal view of
        50 years of international cooperation*, ECDPM Policy Management Report 15
        [Online: European Centre for Development Policy Management]. Available at:
        www.ecdpm.org/pmr15.
ICCO 2008. Dialogue of the deaf – An assessment of Europe's developmental
        approach to trade negotiations [Online: ICCO]. Available at: http://www.icco.
        nl/documents/pdf//31-10.Dialogue-Deaf.pdf.
ICTSD 2009. News and Publications: 'EU decisions on GSP+ applications'. *Trade
        Negotiating Insights*, 8(1). Available at: http://ictsd.org/i/news/tni/39401/.
ICTSD and ECDPM 2007. EPAs: There is no Plan B – An interview with Peter
        Mandelson. *Trade Negotiations Insights*, 6(5). Available at: www.acp-eu-
        trade.org/tni.
ICTSD and ECDPM 2008. Interview with ACP Secretary General Sir John
        Kaputin. *Trade Negotiations Insights*, 7(1). Available at: http://www.acp-eu-
        trade.org/library/files/TNI_EN_7-1.pdf.
IPS News 2008. Q&A: 'We Are Generous but Not Naïve' – Interview with Louis
        Michel, EU Development Commissioner, 11 January 2008. Available at: www.
        ipsnews.net/news.asp?idnews=40762.
Jessop, D. 2007. All or Nothing: the Caribbean EPA. *Trade Negotiations Insights*,
        6(8). Available at: www.acp-eu-trade.org/tni.
Keet, D. 2010. *Implications of EPA/FTAs Against Developmental Regional
        Integration in Africa* [Online: Transnational Institute]. Available at: www.tni.
        org/article/implications-epaftas-against-developmental-regional-integration-
        africa.
Laporte, G. 2007. *The Cotonou Partnership Agreement: What role in a changing
        world? Reflections on the future of ACP-EU relations*, ECDPM Policy
        Management Report 13 [Online: European Centre for Development Policy
        Management]. Available at: www.ecdpm.org/pmr13.

Lui, D. and Bilal, S. 2009. *Contentious issues in the EPAs: Potential flexibility in the negotiations*, ECDPM Discussion Paper 89 [Online: European Centre for Development Policy Management]. Available at: www.ecdpm.org/dp89.

Makhan, D. 2009. *Linking EU Trade and Development Policies: Lessons from the ACP-EU trade negotiations on economic partnership agreements*, Studies 50 [Online: Deutsches Institut für Entwicklungspolitik / German Development Institute]. Available at: www.die-gdi.de/CMS-Homepage/openwebcms3.nsf/ (ynDK_contentByKey)/ANES-7YUFTE?Open. ODI 2007. *The costs to the ACP of exporting to the EU under the GSP*, Report prepared for the Dutch Ministry of Foreign, March 2007 [Online: Overseas Development Institute]. Available at: www.odi.org.uk.

Oxfam 2008. *Partnership or Power Play? How Europe should bring development into its trade deals with African, Caribbean, and Pacific countries* [Online: Oxfam International]. Available at: http://www.oxfam.org/en/policy/bp110_ EPAs_europe_trade_deals_with_acp_countries_0804.

Painter, A. 2009. The Washington consensus is dead. *The Guardian,* 10 April 2009. Available at: http://www.guardian.co.uk/commentisfree/cifamerica/2009/ apr/09/obama-g20-nato-foreign-policy.

Persson, M. and Wilhelmsson, F. 2006. Assessing the Effects of EU Trade Preferences for Developing Countries, in *The European Union and developing countries: Trade, aid and growth in an integrated world*, edited by Y. Bourdet, J. Gullstrand and K. Olofsdotter. Cheltenham: Edward Elgar Publishing Ltd, 29-45. Available at: www.nek.lu.se/nekmpe/EU%20trade%20preferences.pdf.

Primack, D. 2007. EPA Fails to Draw the Pacific Closer to the International Trading System. *Trade Negotiations Insights*, 6(8) [Online: ECDPM-ICTSD]. Available at: www.acp-eu-trade.org/tni.

Reid Smith, S. 2009. EPA Provisions may impact the ability of some developing countries to respond to the crisis. *Trade Negotiations Insights*, 8(4) [Online: ECDPM/ICTSD]. Available at: www.acp-eu-trade.org/tni.

Reinert, E.S. 2007. *How Rich Countries Got Rich and Why Poor Countries Stay Poor.* London: Constable and Robinson.

Rodrik, D. 2007. *One Economics, Many Recipes: Globalization, Institutions, and Economic Growth*. Princeton, New Jersey: Princeton University Press.

Sauvé, P. and Ward, N. 2009. *The EC-CARIFORUM Economic Partnership Agreement: Assessing The Outcomes on Services and Investment*, ECIPE Paper. Available at: www.ecipe.org/publications/ecipe-working-papers/the- ec-cariform-economic-partnership-agreement-assessing-the-outcome-on- services-and-investment.

Serra, N. and Stiglitz, J.E. (eds) 2008. *The Washington Consensus Reconsidered: Towards a New Global Governance.* Oxford: Oxford University Press.

Sharman, T. 2005. *The Trade Escape: WTO rules and alternatives to free trade Economic Partnership Agreements* [Online: ActionAid International]. Available at: www.actionaid.org.uk/media/images/trade_escape.pdf.

South Centre 2010. *EPAs: The wrong development model for Africa and options for the future*, Analytical Note SC/TDP/AN/EPA/23, March, Geneva: The South Centre. Available at: www.southcentre.org/index.php?option=com_docman&task=doc_download&gid=1807&Itemid=182=en.

Stabroek news 2008. *The Caribbean lost in the negotiations with Europe-Jagdeo*. 6 January 2008. Available at: http://www.stabroeknews.com/2008/news/stories/01/06/the-caribbean-lost-in-the-negotiations-with-europe-jagdeo/.

Stevens, C. 2007. Economic Partnership Agreements: What happens in 2008?, ODI Briefing Paper No. 23. Available at: www.odi.org.uk/publications/briefing/bp_june07_EPAs2008.pdf.

Stevens, C., Kennan, J. and Meyn, M. 2009. *The CARIFORUM and Pacific ACP Economic Partnership Agreements: Challenges Ahead*, Economic Paper Series, London: Commonwealth Secretariat. Available at: http://publications.thecommonwealth.org/the-cariforum-and-pacific-acp-economic-partnership-agreements-681-p.aspx.

Ukaoha, K. 2009. The ECOWAS EPA: A 'Funeral Oration' to Regional Integration? *Trade Negotiations Insights*, 8(5) [Online: ECDPM-ICTSD]. Available at: www.acp-eu-trade.org/tni.

Ulmer, K. 2007. The Emperor's new clothes. *Trade Negotiations Insights*, 6(8) [Online: ECDPM-ICTSD]. Available at: www.acp-eu-trade.org/tni.

United Nations 2009. International Institutions, in *The Preliminary Draft of the Full Report of the Commission of Experts on Reforms of the International Monetary and Financial System*, by the Commission of Experts of the President of the UN General Assembly on Reforms of the International Monetary and Financial System. Available at: www.un.org/ga/president/63/interactive/financialcrisis/PreliminaryReport210509.pdf.

Watson, J. 2007. East Africa: a splintered picture. *Trade Negotiations Insights*, 6(8) [Online: ECDPM-ICTSD]. Available at: www.acp-eu-trade.org/tni.

Weller, C. and Ulmer, K. 2008. Trade and Governance: Does governance matter for trade? [Online: Aprodev]. Available at: www.aprodev.net/trade/Files/Events/Trade-and-gov.pdf.

World Bank 2009. *Full Report on Implementing Interim EPAs.* Washington, D.C.: The World Bank. Available at: http://go.worldbank.org/31D32J2LN0.

World Bank – OAS 2009. *Caribbean: Accelerating Trade Integration - Policy Options for Sustained Growth, Job Creation, and Poverty Reduction*, Document of the World Bank and the Organisation of American States, co-produced with the Governments of CARIFORUM Countries. Available at: http://siteresources.worldbank.org/INTLACINSPANISH/Images/CaribeReporte.pdf.

Chapter 4

Comparative Asymmetric Trade Negotiations in the Southern Cone: FTAA and EU-MERCOSUR

Mercedes Botto and Andrea C. Bianculli

Introduction

During the 1990s, regional initiatives received an enormous boost in Latin America, giving way to what has been denominated 'new regionalism' or 'strategic regionalism' to show their qualitative departure from the regional initiatives that had taken place during the 1950s and 1960s. In contrast to this first wave, these new regional negotiations would include a much broader and deeper economic agenda, which, apart from the traditional trade liberalisation, would now embrace regulation in new policy areas. Secondly, new regionalism spanned the divide between developed and developing countries: these initiatives would bind countries with strong asymmetries in terms of their economic, social and political development, though no compensation mechanism was included to neutralise these asymmetries.

Explanations regarding the 'why' and 'what for' of these new regionalism initiatives are many and not necessarily contradictory. Initially some authors argued that the peculiarity of these processes lies in the decision of elites to deepen the structural reform programs launched during the 1980s (Ethier 1998, Bhagwati 1999, Devlin and Estevadeordal 2001, BID 2002). Other authors have highlighted the fact that these regional initiatives were promoted by multinational firms (Deblock and Brunelle 1993, Hettne 1996, Briceño Ruiz 2007).

The stop-go asymmetric negotiations involving MERCOSUR seem to be more readily explained by the second argument. In effect, by the mid-1990s MERCOSUR external agenda involved negotiations with the United States (US) to establish a free trade area along the continent: the Free Trade Area of the Americas (FTAA). Negotiations with the European Union (EU) pursued the same objective. However, after a long process and numerous meetings, neither of the two negotiations was closed. As negotiations advanced, difficulties to come to an agreement are explained not only by the small and insignificant economic gains for middle countries, such as Argentina and Brazil, but by the increasing governance demands and criteria imposed by the northern partners as well. Both the moderate trade gains and the regulatory and standard content have increased the costs of the negotiations, contributing thus to their impasse or even dilution.

In order to develop this argument, the chapter is organised as follows. The next section will examine the emergence of 'new regionalism' in the 1990s and highlight two negotiation processes: the FTAA and the EU-MERCOSUR agreement in this context, together with an analysis of the winners and losers within each scheme. The third section concentrates on comparing similarities and differences between these two processes and finally, a description of the changes and modifications they underwent between 1995 and 2004. The final aim is to determine to what extent national positions were transformed along these 10-year negotiating processes, while procedural and governance demands kept increasing. Finally, the conclusion section presents an initial comparative analysis of the reasons that account for both negotiations processes coming to a halt or impasse.

A preliminary political analysis of the launching of the FTAA and the EU-MERCOSUR negotiations

MERCOSUR and its North-South agenda

The North-South agenda of MERCOSUR involved two challenging negotiations: the creation of a free trade area – FTAA – where the main counterpart was the US, and the establishment of an interregional free trade area with the EU. Launched during the 1990s, both negotiations were important in terms of their international insertion, and strategy, apart from the binding effect of these processes. In the first place, and given their role as 'global traders', negotiations within the FTAA and those with the EU would be of interest for southern countries as their priority was to improve market access conditions in industrialised countries to achieve thus, a better insertion in a globalizing world economy. Secondly, by promoting negotiations with the US and the EU, MERCOSUR countries, particularly Brazil, would engage in a double strategy: they would take negotiations with the EU as one of their strongest weapons in their negotiations with the US in order to extract concessions from the latter. Therefore, MERCOSUR member states have been interested in advancing in parallel toward the FTAA and the free trade agreement with the EU. From the perspective of their northern partners, being 'the most promising integration scheme of the developing world' (Faust 2004: 5) can explain their interest in negotiating with the Southern bloc. For these and other related reasons, both negotiating processes must be analysed together.

The US proposal for an FTAA

In 1995, the US invited all countries in the hemisphere – with the only exception of Cuba – to create a free trade area.[1] This project, certainly the most ambitious ever known, was mainly explicated by the particular global context and the US need to reposition as a geopolitical and geo-economic leader in the global economy (Briceño Ruiz 2007: 11).

The international context was marked by the end of the Cold War and the stagnation that pervaded multilateral trade negotiations just after the formal conclusion of the Uruguay Round. At the regional level, both the Asiatic and European integration processes showed Japan and EU as the new regional leaders.[2] These regionalism processes influenced the US – the champion of multilateral negotiations to liberalise trade since 1945 – to move to a more 'consensual' hegemony and promote the creation of a regional arena in the American continent.

US aspirations were also a fundamental element. First, the US was interested in promoting the trade discussion at the multilateral level. By means of a 'strategy' where the (thematic) 'ceiling' reached at every asymmetric negotiation would turn into the minimum 'floor' for future negotiations, the US included non-trade issues on the regional agenda, pressing thus all regional blocs into the same path, under the threat of being excluded from the trade integration benefits. This was the strategy deployed when negotiating with Chile, Israel, and Mexico. Second, the US intended to regain geopolitical leadership in the region by promoting an agenda based on common interests among the different participating countries, where together with the traditional issues on trade liberalisation and integration, a political and social regional agenda would also be on the table. These agendas focused on strengthening democracy and human rights, combating drug traffic and terrorism, eradicating poverty, and economic reform, among others.[3] Finally, the US intended to expand business and investment opportunities for multinational firms along the region. Thus, the FTAA would turn into the hemispheric expression of the alliance that had been built between the US government and multinational firms already in the 1980s, during the Reagan administration, to promote and assure these companies leadership in the global economy, as a dimension of the country's geopolitical strategy (Briceño Ruiz 2007: 11). Trade liberalisation would lead to

---

1   The geographical area would span from Alaska to Tierra del Fuego, with a population of around 800 million people, a combined GDP well over US$11 trillion, and total annual exports of more than US$1.5 trillion.

2   While Japan was already leading the Asia-Pacific economy by means of a regional process not institutionalised but fostering increasing interdependence, the EU had finally achieved the Single Market in 1992, and intended to re-launch regionalism through the establishment of free trade agreements with third countries, namely, Chile, Mexico, and the MERCOSUR countries, and South Africa.

3   Masi and Wise (2005) argue that the trade issue was only included at the last moment, and mainly because of Latin American countries (LACs) insistence and in spite of some reticence on the part of the US.

an immediate expansion of US exports simply by the fact that having one of the lowest tariff structures in the world (2 per cent average tariff rate), the US had a competitive advantage over most of Latin American products, being the average tariff in Latin America close to 10 per cent. These benefits would be even larger for industrial goods and for high-tech sectors, such as the automotive manufacture, the aeroplane industry, pharmaceuticals, and electronics, in which the US was clearly the leading country in the region. However, this would not be the case with the agricultural sector, in which the US and Latin America had divergent positions given the high competitiveness of the latter. Furthermore, negotiations in this area would include non-tariff barriers, in particular policies such as compensatory duties and antidumping, together with protectionist measures used by the US, all of which were quite difficult to negotiate.

Nevertheless, and despite this trade expansion, by means of the FTAA, the US intended to regulate the so-called 'non-trade issues'. The aim was to overrule those national norms that discriminated against foreign investments and the protection of intellectual property, and, at the same time, to be able to compete on equal terms with European firms and investments, which were making big strides. Thus, the main objective was no longer to deregulate, but to regulate open markets (Bull 2005). For these and related reasons, the FTAA and the EU-MERCOSUR negotiations have to be understood and analysed with respect to each other. These two negotiating processes are not totally independent; in fact, they mutually reinforce and limit each other. MERCOSUR turned out to be an area of commercial rivalry between the EU and the US, a region where two of the most important countries of South America are involved.[4] Consequently, the interest of the EU in MERCOSUR can be explained as a strategic response to the FTAA, particularly driven by concerns about the dominance of the US in the future hemispheric process, which, in turn, could lead to a drop in European investments and trade with these countries (Phillips 2003, Faust 2004, Grugel 2004).

The EU and the ideal of inter-regionalism

The initiative to establish a free trade area between the EU and MERCOSUR followed the US initiative, though the idea of creating the first-ever case of inter-regionalism was certainly previous to that of the FTAA. The EU has always supported mirror images of itself (Botto 2009). Nevertheless, the EU had to wait

---

4   Until the 1990s, Latin America had not been of great importance for the EU. In fact, during the 1970s, relations advanced mainly in the economic field: while the European bloc sought to expand markets for its exports and investments, as well as guarantee supplies of raw materials, LACs had begun a process of diversification of their partners, though these initiatives never went too far. A decade later, while economic ties deteriorated, political alliances, on the contrary, strengthened. In the mid-1980s, the EU turned to Latin America, inaugurating thus an era of substantive political relations, but only in the 1990s did Europe become interested in the region from a commercial point of view.

until 1995 to formalise this proposal, when MERCOSUR finally attained legal status in international law, being this a strong demand of the EU.[5] Thus, while this status allowed the bloc to sign international agreements and trade conventions, the EU was confirmed as an 'external federator' for regional initiatives (Santander 2005).

The EU's interests did not differ from those of the US. First, the EU intended to dispute the growing leadership of the latter on a regional scale, and to attenuate the threat of losing their role as a leading partner of MERCOSUR countries. In terms of the trade relations, Europe's exports to MERCOSUR grew from 14 to 21 per cent between 1990 and 1998. Main exports included manufactures and industrial goods, and just 1.7 per cent accounted for agricultural products, namely wine, liquors, cheese, and olive oil. However, the most interesting element did not lie in the growth in exports. In fact, and given that MERCOSUR exports to the EU were mainly composed of low-added value products, there would be an increasing trade deficit for the Southern Cone economies. Nevertheless, and by promoting a further liberalisation of trade in the region, the EU intended to gain better access for industrial products in MERCOSUR market. Even if the average rate of the common external tariff between the two regions was relatively low (9.4 per cent in the case of the EU, and 12.5 per cent for MERCOSUR), both blocs were protecting their respective key sectors. The car industry was a priority for the EU, an area in which protection is still high.

The presence of the EU in the region was paramount in the area of investments. It was the main beneficiary of privatisation, first, in Argentina, and later on in Brazil. MERCOSUR captured 60 per cent of the investments made by European enterprises in Latin America, which hence turned out to be the main global destination (Giordano and Santiso 2000). This element leads us to the second aim the EU pursued through this interregional agreement: the promotion of liberalisation and regulation of non-trade issues, especially in the area of investments, but also in services and government procurement. Thus, the UE intended to protect existing investments – in telecommunications and financial services – and to extend into other sectors such as transportation, insurance, and engineering.

To dispute political leadership vis-à-vis the FTAA, the European proposal was based on three pillars.[6] The first pillar institutionalised a political dialogue for bi-regional consultations and coordination of the partners' positions on multilateral questions in the international bodies. The second foresaw cooperation in fields, such as war on drugs, culture, information, and communication, as well as training in regional integration with a focus on the social dimension. The third and last pillar focused on strengthening economic and commercial cooperation which

---

5   Following a demand made by the EU, the Additional Protocol to the Treaty of Asuncion on the Institutional Structure of MERCOSUR (Ouro Preto Protocol), signed in 1994, granted MERCOSUR legal status in international law.

6   The EU proposal was based on the Interregional Framework Cooperation Agreement (EMIFCA) signed between the European Commission (EC) and its Member States, and the MERCOSUR and its Party States in 1995.

would include liberalization of all trade in goods and services in conformity with World Trade Organization (WTO) rules (EC 1995).

MERCOSUR responses to asymmetric negotiations

MERCOSUR was mainly interested in improving agricultural access, while its northern partners were concerned with deregulation and investment protection. In the case of the FTAA, market access turned out to be an area of crucial importance since many of MERCOSUR's exports were subject to high tariffs in the markets of many of their potential hemispheric partners; moreover, these products were also subject to non-tariff barriers in the US market. Thus, for instance, MERCOSUR exports of textiles, clothing, and footwear faced discrimination compared to those coming from Central America and the Caribbean, which enjoyed preferences in this market. Even if MERCOSUR exports to the US were not concentrated in agriculture as those directed to the EU, trade in this area remained controversial. Although exports to the US are mostly manufactured products, it would be difficult for the latter to obtain improved access for its offensive interests if it was not willing to make considerable concessions in the core of its protectionist structure: agriculture and traditional manufactures (Lorenzo and Vaillant 2005). The opposite is true for MERCOSUR.

In terms of the free trade agreement with the EU, MERCOSUR took this as an opportunity for securing market access for highly competitive exports of foodstuffs, reducing the historical trade deficit with the EU. In effect, by then, trade flows between both regions were not so dynamic and the relevance of EU as a market had been declining. In 1990, MERCOSUR enjoyed a large trade surplus with the EU, which disappeared four years later, and worsened through the 1990s. At the end of the decade recession compressed import demand, which in turn, affected EU exports (Bulmer-Thomas 2000). However and rather mirroring the case of the FTAA, MERCOSUR's position was that EU concessions on the agricultural front were a sine-qua-non condition for further opening the Southern bloc's economy.

The main products within the agricultural and food sector affected by European protectionism, an area where MERCOSUR governments expected a high increase once the free trade area would be accomplished, were cereals, sugar, tobacco, meat, dairy products, and poultry. These products and their derivatives (over 600 tariff lines) had tariffs over 30 per cent, apart from other quotas, subsidies, and other types of non-tariff measures. MERCOSUR exports were put to a particular disadvantage by these protectionist measures, and also vis-à-vis other non-European competitors that had already been granted preferential access, namely ex European colonies in Africa, Central America and the Caribbean; all these different elements account for the widening of the MERCOSUR trade deficit with the EU since 1995.

The governments' enthusiasm to promote a bi-regional agreement was based on rather contradictory evidence. While some analyses showed that the elimination of trade barriers would lead to an increase in European exports to MERCOSUR, which would rise more significantly than EU imports from the Southern bloc (Bulmer-Thomas 2000), others, on the contrary, argued that full trade liberalisation would entail more concentrated gains in specific MERCOSUR sectors (Flores Jr. 2004).

In terms of non-traditional trade issues, such as services, government procurement and investments, MERCOSUR showed a rather ambiguous stance, and, in some cases, not necessarily homogeneous. Negotiators expected that the interregional agreement would support the necessary reforms to enhance the competitiveness of their economies, and attract, thus, more investments from EU firms. This was not the case in services, where the domestic regulatory frameworks showed important divergences among MERCOSUR countries. While Argentina had already liberalised this sector, Brazil still showed a strongly defensive approach to the issue. Therefore, the final decision of the bloc was to keep these issues out of the negotiation agenda, and to use them in exchange for the liberalisation of goods, in case this would be finally untied.

However, and apart from the implied trade benefits, the bi-regional negotiation was also intended to promote MERCOSUR's strategic interests both at the regional and multilateral level. At the regional level, southern countries intended to control for asymmetry by conducting negotiations with the EU and those of the FTAA in parallel so that negotiations with the EU could be used to extract concessions from the US, and vice versa. At the multilateral level, the possibility of moving forward the issues related to market access for agricultural products would also empower MERCOSUR as a global player.

The departure line: similarities and differences between the FTAA and the EU-MERCOSUR processes

Even if the main interests underlying both negotiation processes were identical – regulations vis-à-vis market access – the various agendas included, the institutional mechanisms devised to achieve consensus, and the channels opened to non-state actors' participation showed some degree of variation.

The agendas

The initial proposal put forward by the US was strictly economic and did not contemplate, as had been the case in the previous Enterprise for the Americas Initiative, the inclusion of neither incentives nor chapters providing economic cooperation for less developed countries. The agenda included the negotiation of an ample array of issues. Even if the US led the process from its very inception, it did leave room for other voices and initiatives coming from the 34 countries at the negotiation table. No initiative was left aside. Working groups were created to deal with those issues upon which there was consensus. The final list included nine

Negotiating Groups (NGs) to deal with fundamental trade issues: market access; investment; services; government procurement; dispute settlement; agriculture; intellectual property rights; subsidies, antidumping and countervailing duties; and competition policy. In those areas in which countries maintained important differences, three ad-hoc consultative groups were created: the Consultative Group on Smaller Economies, the Committee of Government Representatives on the Participation of Civil Society, and the Joint Government-Private Sector Committee of Experts on Electronic Commerce.

When comparing this agenda to the one proposed by the EU to MERCOSUR in 1998, it is clear that the latter was much more reduced in economic terms, but broader in political issues. The proposal was made of three pillars: trade issues, political dialogue, and cooperation. As regards its final scope, the agreement was intended to constitute an alternative governance model rather than just a trade agreement. In effect, the proposed agreement provided substance to EU claims of a distinctive approach to its relation with developing countries, which emphasises democracy, human rights, citizenship, and regional integration based on equality and cooperation, rather than power inequalities, to project European values globally (Grugel 2004).

This equation should not be taken as a sign of strength but of weakness, instead: restrictions imposed on the economic agenda had to be compensated with the inclusion of political and economic incentives. The initial liberalisation proposal presented by the EC was later on neutralised by the differences that emerged across the different member countries and across the various economic sectors as well. Main opposition arose within the Council of Europe, committed to the elaboration of a negotiating mandate, sine-qua-non to move forward with the international negotiation. The main objection came from the French, Irish, and Dutch ministers of agriculture and fisheries. On the contrary, those countries having large investments and firms already established in MERCOSUR countries supported the mandate. A third position – and the one that would finally prevail – was that of the United Kingdom, for whom the agreement was not an end in itself, but a way of putting additional pressure on member governments to accept a reform of the EU's Common Agricultural Policy (CAP), highly costly for the whole bloc, and mainly benefiting French interests. The UK government proposed conceding the negotiating mandate, though limiting its scope and rhythm to negotiations at the multilateral level – the WTO. There was also disagreement within the Santer Commission (1995–1999), though, in this case, opposition was neutralised by the explicit support of the German presidency of the EU and the governments of Italy, Portugal, and Spain, who were feeling the pressure of their own industrial lobbies.

While the EC worked on a draft mandate, an EU-MERCOSUR working group was established to examine three key areas – trade in goods, in services, and related standards and disciplines – to elaborate a complete report on trade flows with a 'photograph' of institutional practices and regulations over competition, anti-dumping, technical standards, norms of origin, and import licences. Both the EC and the MERCOSUR governments launched a series of studies to collect data and prepare the analysis of their mutual trade relations and regulations. As the process advanced, the number of items on the agenda expanded: both parties exchanged and analysed each other's information, including not only trade in goods and services, together with technical standards, but also investment, government procurement, agriculture, competition policy, intellectual property rights, veterinary and phytosanitary rules, and general trade. By the end of 1998, the EC urged negotiators to come to an agreement to launch bi-regional negotiations. Clearly, the EU needed to make a stance vis-à-vis progress in the FTAA and the oncoming Doha Round at the WTO.

However, progress on trade was scant: the EU imposed several restrictions in the scope of negotiations, which made the agreement less attractive for MERCOSUR.[7] To sign the final document, MERCOSUR ministers demanded the inclusion of regional cooperation within the so-called 'second pillar' to allow the Southern bloc to benefit from the European experience (Santander 2005).

The methodology

Following the Miami Summit (1994), there was a preparatory phase, along which the institutional structure and the dynamic of the hemispheric process were set up. The FTAA organisation chart assumed a rather complex character, which included a dense routine of public officials meetings. The Ministers Responsible for Trade would gather every 18 months to build consensus on the directives to be translated into the domestic arena. The Trade Negotiations Committee (TNC) would bring together the Vice Ministers Responsible for Trade as required, but no less than twice a year, to examine and evaluate the workings and difficulties within the nine NGs. Technical experts and second-line public officials would also be part of these meetings. To assure continuity and prevent negotiations from coming to a halt, the FTAA negotiation structure and dynamic were based on a work plan establishing concrete dates for Ministerial meetings together with the designation of the governments in charge of these. Moreover, the 1998 Santiago Summit set the year 2005 as the deadline for ending all negotiations.

Intense negotiations preceded the establishment of rules of consensus building. MERCOSUR, led by Brazil, was successful at establishing the principle of 'single undertaking', which replaced the US proposal of an 'early harvest' or the implementation of partial agreements for tariff reductions, which could have enabled the US to achieve incremental liberalisation in sensitive sectors through provisional agreements. In addition, it was agreed that the FTAA would be built

---

7   Three important restrictions were imposed regarding the scope of the negotiations: 1. only non-tariff barrier negotiations would begin immediately; 2. tariff reductions and services would be delayed until July 1, 2001; 3. no date was set for tariff negotiations, services, and agriculture. In the meantime, parties would hold a 'dialogue' on these issues in the light of the Seattle Round due in December 1999; negotiations were thus tied to progress at the multilateral level.

on existing bilateral and sub-regional trading blocs, rather than being negotiated through bilateral deals and as an extension of the North American Free Trade Agreement (NAFTA), just as the US had initially anticipated. In other words, MERCOSUR countries would be able to negotiate as members of a sub-regional trading bloc; this decision legitimised the bloc's stance in the regional negotiations: members saw their leverage increased while asymmetries in their negotiation power were reduced (Carranza 2004, Masi and Wise 2005). Nevertheless, the US would still attempt at dividing MERCOSUR. After negotiations were formally launched in 1998, the US offered Argentina and Uruguay the possibility of negotiating outside the MERCOSUR framework.[8]

A third conflictive issue between the Southern bloc and the US related to liberalisation rhythms and timing. A model based upon radical liberalisation – that is, showing a strong free trade bias – would have a quite negative impact on Brazilian development strategy, being this more acute in the case of electronics, capital goods, chemicals, automobiles, and machinery. Contrariwise, steel and petroleum producers, together with the agroindustry and exporters of agricultural commodities favoured a hemispheric free trade area and supported the expansion of new investments and joint ventures with foreign economic agents.

The launching of the negotiations between the EU and MERCOSUR would also involve the definition of the negotiation structure, methodology, and calendar. However, and contrary to the FTAA, the main forum for trade negotiations would be the EU-MERCOSUR Bi-regional Negotiations Committee (BNC), integrated by Council members, members of the EC's general directorates of Trade and Foreign Policy, and the Ministers of Foreign Affairs of MERCOSUR countries. In addition, a Subcommittee on Cooperation (SCC) was established to conduct negotiations on cooperation while three Technical Groups (TGs) would deal with specific issues: trade in goods and tariffs, service and intellectual property, and competition and regulated markets. In terms of the schedule, the BCN established its own timing and frequency, though this also included three meetings a year to discuss progress in the negotiations, with a focus on the trade agenda. The same accounts for the SCC, which met periodically to deal with a wide array of issues: institutional support, customs harmonisation, technical norms and standards, statistical harmonisation, veterinary and phytosanitary rules, and civil society support. The TGs would meet in conjunction with the BNC, and maintain informal contacts in order to further their activities. In contrast to the FTAA model, this structure revealed that cooperation had a prominent place on the bi-regional agenda. In fact, it was intended to ensure consistency between both agendas, namely trade and cooperation.

The process took up the principle of the single undertaking whereby the package would be closed in all areas at the same time. However, in practice,

---

8   The US would try similar strategies with Central America, and with the Caribbean countries and Andean countries as well, as it re-launched negotiations for a bilateral free trade agreement with Chile.

this turned out to be difficult to achieve. Despite the long preparatory phase that preceded the launching of negotiations and the subsequent bargaining, negotiators could not resolve basic technical issues, namely, definition of the methods and modalities of tariff offers. This resulted in mismatched offers that would have to be untangled, further complicating negotiations (Rios and Doctor 2004).

A key difference between the FTAA and the EU-MERCOSUR process was the European condition of sticking to the bloc format. Members would have to build consensus at the regional level to act with a single voice. This requirement faced member countries with the need of harmonizing their national positions within the bloc before advancing negotiations with the European counterpart. This would certainly lead to a learning process and promote the negotiation capabilities of the Southern countries, which could be directly transposed into the negotiation process with the US within the FTAA. In addition, it forced member countries to discuss issues and norms that were not part of the common agenda, as in the case of government procurement. However, this single-voice requirement would introduce another tier of asymmetry, this time at the level of the bloc's intra-regional relations as shown in the negotiation of services. Being this an area where Argentina and Brazil showed important discrepancies, regional harmonization led to the prevalence of Brazil's interests in the final offer presented to the UE.

Involvement of non-state actors

During the preparation phase of both negotiation processes, the activation, mobilisation, and collective action strategies were channelled through informal mechanisms and traditional lobby pressure at the national level and also at the regional level, when regional institutions were available.

In the case of the FTAA, the first reaction came, rather surprisingly, from multinational firms with a clear interest in the hemispheric process. These actors focused on providing support to the process and the organisation of transnational networks that would reinforce their members' stance at the domestic level given that defensive interests would be strong and active too. Composed of a small number of powerful firms, this group had supported the negotiation process since the first meeting of Trade Ministers (Denver 1995). During the design of the organisation chart, all governments agreed on the need of involving business actors in the negotiation process. Thus, the Business Network for Hemispheric Integration (REIH, Red Empresarial para la Integración Hemisférica) was invited to participate through the Americas Business Forum (ABF), which would hold meetings just before the trade ministers' gatherings, following a scheme analogous to that of the NGs. Their aim was to come to internal agreements and to make their demands explicit through recommendations to be then presented to the governments for their consideration. Civil society organisations (CSOs) would not be given the same status. Even if CSOs were already mobilised through the articulation of national networks created during the negotiations of the NAFTA and the Canada United States Free Trade Agreement (CUFTA), most of Latin American negotiators rejected the idea of granting them mechanisms of participation within the FTAA negotiation process. Certainly, this stance was not homogeneous across all countries. Nevertheless, and given that decisions followed the unanimity rule, the rejection of CSO participation would remain in place. Thus, trade unions and non-governmental organisations (NGOs) representatives were not included in the negotiation process during the initial stage. To observe formalities, governments created the so-called 'Committee of Government Representatives on the Participation of Civil Society' (SOC). Composed of public officials, this Committee was in charge of proposing initiatives and mechanisms to reflect civil society interests.

Within the EU-MERCOSUR process, the idea of opening up the dialogue between both blocs triggered the rejection of European agricultural lobbies, organised under the Committee of Professional Agricultural Organisations (COPA) – General Confederation of Agricultural Cooperatives in the European Union (COCEGA). As the sector rejected the freeing of trade in agriculture, it heavily lobbied governments and EU institutions – mainly through the ministers of agriculture and fisheries – against the interregional initiative (Faust 2004, Sanchez Bajo 2005). Still, their aspirations were partially frustrated when the EC finally got the negotiating mandate. Negotiations were strongly supported by EU economic interests experiencing booming trade and investment relations with MERCOSUR, mainly in industry and services. Spanish, German, French, Dutch, and Italian firms were the most active actors, though Spain would quickly move to the head to protect its expanding investments (ECLAC 2000).

Facing both supportive and opposing voices, EU-MERCOSUR negotiations were formally launched in 1999, showing a rather more equitable and egalitarian stance towards non-state actors participation, when compared to the FTAA (Bianculli 2005). The negotiation structure did not include a formal and institutionalised space for the inclusion of business and civil society actors. Dialogue and participation with bi-regional networks was promoted through informal meetings. Both European and MERCOSUR public officials recognised that business actors played a key role in providing information and expertise. Hence, participation was actively promoted, but not institutionalised. A powerful supporting lobby was the MERCOSUR-European Business Forum (MEBF) created in early 1999, which comprised large firms anchored in highly protected sectors and privatised services, being small and medium enterprises excluded from the forum. The MEBF included an Executive Board representing both EU and MERCOSUR firms, and three working groups – 'Market Access', 'Services and Investment', and 'Cooperation Programs between MERCOSUR/EU Business Facilitation Measures'. The MEBF was able to speak with one voice to the EC and to MERCOSUR governments during this first phase, but as negotiations advanced and particular sector-specific issues were tabled, their internal consistency was affected by divergent interests. Given these discrepancies, the MEBF would then develop an active work plan on trade facilitation measures, an area where consensus seemed easier to achieve, and one deemed as fundamental in view of the final agreement (Bianculli 2010).

Changes along the negotiation processes

By the end of 1999, both negotiation processes were well on track, though success was still uncertain. A decade later, both negotiation processes had undergone several phases under a changing global environment. The widespread optimism of the 1990s had been replaced by stagnation, disillusionment, and increasingly discrepant opinions and views regarding a 'free trade' agreement and its content. As negotiations advanced, interests and national positions changed. Whereas market access, especially for agricultural products, turned out to be a controversial and rather nonnegotiable issue, other agendas gained notoriousness, leading to an increase in procedural demands. Interestingly, as these changes and transformations gained terrain, both negotiation processes converged into a similar model of regional governance.

The FTAA

The whole negotiation process (1995–2005) can be divided into four different stages: preparatory stage (1994–1998), launching of negotiations (1998–2001); initial exchange of offers (2001–2002), and ending of negotiations (2002–2005) (Table 4.1). The year 2005 was settled as the deadline for ending all negotiations and for launching a schedule for tariff reductions and a work plan for liberalisation in three key sectors: services, investment, and government procurement. However, this deadline was not met as negotiations became diluted, finally coming to a halt.

Once formal negotiations were launched in 1998, the nine NGs were instructed to draw up a draft text of their respective chapters, bringing to light consensus and conflicts in each issue area, which was to be presented for preliminary agreement at the Summit of Quebec (April 2001).

The NGs did not take long to identify the key issues and to settle how positions would be aligned among the different 34 countries. While the US agenda concentrated on tariff reduction and trade liberalisation in three main sectors – services, investments, and government procurement – MERCOSUR countries, led by Brazil, focused on agricultural trade liberalization and the elimination of US non-tariff barriers and antidumping regulations. The US consistently refused to negotiate this issue within the FTAA framework, and privileged instead the WTO. However, no substantial progress was made in this area, especially in terms of non-tariff barriers. Market access to the US remained as a central, but difficult issue to solve, especially for agricultural products.

Table 4.1 The FTAA negotiation phases (1995–2005)

Ministerial Meeting	Date	Location	Phases and Issues
First Summit of the Americas	1994	Miami	**Preparatory phase**
1st Trade Ministerial Meeting	1995	Denver	
2nd Trade Ministerial Meeting	1996	Cartagena	
3rd Trade Ministerial Meeting	1997	Belo Horizonte	
4th Trade Ministerial Meeting	1998	San José	– Structure of negotiations – General principles and objectives
Second Summit of the Americas	1998	Santiago de Chile	**Launching phase**
5th Trade Ministerial Meeting	1999	Toronto	– Business facilitation measures on customs procedures and enhanced transparency
6th Trade Ministerial Meeting	2001	Buenos Aires	– Acceptance to make public the draft text of the FTAA Agreement – Corporate Social Responsibility
Third Summit of the Americas	2001	Quebec	**Interchange of offers phase** – Deadlines for the conclusion and implementation of the FTAA Agreement – Initiation of market access negotiations
7th Trade Ministerial Meeting	2002	Quito	**Ending of negotiations phase** – Second draft of the text of the FTAA Agreement – Establishment of the Hemispheric Cooperation Program
8th Trade Ministerial Meeting	2003	Miami	– Negotiations "*à la carte*" – Meeting with CSOs representatives

Given the difficulty to attain substantive agreements, governments agreed on promoting procedural issues, and defining agreements and common rules in the area of trade facilitation. An ad-hoc Committee was thus created to oversee the implementation of approved business facilitation measures and identify new instruments. Composed of technical experts and academics related to the private sector, this Committee reported directly to the TNC. The private sector was thus acknowledged as having an important role in the negotiation process. A new window of opportunity was opened for these actors participation, through the provision of information and the monitoring of hemispheric agreements implementation.

The Third Summit (Québec 2001) opened the third phase of the FTAA process. During this stage, which covered a period of 18 months (April 2001–November 2002) negotiations did not go very far. The main objective was to polish the draft of the text of the FTAA Agreement that the ministers had received in the Sixth Trade Ministerial Meeting (Buenos Aires 2001). In terms of the scope and issues under negotiation, this first draft was still too far away from what should be the final version of the agreement. At least two opposing visions emerged in each of the issues and items under negotiation. Trade negotiations were slowed down, as the agricultural agenda would now be tackled at the WTO, a decision clearly showing US preferences and priorities.

The main changes along this phase were related to the need of providing social legitimacy to the trade negotiation process given the increasing animosity coming from different actors. To face this, the FTAA introduced two main innovations. The first had to do with the explicit backing of the ABF to promote voluntary standards through Corporate Social Responsibility. The second innovation referred to the unprecedented move designed to increase both the legitimacy and transparency of the process. In response to the demand put forward by different groups and CSOs during the 2001 Summit of the Peoples, the draft text of the FTAA Agreement was made publicly available through Internet.

CSOs and trade unions, whose organisation preceded the launching of the FTAA negotiations,[9] but that were neither acknowledged nor included in the negotiation process, would rapidly articulate to create a hemispheric network under the name of the Hemispheric Social Alliance (HSA). This new collective action strategy was built around a core agreement, which had to do more with how negotiations should be conducted than with the agendas under discussion.

---

9   These actors comprised both sectoral and multisectoral networks that were organised in response to the different free trade negotiations launched in the region during the 1990s. In North America, these first networks included those established in Canada to face the CUFTA negotiations, and those comprising American and Mexican organizations to oppose NAFTA. Within the Southern Cone, on the contrary, the most important networks were sectoral, such as the Coordinating Group of Trade Unions of the Southern Cone (CCSCS as per its Spanish acronym from Coordinadora de Centrales Sindicales del Cono Sur) (Botto 2001).

Because of the strong pressure placed by the HSA, some national governments – namely, the Canadian – were forced to acknowledge the hemispheric network, to implement different consultation mechanisms and, even, to provide funding for their activities.

Changes were also introduced in terms of the conclusion and implementation of the FTAA Agreement, and the provision of differential and special treatment – namely, technical assistance – to smaller economies in the region. In both cases, the underlying motivation was to energise the negotiations in the face of the transformations already affecting the global scenario, which seemed to endanger the efforts of previous years. Both the failure of the Doha Round talks and the 9-11 terrorist attacks gave way to important changes in the US trade approach: in order to make fast moves, the US would deploy a 'seductive' strategy through the establishment of bilateral free trade agreements across the region.

As negotiations slowed down, several steps were taken to accelerate the process at the Seventh Ministerial Meeting (Quito, November 2002). In the first place, deadlines were ratified for both the conclusion and implementation of the FTAA agreement: negotiations were to be concluded no later than January 2005, and entry into force would be sought as soon as possible thereafter, but not later than December 2005. Second, measures benefiting smaller economies were introduced. Even though this issue had been on the agenda ever since the negotiations started, disagreement among the countries had prevented these from being implemented. The main detractors were countries of mid-development, such as MERCOSUR countries, as they perceived they would have to concede preferences to smaller economies without receiving particular benefits in exchange. Finally, differences were overcome with the establishment of the Hemispheric Cooperation Program (HCP). Nevertheless, this program was of limited scope as it was mainly aimed at strengthening the capacities of less developed and smaller countries to effectively participate in the negotiations, implement their trade commitments, and address the challenges and maximise the benefits of hemispheric integration. Finally, Ministers confirmed the timetable established by the TNC for market access-related negotiations to exchange initial offers between December 15, 2002 and February 15, 2003; to review offers and submit requests for improvements to offers between February 16 and 15 June 15, 2003; and initiate the presentation of revised offers and subsequent negotiations on improvements as of July 15, 2003.

The fourth stage, starting in November 2002, was intended to end negotiations. However, the negotiation of market-access offers put the hemispheric process under severe stress to the extent that changes in the negotiation methodology and format had to be introduced to reach consensus. Difficulties emerged not only because of the US stance of not opening negotiations in the agricultural agenda, but also because within MERCOSUR, building a common position to present concrete offers and coordinate participation in the hemispheric negotiation process proved to be difficult.

As negotiations evolved and decisions required identifying common and complementary interests, and arbitraging existing differences, MERCOSUR showed the fragility of its institutional and political mechanisms[10] in shaping a common position. The bloc's independent and gradualist strategy would be useful during the first phases of the hemispheric negotiation process. When discussions were mainly focused on defining the FTAA's guiding principles and framework, MERCOSUR negotiators were then able to maintain a unified posture. However, as the negotiation agendas gained in complexity and challenge, the bloc's participation turned out to be defensive and reactive. These weaknesses were particularly evident during the exchange of market access offers for goods in 2003. Whereas these initial offers excluded investment and government procurement proposals, only Uruguay and Paraguay submitted offers in services. Argentina and Brazil failed to do so. Even if it had been agreed that each member state would submit its own list of offers in services, it was implicit that the submission of the four lists would be simultaneous. Being services an important and contentious issue because of existing asymmetries among MERCOSUR countries, the Southern bloc failed to build a common position. Clearly, negotiating as a bloc vis-à-vis third countries became an elusive objective without going through a process of regional harmonisation. Faced with this complex scenario, governments made three key decisions in the Eighth Trade Ministerial Meeting (Miami 2003) to introduce greater flexibility in the FTAA strategy. The principle of single undertaking was left aside, and countries would now be able to assume different levels of commitment in terms of the agenda, that is to say, regarding the specific sectors and products they intended to open up for negotiation.

This 'FTAA à la carte' or 'FTAA light' implied a two-tier approach, involving a common tier of mutual but minimal obligations focused on market access, and an upper, voluntary tier of strengthened obligations in various trade-related disciplines. The framework established a core of concessions in the area of market access: lower tariffs and non-tariff trade barriers on goods, including agriculture. In addition, minimum obligations would be required from all countries in the other negotiating areas, together with a discretionary adherence to deeper and more far-reaching obligations in areas of their choice, i.e. trade in services, intellectual property, government procurement, and investment.

A third change referred to civil society participation. The TNC instructed the SOC to organise a series of issue meetings, which should be open to civil society representatives before or after its regularly scheduled meetings in 2003 and 2004. A limited number of non-governmental representatives would thus gain access to the regional process. Actually, the decision to send representatives would be at

---

10   National negotiation positions frequently differed on substantive issues. Given the inexistence of supranational institutions, the identification of common and complementary interests, and the analysis and assessment of alternative trajectories remained in the hands of national officials, who, as expected, tended to be rather entrenched in their perceived national views. Thus, rather than being the result of mutually accepted trade-offs, regional negotiating positions have frequently been based on the minimum common denominator of national views (Bouzas 2004).

national government's discretion. The underlying objective was to discuss issues identified by the SOC as being of special relevance out of the more comprehensive negotiation agenda. At the end of each meeting, the Chair, with the assistance of the Tripartite Committee, would draft a factual report reflecting the different visions and positions presented, which should then be submitted to the TNC for consideration. Three different meetings were conducted following this scheme and methodology. A first meeting was held in Sao Paulo (June 2003) to discuss 'agriculture', while 'services' was the key issue under analysis in the second meeting in Santiago de Chile (September 2003). The last meeting took place in Santo Domingo (January 2004) where the agenda concentrated on 'intellectual property rights'. The results of these meetings did not satisfy any of the involved parties. On the one hand, negotiators found that these discussions were out of focus as countries were merely interested in promoting their own national negotiating position.[11] On the other hand, given that only a reduced group of CSOs took part in these meetings, conclusions could hardly been taken as standing for the position of the Americas civil society.[12]

The TNC also instructed the SOC to study the possibility of devising a civil society committee within the FTAA institutional framework, which was to be established after the entry into force of the free trade agreement. However, as the new spirit of Miami faded away, proposals such as these seem to have followed a similar path. In fact, this new Miami spirit did not even survive the next round of vice-ministerial meetings held in Puebla (February 2004).

During the XVII Meeting of the TNC, a 'G14' group emerged, which was committed to negotiate a WTO-Plus agreement granting a higher level of market access in services and investment. Led by the US, the 'G14' was formed by a group of countries with which the US had already negotiated or was about to negotiate free trade agreements: Canada, Mexico, Chile, Guatemala, El Salvador, Honduras, Nicaragua, Costa Rica, Panama, the Dominican Republic, Columbia, Ecuador, and Peru. On the other hand, under the lead of Brazil, MERCOSUR countries insisted on a gradualist approach to hemispheric integration and on negotiating as an independent sub-regional bloc. Two elements account for this gradualism. First, this strategy would allow more time for MERCOSUR's internal consolidation. Second, it would strengthen the bloc's negotiating position with the EU. Moreover, Brazil proposed the creation of the South American Free Trade Agreement (SAFTA), a project that saw MERCOSUR as a common market and

---

11   During the Sao Paulo meeting, the Canadian representative argued that: 'the FTAA negotiations are not meant as a means to advance development or resolve other problems in developing countries' (Weinberg 2003).

12   As observed by Stephanie Weinberg (2003), an Oxfam America representative attending the Sao Paulo meeting: NGOs 'took the position that such a meeting could not be considered as a civil society consultation in the FTAA process but rather as a dialogue with certain representatives of civil society'.

as grouping expanding to embrace the whole of South America so that the region would gain more bargaining power vis-à-vis the US.

As the FTAA failed in its attempt to establish a free trade area along the region, MERCOSUR would bring back the idea of promoting and furthering the agreement on trade complementation known as the Rose Garden Agreement or 'Four plus One' Agreement signed by MERCOSUR countries and the US in June 1991. The option of starting negotiations under this '4+1' pattern would reappear in February 2003 after the unsuccessful change of offers within the FTAA. In contrast to the hemispheric initiative, this agreement was not perceived as a menace by the main countries of the Southern bloc given that the aim was not to achieve trade liberalisation, but to advance in those areas of 'mutual interest': agricultural and industrial trade, investment development, and electronic commerce.

EU-MERCOSUR negotiations

Just an in the FTAA negotiation process, interregional relations between the EU and MERCOSUR evolved along four stages: preparatory phase (1995–1999), the formal launching of negotiations (1999–2001), the substantive bargaining (2001–2004), and efforts to conclude the agreement (since 2004).

Once negotiations were formally launched, the first four meetings of the BNC were limited to solving methodological issues and exchanging information and analyses on the basic requirements to start the concrete tariff bargaining. Despite existing differences between the EU and MERCOSUR in these more substantive issues, negotiations would still move forward in areas of political and strategic concern. While the EU was interested in showing a repositioning in the region in the face of the progress towards the establishment of a free trade area led by the US and the failure of the WTO meeting in Seattle, MERCOSUR showed increased optimism and required more cooperation in exchange.

Therefore, whereas negotiations made small progress in terms of the methodology and the deadlines that would rule the process of exchange of offers to avoid deadlocks in the inter-regional dialogue, the initiative would promote the involvement and support of civil society actors. The EU allocated further funds to promote financial and technical cooperation with the Southern bloc during 2000–2006, 30 per cent of which would be directly assigned to civil society actors in MERCOSUR (ALOP 2003). This was part of the European model of governance (Grugel 2004).[13]

---

13   The Civil Society Dialogue can be taken as part of this model as well. Following an initiative of Pascal Lamy, who in 1999 invited an advisory group of civil society representatives to form part of the EU delegation to the WTO meeting in Seattle, the Civil Society Dialogue was finally established within EU's bilateral trade negotiations with Latin American and Caribbean countries. For further details on this, see Doctor (2007) and Jordana and Bianculli (2007).

Table 4.2 The EU-MERCOSUR negotiation phases (since 1995)

Negotiation Round	Date	Location	Phases and Issues
	Dec. 1995	Madrid	**Preparatory phase** – Interregional Framework Cooperation Agreement
1st EU-Latin America Summit	1999	Rio de Janeiro	**Launching phase**
1st Round	April 2000	Buenos Aires	– Establishment of general principles – Creation of Technical Groups on Trade, and working subgroups
2nd round	June 2000	Brussels	– Identification of obstacles and objectives
3rd Round	Nov. 2000	Brasilia	– Exchange of technical data – Draft on economic cooperation, political dialogue, and institutional framework
4th Round	March 2001	Brussels	– Cooperation and business facilitation measures – Horizontal issues
5th Round	July 2001	Montevideo	**Exchange of offers phase** – First European tariff offer
6th Round	Oct. 2001	Brussels	– MERCOSUR's counter-offer
7th Round	April 2002	Buenos Aires	– Political cooperation – Business Facilitation Action Plan
8th Round	Nov. 2002	Brasilia	– Methods and modalities for negotiations on goods and services, technical barriers to trade, rules of origin, competition, customs, and dispute settlement

9th Round	March 2003	Brussels	– Substantive tariff offers – MERCOSUR's improved offer – Progress in government procurement and investments
10th Round	June 2003	Asunción	– Discussion on methods and modalities for government procurement – Sustainable development
11th Round	Dec. 2003	Brussels	– Agricultural modes – Common text on services, government procurement, investments, competition, among others
12th Round	March 2004	Buenos Aires	**Ending of negotiations phase** – Political and cooperation – Technical barriers to trade – Competition – Customs
13th Round	May 2004	Brussels	– Exchange of views on future improved tariff offers
14th Round	June 2004	Buenos Aires	– Attempt to conclude negotiations
15th Round	July 2004	Brussels	– Attempt to conclude negotiations

Meetings with civil society, which were held in parallel to the presidential meetings, were attended by a wide array of organisations, including academic, environmental, cultural and immigrants associations' representatives, among others. European organisations were also involved in these meetings. Trade unions bi-regional meetings were held on a more regular basis and were attended by the main trade networks: the European Union Trade Confederation (ETUC) and the CCSCS.

Market access negotiations were formally inaugurated during the Fifth BNC meeting (Montevideo 2001), with the actual exchange of negotiating texts for goods, services, and government procurement. Given that deadlines had not been explicitly established, offers turned out to be only unilateral in character. In this sense, the EU proposal clearly reflected the European intention of accelerating negotiations to fulfil the mandate. Moreover, this unilateral dynamic was intended to prevent bilateral agreements between the US and Argentina and Uruguay.[14] By means of this offer, the EU intended to make clear that if the Southern bloc were to be dismantled, the biregional agreement would not be replaced by bilateral agreements between the EU and individual countries.

The European offer comprised all sectors – including fishing, services, industry, and agriculture – but it also incorporated important restrictions. In the first place, it proposed a gradual liberalisation schedule of 10 years – very compatible with the WTO, while the CAP would not have to be immediately compromised; and second, the liberalisation program would include 100 per cent and 90 per cent of industrial and agricultural goods, respectively. The remaining 10 per cent was composed of the so-called sensitive products, where MERCOSUR's main competitive exports lay.[15] Even if the European proposal did not offer cuts in subsidies, it did foresee greater liberalisation by means of the increase in tariff quotas for products in which MERCOSUR countries were interested. The innovative character of this offer was not related to the quota system itself, but rather with the fact that it contemplated an improvement for MERCOSUR exports to the EU.

MERCOSUR members' disappointment was reflected in their counter-offer. Whereas the Southern bloc did not reject the European offer, even if it was perceived as being rather limited, MERCOSUR acted consequently, mainly limiting the scope of the liberalisation program, especially in those areas of European interest. The Southern bloc agreed on a 10-year gradual liberalisation program, covering 86 per cent and 90 per cent of manufactured and agricultural goods, respectively, but it excluded the automotive industry, certainly a sensitive area for these countries and one of high priority for the EU. MERCOSUR countries, led by Brazil, were also reluctant to offer concessions in services, investments, and government procurement to foreign competitors.

This phase introduced a major change as a by-product of MERCOSUR's difficulty to 'speak with one voice'. Building consensus on the bloc's offer and on the distribution of costs and benefits among member countries proved to be a highly complex task, being this a reflection of MERCOSUR's institutional deficits. Complexity was even stronger in those areas where member countries showed important discrepancies, as in the case of trade regulation: while Argentina offered this as a trade-off to attain better market-access, Brazil has consistently opposed the introduction of this issue on the negotiation agenda.

This deficit opened a window of opportunity for the participation of the private sector, who was called on to contribute to the design of the regional offers, by

---

14   In 2001, the 'Four plus One' Agreement was reactivated under the auspices of Argentina and Uruguay, who then favoured the establishment of bilateral agreements with the US.

15   The EU offer stood for just 40 per cent of the products exported from MERCOSUR to the European market. The remaining 60 per cent of excluded goods, comprised agricultural products or manufactures with low technology (Heidrich and Oliveira 2005).

harmonizing the various positions and interests within their corresponding sectors. Thus, and before each meeting, MERCOSUR promoted business sectors meetings both at the national and regional level to build the four national positions, which would then be harmonised in the regional arena. Nevertheless, as differences seemed to be difficult to conciliate even within specific economic sectors, governments would have to take up again the leadership, and work on the final harmonisation of the offers.

Another instrument the EU has relied on to facilitate bi-regional negotiations was financial cooperation and technical assistance, directed either to the governments or to civil society actors – namely, NGOs and academics. In 2002, under the Regional Indicative Programme with MERCOSUR, the EU located €48 million to promote agreements and advance different areas related to the negotiations: internal market, institution building, and civil society (EC 2002).

Thus, the EU has managed to keep in the interregional discussion sensitive issues, namely the so-called 'Singapore issues' – transparency in government procurement, trade facilitation, investment, and competition – which showed no progress at the Doha Round.

The final stage was opened by the end of 2003, when the deadline for concluding biregional trade negotiations had already been missed. Following the then EU Trade Commissioner's determination – Pascal Lamy – to meet the EC mandate, the trade ministerial meeting (Brussels 2003) approved a new work programme intended to close all talks in October 2004. The formal announcement was made in the EU-Latin America Summit held in Guadalajara in May 2004.

Even if the trade liberalisation proposals fell short of both regions' expectations, they constituted an important platform for negotiators and allowed them to make progress in successive talks. The EC plan for the conclusion of the bi-regional agreement – the so-called 'Brussels Program' – was certainly an ambitious one, establishing additional five negotiation rounds and two ministerial meetings to sign the bi-regional agreement before the end of the Prodi Commission's mandate in 2004. In a way, the Brussels Program marked a differentiation between the EU-MERCOSUR process and the FTAA: while the latter seemed to be fading away after the WTO meeting in Cancun and the 9-11 terrorist attacks, the EU-MERCOSUR agreement seemed to be coming to a end in the short term. Nevertheless, progress would not last long; and difficulties to come to an agreement would soon become evident. The finalisation of the Prodi Commission's mandate together with the 2004 EU enlargement process added new elements of complexity to this long and difficult negotiation process. Even if the window of opportunity for the finalisation of the agreement would vanish, negotiations continued. However, these included now informal technical meetings between the EU and MERCOSUR, together with ministerial level meetings and other activities aimed at deepening the agendas on political dialogue and cooperation. After further informal contacts in 2009 and 2010, negotiations were re-launched at the VI EU-LAC Summit (Madrid 2010).

Some final remarks

This article has analyzed the evolution of two asymmetric negotiations, involving countries or blocs showing important differences in terms of their development level, but showing great economic, and trade potential. Certainly, had the agreements been sealed, they would have created the largest economic regions in the world. However, this was not the case and this chapter has looked precisely into the factors that account for this non-development. Different reasons combine to explain the difficulties to come to a free trade agreement.

The literature frequently swings between the relevance of contextual factors – namely, the multilateral scenario – and that of domestic institutional variables – the institutional and governance deficits in developing countries that hinder common and coherent positions at the regional level. By contrast, building on the analysis of the particular negotiation dynamics, this chapter has argued that as substantive trade offers lost interest, these were replaced by increasing procedural and governance demands, leading thus to a deadlock or virtual emptiness in the negotiation agenda.

Led by northern countries, both negotiation proposals – the FTAA and the EU-MERCOSUR process – were warmly received by the southern counterparts. Even if in terms of the economic strategy, the objectives pursued by the northern partners were comparable, divergences were more evident in terms of the political incentives. While the FTAA was limited to political dialogue, the European proposal, on the contrary, was intended to promote democracy, being this accompanied by substantial financial and technical support. In turn, these last incentives would sustain the interest and enthusiasm of both governmental actors and civil society representatives in the southern countries.

Despite this initial differentiation, our narrative has shown that as the negotiations advanced, the dynamics of both negotiation processes slowly converged into a common pattern. As southern counterparts lost interest in liberalisation offers, the US and the EU would leave aside issues such as market access for agricultural products and non-tariff barriers, which were to be discussed at the multilateral level. Thus, regional negotiations would depend on concessions within the Doha Round. Consequently, northern interests were reduced to market access in manufactures and the creation and/or harmonisation of regulatory frameworks, especially in the areas of services, government procurement, and investments. MERCOSUR's strategy followed the same path: these countries main interests now lay in agriculture while at the same time attempted at connecting this to the negotiation of regulatory issues.

In terms of the procedural agenda, and when considering the consensus rules established, in both cases, either on the basis of option or coercion, parties agreed on negotiating a trade package. However, when looking deeper into the negotiation methodology, we find that in practice, the single undertaking principle was overlooked, and instead, partial consensus was promoted. Important changes were also introduced regarding the timing of the negotiation processes. Based on the interests of northern partners, initially agreed schedules and deadlines were delayed and postponed as they attempted to connect regional processes to the timing of WTO negotiations.

Convergence was also evident in the pattern of civil society involvement in the negotiation process. In both cases, governments accepted and promoted the participation of business actors as 'listeners' as this could work as a selective incentive to further negotiations. Similar inclusion for civil society actors failed to consolidate; even within the inclusive model proposed by the EU, fostering convergence in this dimension as well. Clearly, the promotion of spaces and channels of participation within the FTAA were intended to promote legitimacy. Business actors' perception and strategies were transformed along the negotiation dynamics: the unification of positions within business networks during the rule-definition phase would then turn out to be a motive of dispute when offers were to be exchanged.

In real terms, both the FTAA and the EU-MERCOSUR negotiations have turned out to be lengthy, complicated, and rather slow motion processes. The dense agendas involved, which included sensitive issues, upon which northern and southern partners' perceptions differed greatly, in the context of marked asymmetries in their negotiation capacities are important factors explaining this complexity and timing. This brings us then to the nature of asymmetry and its impact on trade negotiation processes.

The underpinning of this chapter is that asymmetries are dynamic and that these change and transform as negotiation processes evolve, bringing in not only new issues and requirements, but also new opportunities. In this sense, our analysis confirms the argument put forward by Tussie and Saguier (Chapter 1 in this volume): asymmetry should not be viewed as static. However, in doing so, our findings seem to call for a more nuanced approach to the study of asymmetry in trade negotiations.

Clearly, when addressing their vulnerabilities, southern governments can promote the inclusion of non-state actors. Still, the extent to which this alignment can effectively promote state's capabilities is not automatic or linear across asymmetric trade negotiations, as evidenced when comparatively analyzing the FTAA and the EU-MERCOSUR processes. In the case of the FTAA, a positive relation emerged between state and those non-state actors opposing the agreement – as shown by the articulation between the Brazilian government and trade unions. Contrariwise, within the EU-MERCOSUR process opposition by trade unions remained rather opaque and fragmented to the extent that only large economic actors holding strong stakes in the agreement would stand by the government, whose negotiation position was thus weakened. Clearly, the analysis of the political economy of asymmetric trade negotiations requires a closer examination of the actors, their interests, and strategies in the context of particular negotiation scenarios.[16] In a similar vein, further research is needed

---

16   Similar variation could certainly be observed when analyzing the use of knowledge in trade negotiations, and its impact on governments' capabilities (Botto and Bianculli 2009).

on the conditions that lead to the emergence of new tiers of asymmetry – among southern countries – because of asymmetric processes, as shown in the case of the negotiations of services, where finally the position of Brazil would predominate.

Certainly, as social transformation processes, integration initiatives are socially constructed and politically contested. Our analytical narrative has confirmed this assumption and has shown that as both negotiation processes evolved, difficulties to build consensus among southern and northern partners, plus the increasing procedural and governance demands placed by the latter have altered the initial cost-benefit perceptions of the actors involved. One could reasonably argue that these elements which were displayed as the processes advanced could have not been envisaged at the moment of launching negotiations. Only as these developed, asymmetries would offer new opportunities but also additional constraints to the various actors at play.

References

ALOP. 2003. *Las relaciones MERCOSUR - Unión Europea - Chile: un estudio desde la perspectiva de la sociedad civil.* Montevideo: ALOP.

Bhagwati, J. 1999. Regionalism and Multilateralism: An Overview, in Bhagwati, J. Pravin, K. and Panagariya, A., *Trading Blocs. Alternative Approaches to Analyzing Preferential Trade Agreements.* Cambridge and London: The MIT Press.

Bianculli, A.C. 2010. *Trade Governance in Latin America. Interest Articulation and Institutions across Negotiations in Argentina and Chile.* PhD Dissertation, Department of Political and Social Sciences, Universitat Pompeu Fabra.

Bianculli, A.C. 2005. *Social agendas within new regionalism initiatives. A comparative approach to the FTAA and the EU-MERCOSUR process.* Third annual conference of the Euro-Latin Study Network on Integration and Trade (ELSNIT), Kiel.

BID. 2002. *Más allá de las fronteras: el nuevo regionalismo en América Latina.* Washington, D.C.: BID.

Botto, M. 2009. The role of epistemic communities in the makability of MERCOSUR, in *The EU and World Regionalism. The Makability of Regions in the 21ˢᵗ Century*, edited by De Lombaerde, P. and Schulz, M. Farnham: Ashgate, 171–185.

Botto, M. 2001. *La participación de la sociedad civil en los procesos de integración comercial: los casos del TLCAN, MERCOSUR y ALCA.* Buenos Aires, FLACSO-Argentina. Serie Brief 2.

Botto, M., and Bianculli, A.C. 2009. The case of Argentine Research in the Building of Regional Integration, in *The Politics of Trade: The Role of Research in Trade Policy and Negotiation*, edited by Tussie, D.: Brill Academic Publishers, 81–120.

Bouzas, R. 2004. *MERCOSUR*'s experiences of preparing trade negotiations with the EU. *A memorandum.* Maastricht: ECDPM/ODI.

Briceño Ruiz, J. 2007. *Strategic Regionalism in the Americas: MERCOSUR-CSN and FTAA in Comparative Perspective.* Helsinki: European Consortium for Political Research (ECPR) Joint Sessions.

Bulmer-Thomas, V. 2000. The European Union and MERCOSUR: Prospects for a Free Trade Agreement. *Journal of Interamerican Studies and World Affairs*, 42(1), 1–22.

Bull, B. 2005. *Regional integration and regional regulation in Latin America.* Paper to the General European Consortium for Political Research (ECPR) Conference, Budapest.

Carranza, M.E. 2004. MERCOSUR and the end game of the FTAA negotiations: challenges and prospects after the Argentine crisis. *Third World Quarterly*, 25(2), 319–337.

Deblock, C. and Brunelle, D. 1993. Une intégration régionale stratégique: le cas nord-américain. *Revue Etudes Internationales*, XXIV(3), 595–629.

Devlin, R. and Estevadeordal, A. 2001. *What's new in the new regionalism in the Americas?* Buenos Aires: Banco Interamericano de Desarrollo - Instituto para la Integración de América Latina y el Caribe.

Doctor, M. 2007. Why bother with inter-regionalism? Negotiations for a European Union-MERCOSUR agreement. *Journal of Common Market Studies*, 45(2), 281–314.

EC. 1995. *Free Trade Areas: An Appraisal.* Brussels: European Commission.

EC. 2002. *EU-MERCOSUR: European Commission adopts regional programme in support of further MERCOSUR integration.* Brussels: European Commission.

ECLAC 2000. Spain foreign investment and corporate strategies in Latin America and the Caribbean, in ECLAC, *Foreign investment in Latin America and the Caribbean 1999.* Santiago de Chile: ECLAC.

Ethier, W.J. 1998. The New Regionalism. *The Economic Journal*, 108: 1149–1161.

Faust, J. 2004. Blueprint for an interregional future? The European Union and the Southern Cone, in Aggarwal, V.K. and Fogerty, E.A., *EU Trade strategies: between regionalism and globalism.* London, New York: Macmillan, 41–63.

Flores, Jr., R. 2004. Main results of the study, in Valladão, A., *The EU-MERCOSUR Association Agreement: Mutual Advantages for Business and the Cost of Failure.* Paris: Chaire MERCOSUR de Sciences Po.

Giordano, P. and Santiso, J. 2000. La course aux Amériques: les estratégies des investisseurs Européens dans le MERCOSUR. *Problèmes d'Amérique latine*, 39: 55–87.

Grugel, J. 2004. New Regionalism and Modes of governance: comparing US and EU strategies in Latin America. *European Journal of International Relations*, 10(4), 603–626.

Heidrich, P. and Oliveira, G. 2005. Negociaciones entre MERCOSUR y la Unión Europea. *La Chronique des Amériques, L'Observatoire des Amériques*, Centro de Estudios Internacionales y Mundializaciones (CEIM), 30.

Hettne, B. 1996. Development, security, and world order: A regionalist approach. *The European Journal of Development Research*, 9(1), 83–106.

Jordana, J. and Bianculli, A.C. 2007. Trade policy in the European Union, in Sawaya Jank, M. and Davi Silber, S., *Comparative Trade Policies. Organizational Models and Performance.* São Paulo: Editora Singular, 375–434.

Lorenzo, F. and Vaillant, M. 2005. Exploring the link between decentralization and democratic governance, in Lorenzo, F. and Vaillant, M., *MERCOSUR and the Creation of the Free Trade Area of the Americas.* Washington, DC: Woodrow Wilson International Center for Scholars, 1–28.

Masi, F. and Wise, C. 2005. Negotiating the FTAA between the main Players: the United States and MERCOSUR, in Lorenzo, F. and Vaillant, M., *MERCOSUR and the Creation of the Free Trade Area of the Americas.* Washington, DC Woodrow Wilson International Center for Scholars, 305–347.

Phillips, N. 2003. Hemispheric integration and subregionalism in the Americas. *International Affairs,* 79(2), 327–349.

Rios, S. and Doctor, M. 2004. Scenarios for untying the knots in market access, in Valladão, A. and Messerlin, P., *Concluding the EU-MERCOSUR agreement: feasible scenarios.* Paris: Chaire MERCOSUR de Sciences Po.

Sanchez Bajo, C. 2005. European Union-MERCOSUR interregionalism: negotiations, civil society and governance, in Bøås, M., Marchand, M. H. and Shaw, T., *The Political Economy of Regions and Regionalism.* Basingstoke: Palgrave Macmillan, 33–57.

Santander, S. 2005. The European partnership with MERCOSUR: a relationship based on strategic and neo-liberal principles. *Journal of European Integration*, 27, 285–306.

Weinberg, S. 2003. *Summary report on the first thematic meeting (on agriculture) of the Committee of Government Representatives on the Participation of Civil Society in the FTAA (SOC)*, Sao Paulo, 25 June 2003.

Chapter 5

Venezuela in Asymmetric Trade Negotiations: The Cases of Negotiations in the FTAA and with the EU

Rita Giacalone

Introduction

The decision of the Venezuelan government to leave the Andean Community (CAN) in April 2006, to become a member of the Southern Common Market (MERCOSUR), was the continuation of a process of change in its foreign policy that started in 2001, and had implications for its negotiations with the European Union (EU). Both these aspects are considered here, because the present chapter aims at: (1) making explicit the objectives, strategies, and political economy interests of the Venezuelan government during asymmetric trade negotiations, in the Free Trade Area of the Americas (FTAA) and with the EU as a member of CAN (1995–2006), and (2) evaluating those aspects, as well as future scenarios for Venezuelan-European negotiations.

To achieve these objectives, the chapter is divided in five sections, plus a conclusion. Section two, following the introduction, describes our case study – Venezuela in FTAA negotiations and in CAN-EU negotiations. The third section looks at the motivations of Venezuela, the strategies applied (alliances, linkage with energy questions) and the political economy aspects (sector interests) behind them. Section four outlines the changes that took place along the process and attempts to evaluate the outcome of negotiations and the negotiation strategy of Venezuela. In the fifth section, we discuss the possibility of Venezuela's participation in MERCOSUR-EU negotiations. A summary of the findings will lead us to sketch alternative future scenarios for Venezuela-EU negotiations in the conclusion.

Our efforts to gather information from primary and secondary sources, as well as quantitative and qualitative data, were hindered by strong limitations in access to information from governmental sources. Some of the persons interviewed manifested their opposition to be quoted, and some others did not want to be mentioned. Anyway, the data provided by these persons were validated by other sources.

Description of case study

When the North American Free Trade Agreement (NAFTA) came into effect in January 1994, the hub-and-spoke pattern appeared to be the United States (U.S.) favorite mechanism for signing trade agreements with nations of the hemisphere. However, in December of that year, at the Miami Summit Meeting of Hemispheric Heads of State, the US launched the proposal for a FTAA. At the beginning of the process member nations of CAN (Bolivia, Colombia, Ecuador, Peru, and Venezuela) expressed their willingness to establish a joint voice, faced with the dilemma of delegating sovereignty within the FTAA or within their integration group (da Motta Veiga 2001: 94). But, at that time, CAN was facing a political and institutional crisis that lasted until the reincorporation of Peru in 1997, so coordination was nil before the Ministerial Meeting in San Jose (Costa Rica, 1998). From then on, the Secretariat in Lima established position papers on the basis of the lines suggested by the vice ministers of commerce of member nations; whenever disagreements developed, the position of vice ministers prevailed over that of the Secretariat (Rico Frontaura 2004: 22–23). This meant that national interests prevailed over regional interests, and, by the last stages of the process, when negotiations floundered in December 2004, the former have overridden group considerations.

In Venezuelan negotiations of the FTAA, two stages can be observed: (1) roughly between 1995 and the year 2000, and (2) from 2001 on. Since 1994 the government of Rafael Caldera (1994–1998) changed its emphasis in trade and integration from CAN to Brazil, following the same strategy already observed in the first presidential term of Caldera (1964–1968). Together with the beginning of the construction of the hydroelectric interconnection between Venezuela and Brazil, the Venezuelan government announced, for the first time, its willingness to enter MERCOSUR,[1] and its support to Brazil to obtain a permanent seat in the Security Council of the United Nations.[2] When the rest of the Andean nations protested against Venezuelan intentions regarding MERCOSUR, this idea was substituted by the notion of turning Venezuela into a 'hinge' between CAN and MERCOSUR.[3]

During the first years of the FTAA negotiations, Venezuela participated in all meetings, developed a highly technical staff within the Ministry of Industry and Commerce, which substituted the Institute of International Trade (ICE) in 1997, incorporated members of the private sector, and tried to adequate its institutional and economic structure (modernisation of customs, etc.) in preparation for the agreement. At the same time, President Bill Clinton visited Caracas in October

---

1   At that time MERCOSUR looked attractive for business groups.
2   El Universal, November 8, 1996.
3   Brazilian interest in Venezuela was related to the need to secure access to the energy resources of that country. The idea was well received by the Venezuelan government and business groups (Allegrett 1999).

of 1997, in order to promote the FTAA. By then, the so called 'tequila crisis' had forced the Caldera government to retreat from its heterodox program of adjustment and opt for a more orthodox one, with the support of the International Monetary Fund (IMF). Accordingly, a cooperative attitude with the US government was expected.

The coming to office of Hugo Chávez (1999–2006), supported by a leftist civil-military alliance, did not initially lead to major changes. Until 2001 in a scenario of low oil prices and a preoccupation with steering through changes in the domestic sphere – a new constitution passed in 1999, a new congress, and so on, – the administration continued fulfilling its international obligations, even in the FTAA negotiations, albeit with a new diplomatic style.[4] Also, the new administration maintained the emphasis on relations with Brazil, helped by the strong influence exercised by the Brazilian military upon their Venezuelan counterpart, as evidenced by a history of shared information and sale of armaments (Mendible 2001: 176–77).

The year 2001 marked the beginning of a second stage. In the Quebec Summit Meeting of the FTAA (April 2001), Venezuela signed the final document with reservations – the short time limit for establishing the agreement by January 2005 and the need to submit it to a process of internal consultation (by referendum), but, by the end of the year, the obstruction of the negotiation and the supplanting of the FTAA by a Venezuelan project had become the main objectives of the government. The timing of the change is important because it has been claimed that the Venezuelan government hardened its position vis-à-vis the FTAA negotiations after the strike of the oil industry, and the subsequent events that led to the military and civilian uprising of April 2002, Although this position had already been shaped the previous year, after the uprising the strategy was one of open confrontation, alliance building and the pursuit of strategic influence to alter the course of the negotiations.

In June 2001, Venezuela officially presented a formal request for membership to MERCOSUR, after unsuccessfully calling on CAN to transform itself into a 'Bolivarian Union' (Briceño 2003–2004: 62) with political and military elements.[5] This followed a long list of clashes between Venezuela and CAN, related to the presence in Venezuela of fugitive former Peruvian minister Vladimiro Montesinos, and alleged contacts between the Venezuelan government and the Colombian guerrilla. During these clashes, Venezuela proposed to eliminate the Andean Court of Justice due to the number of pending trials against that country (Cardozo 2006).

---

4   Examples of this first stage of foreign policy are in "La Política Exterior del Gobierno del Presidente, Hugo Chávez Frías Cien días de gestión: transformar la Cancillería y relanzar la diplomacia comercial », 1999 [Online] Available at: www.mre.gob.ve/metadot/ index.pl?id=2348;isa=Newsitem;op=show.

5   The promotion of a supranational union of Latin American nations was incorporated into Article 153 of the 1999 Venezuelan constitution (Morales Manzur and Naim Soto, 2002).

The last effort at coordination between the Venezuelan government and the rest of the Andean nations was made in preparation for the Quebec summit. During the following vice ministerial meetings of the FTAA, Venezuela adopted an individual stand. Finally, in 2003, CAN did not present a single joint offer of market access for the FTAA but five different ones (CAN Secretariat 2003). However, at that time, MERCOSUR did not grant membership to Venezuela, so the latter had to remain in CAN and continue with it in asymmetric negotiations.

The negative Venezuelan position towards the FTAA after 2001 was not accepted by the other CAN members. So Bolivia, Colombia, and Peru signed the document in support of the FTAA, presented in the Port-of-Spain Meeting of the Committee of Trade Negotiations (October 2003), and Colombia, Ecuador, and Peru accepted the offer to negotiate bilateral free trade agreements with the US, with Bolivia participating as an observer (Taccone and Nogueira 2005: 87). Moreover, the negotiations of Colombia and Peru with the US ended with the signing of two bilateral free trade agreements that triggered the decision of Venezuela to exit from the Andean customs union in April 2006.

Regarding negotiations with the EU, Venezuela became a beneficiary of the Andean Generalised System of Preferences (GSP) of the EU in 1995, which until then had only been granted to the rest of the Andean nations. In order to be included, Venezuela argued that the Andean Group was a customs union, and the granting of a preferential reduction of tariffs to the other members of the union, from which Venezuela was excluded, constituted a form of discrimination against this country. In July 2005, the 1995 GSP was substituted by the GSP-Plus, after the World Trade Organisation (WTO) declared the previous preferential trade scheme illegal. Since then, Andean nations have had to ratify and complied with some 27 international conventions regarding labor, sustainable development and governance (Grisanti 2005: 2–13).

In the III EU-Latin America-Caribbean Summit in Guadalajara (May 2004), the EU, under pressure from Peru and Colombia to start negotiations of an association agreement between the two groups, launched a joint process of evaluation of CAN. Probably the fact that the two Andean countries had already opened negotiations to establish bilateral trade agreements with the U.S. influenced the European decision. The joint evaluation was approved by the Mixed Commission EU-CAN in January 2005, and included: (1) the state of the Andean custom union; (2) the level of free trade in goods and services within CAN; and (3) the state of integration institutions (Adiwasito et al. 2005).[6] The EU insisted that Andean governments delegated in the CAN Secretariat their participation in the process, and this was accepted though it had not been done before. The last evaluation meeting took place in Venezuela in December 2005. After that, the Venezuelan government – in charge of the *pro tempore* presidency of CAN – first postponed

---

6   Valoración Conjunta CAN-Unión Europea, Bruselas, 25 y 26 de Julio de 2005, in Venezuela. Ministerio de Relaciones Exteriores. 2006. *Libro Amarillo 2005* Caracas: MRE, 394–95.

the meeting to present the final document, and then suspended it, until in Brussels (19–20 April 2006) Venezuela officially disapproved the document and announced its exit from CAN. Finally, in May 2006, at the IV EU-Latin America-Caribbean Summit in Vienna, the document was approved by the rest of the negotiators, and by the end of the year Bolivia, Colombia, Ecuador, Peru, and the EU decided to start the negotiation of a trade and cooperation agreement in 2007.

The Venezuelan withdrawal from CAN was not wholly unsuspected by the other Andean governments, and by CAN General Secretary, Allan Wagner, who months before had toured each country to establish which governments were interested in participating in an agreement with the EU. The five governments, including Venezuela, had then confirmed their interest. The EU had probably suspected it too, because quite soon the Chief of the European Commission Office for Colombia and Ecuador was announcing that the Venezuelan decision would not affect European negotiations with CAN. This did not prevent then Peruvian President Alejandro Toledo from publicly blasting the Venezuelan decision in Vienna (www.elcomercio.com.pe 12 May 2006).

In 2006, Venezuela's exit from CAN posed the question of how Venezuela would negotiate with the EU in the future. Accordingly, the analysis of its behavior in failed FTAA negotiations may provide clues regarding its future behavior.

Motivations of Venezuela to engage in negotiations

Political economy aspects

During the first stage of FTAA negotiations, the Venezuelan government kept the private sector informed and included in the process by means of informal consultation and discussion of subjects of special interest to them. Not all sectors, however, were equally interested. As expected the Venezuelan-American Chamber (Venamcham), made up by big importer and exporter companies, supported the possibility of enlarging business with the US through the FTAA. The umbrella organisation for Venezuelan business (Fedecamaras) also had a positive attitude and called for Caracas to be the seat of the FTAA Secretariat, but, after most of its members were harshly affected by the Venezuelan banking crisis of 1995, the association limited its activities to watching developments until 1999, leaving to sector organisations a more active participation.

Of the sector organisations, Conindustria (industry) and Fedeagro (agriculture and cattle) were the most active. Both had a defensive position, conscious of the limitations of their ability to compete in an open economy. Thus, they wanted access to the process in order to secure that some level of protection was maintained, longer chronograms were established, and/or the government would offer them some form of compensation. Fedeagro was the most defensive, but even their representatives viewed the sector shortcomings emanating more from within the Venezuelan economy – lack of incentives, and high cost of doing business in Venezuela, for example – than from the FTAA. In fact, they stated that the negative effects for the sector would be the same if Venezuela signed the hemispheric agreement or if it joined MERCOSUR (Giacalone 2005: 262–270).

An analysis of the pattern of trade between Venezuela and the US (Genúa 2001–2002) shows that 80 per cent of that trade is explained by differences in labour productivity. Accordingly, Venezuela at that time had advantages in only four industrial sectors – food, beverages, and tobacco; chemical substances; oil derivatives; and basic iron and steel industries – while the US had advantages in all the other sectors (textiles, garments, leather products and shoes, paper and paper pulp, metal goods, machinery, transport material, electric equipment, other manufactured industry, and so on). The lowering of bilateral tariffs within the FTAA would have little impact on that pattern. Only a systemic effort to improve Venezuelan productivity would alter this situation and, in order to make this possible, special and preferential treatment for Venezuela would be necessary.

So no sector or business, or just a very small proportion, could be clearly established as a winner due to the establishment of the FTAA. In spite of this, most of their statements show the shared conviction of the private sector that a trade agreement with the US would be beneficial, because it would force the government to streamline its public procurement programs and grant more transparency to its judicial system. These are high priorities in the list of demands that Venezuelan business has presented to the government since the mid 1980s (Giacalone 1999). The general benefit would be a more secure and stable framework for private property and business operation. Additionally, Venezuelan business wanted the entry of US investment after the banking crisis of 1995.

It is difficult to follow the participation and position of Venezuela in FTAA negotiations after 1999. Porcarelli and Garófalo (2005: 124) have classified these difficulties in: (1) external, such as the facts that there are no records of meetings, and drafts include both positions approved and not yet approved without mentioning who proposed them; (2) internal to Venezuela, such as changes in the negotiating teams, lack of consistence in participation in meetings, lack of clear strategic lines that granted ministers leverage to impose their personal and ideological preferences, and lack of coordination among ministries. But, for them, the most important aspect was the transformation and upheaval of the institutions in charge of foreign economic negotiations.

In the previous years, the Ministry of Industry and Commerce, and before that a highly specialised technical office (ICE), had led the process of preparation and participation in the FTAA meetings, in consultation with the private sector. When the new administration came to office in 1999, within the Ministry political appointees replaced technical personnel. A 'parallel diplomacy' structure was set up around the Executive. The creation of a FTAA Consulting Committee in Congress, controlled by members of the government party, marked the beginning of this movement. Its expressed aim was to conduct a process of consultation with civil society and to inform the public about the process of negotiation. In fact, the committee engaged in propaganda against the FTAA.[7] Later on, the Congressional Committee disappeared when an ad-hoc negotiating team (the Presidential Committee for FTAA Negotiation) was formed in February 2003. Part of the ad-hoc team had been previously affiliated with the president within the advisory group (Porcarelli and Garófalo 2005: 127), which included the minister of commerce, together with representatives of the ministries of Foreign Affairs, Agriculture and Land, and Higher Education, plus the president of the state oil company Petróleos de Venezuela S.A. (PDVSA), academics and military.

At the beginning of 2004, the FTAA technical negotiators linked to the Presidential Committee were removed from the Ministry of Industry and Commerce, due to an internal shake up after the appointment of Minister Edmée Betancourt, but they were kept in charge of negotiations after moving to the Foreign Affairs Ministry. This way the FTAA negotiation ended up being conducted directly by the President and a close circle of advisers, and with its technical team working for the Direction of Strategic Analysis of the Ministry of Foreign Affairs, outside the Venezuelan ministry (Industry and Commerce) legally competent for foreign economic negotiations. The high profile of the President in foreign policy negotiations was accompanied by the establishment of direct links between the Executive and business,[8] sidestepping the role of interest associations such as Conindustria, Fedeagro, and Fedecamaras, especially after the 48 hour ousting of President Chavez in April 2002 in which Fedecamaras had played an active role.[9]

The political economy aspects would not be complete without mentioning the different interests of bureaucratic sectors within the Venezuelan government.[10] Though the foreign economic policy of Venezuela formally states the shared objective of diversifying exports, this objective has not been reached and all bureaucratic sectors do not put the same emphasis on it. Part of the sudden changes in the direction of economic ministries demonstrate the existence of clashes of personalities and/or factions, and an ongoing process of disagreement between politically/ideologically oriented groups, with little or no economic knowledge, and 'the technical apparatus'. Both groups have been formed within the present

---

7   The author of this chapter participated in meetings chaired by the Congressional Committee, in which representatives of business, trade unions, and universities listened to lengthy presentations by members of the government party, with no time for questioning.

8   Former minister Giordani, a close adviser of the president, has stated that in Venezuela there are no business people but 'intermediaries' and 'contractors', so the government has to develop a pro-government business sector to complement the activities of foreign business not involved in domestic politics.

9   The president of Fedecámaras became president of Venezuela.

10   In July 2005, a meeting of government offices interested in relations with the EU brought together representatives of the ministries of Foreign Affairs, Commerce and Production, Health, Education, and Transport, the National Electoral Council, the customs service, and many municipalities, showing the variety of Venezuelan bureaucratic interests involved.

government, as anybody associated with previous governments was forced to leave the administration after April 2002.

Thus, it is hard to assess if there are specific interests that favour Venezuelan participation in trade negotiations, such as that of the FTAA or a Venezuelan-EU association agreement with a trade component. The only thing that can be concluded so far is that those opposing this type of agreements (hard line followers of the president, usually without previous diplomatic and/or negotiating experience) have had the upper hand since 2001.

Strategies and alliances for asymmetric negotiations

Different explanations have been provided for the changes in objective and strategy of the Venezuelan government after 2001. Porcarelli and Garófalo (2005: 126) link these changes to an internal debate in the government party that managed to consolidate the anti-FTAA position of members of the National Assembly (Congress) and a small group of academics from the Central University of Venezuela, one of whom had a prominent role in the Presidential Committee and, later on, in the negotiation. This position was first assumed by the Congressional Committee, but later all sectors of the Venezuelan government adopted the banners and repeated the arguments of anti-globalisation groups external to Venezuela.

Naim Soto (2003: 33) sees these changes as a consequence of the fact that the new Venezuelan government supported the idea of a Latin American political and economic bloc, able to undertake external negotiations from a stronger base. And this idea was supported by the resources that since 2001 began to flow into Venezuela due to the international rise of oil prices. Romero (2003: 47–48, 63) gives still another reason – that the existence of a fight for economic hegemony between the US and the EU and the appearance of China as an important economic actor have created an international conjunction in which other economic actors are willing to replace the US as clients and providers of Venezuela; so there was less risk involved in attempting to develop a more autonomous position.

Briceño Ruiz (2003–2004: 61) considers that by December 2001 the Brazilian government had already assumed a hard position vis-à-vis the US in the FTAA negotiations and Venezuela was only following the steps of Brazil. This coincides with analysts who attribute the change to the 'daze with the regional, hemispheric, and world weight of Brazil', and the 'illusion of out of measure influence and lack of vulnerability perceived by the Venezuelan government by the recovery of international oil prices' (Visión Venezolana, 1 July 2001). But this does not explain why representatives of the Venezuelan government participated in an anti-FTAA meeting in Havana (November 2001), in which there was no official Brazilian representation. The meeting, sponsored by Cuba, may be linked to the events of 11 September 2001 in New York, which had fuelled expectations about the political and economic decline of the US.

Accordingly, two external actors worked in favour of Venezuela changing its position regarding the FTAA. One was Brazil, which wanted to slow down the FTAA process in order to have time to increase its bargaining power through the establishment of a free trade agreement between MERCOSUR and CAN;[11] and the other, Cuba which, unable to participate in the negotiation of the FTAA, wanted to disrupt the process. The decision of the government to side with them aimed at obtaining regional and international support for the political changes taking place within Venezuela. In this sense, one recurrent theme of the post 2001 foreign policy has been the building of a network of goodwill in the international community for the revolutionary process, in order to avoid outside intervention and/or the political isolation of Venezuela (Cardozo 2006). Anyway, previous declarations by the government already pointed towards a conceptual and ideological reappraisal of regional integration that would affect its perception of asymmetric trade agreements (see the 1999 Venezuelan Constitution).

The participation of members of the Venezuelan government in the Hemispheric Meeting Against the FTAA in Havana, in November 2001 (Saguier 2007), was the first manifestation of an important change in strategy and objective – from establishing a unitary voice with CAN to negotiate the protection of Venezuelan interests within the FTAA, to associating with the most radical anti-FTAA groups to prevent the signing of the agreement. The following month, the Venezuelan president presented his own project – the Bolivarian Alternative for the Americas (ALBA), at the Summit Meeting of the Association of Caribbean States, in Margarita Island. This counterproposal to the FTAA had a strong ideological component, and it is based upon the use of oil resources and a politically selective opening of Venezuelan trade (Cardozo 2006: 98).

In sum, the decision of the Venezuelan government to change its position in 2001 can be attributed to a mix of internal and external factors to the negotiation. In the first group were the windows of opportunity offered by the hardening of the Brazilian position vis-à-vis the US, the prevalence of national interests among member nations of CAN, and the high visibility of protests by anti-FTAA non-governmental groups. The external developments were the increased possibility of trade and investment access to the EU and China and the influx of oil money into Venezuela. At the same time, the changes in strategy and objective can be attributed to internal developments within the administration, because the decision to side with the Cuban government and anti-FTAA organisations implied the consolidation of anti-US and pro-Cuban groups within the government. Finally, the Venezuelan position became a contributing factor in the failure of the FTAA process towards the end of 2004.

In the negotiations, the post 2001 Venezuelan strategy took the form of introducing new issues in order to stall or disrupt the process before its deadline. New working groups were proposed by the Venezuelan government – one to create

---

11   This fact became more urgent after the Quebec meeting (April 2001), when FTAA trade offers began to take shape (Rojas 2005: 28–29).

compensation funds for asymmetries, and the other to study the legal, constitutional, and juridical aspects of Latin American nations that would be affected by the FTAA. At the same time, the government adopted the arguments and the language of anti-FTAA groups. In general, the political discourse of the government after 2001 became confrontational and the objective of 'destroying US supremacy' was a recurrent subject (Mora Brito 2004: 84). In the regional front, after Venezuela failed to secure support for this position from CAN, its government resorted to: (1) devaluating CAN as a 'neo-liberal' scheme while praising MERCOSUR for its anti-FTAA position; (2) asking for important political changes within CAN while at the same time not fulfilling its duties with the organisation; (3) threatening to leave but remaining until the last moment in order to block other negotiations such as those with the EU; and (4) creating diplomatic rows by provoking a personal clash with Peruvian President Alejandro Toledo.

In the domestic front, the private sector was cut out from participation in informal discussions and from access to governmental information on the process. At that time, all business organisations that had previously participated in FTAA consultations were actively confronting the government. Afraid of being marginalized, they all came out publicly in support of joining the FTAA, if it was established. In parallel, the legally responsible office for the negotiation was substituted by a political advisory group answering to the president himself, and a strong propaganda effort was developed against the FTAA.

What external alliances did the Venezuelan government construct in those years in order to achieve its objective? External alliances from 2001 on were made with governments, such as Brazil, and Cuba. As put forth in Chapter 1 links were also nurtured with Non-Governmental Organisations (NGOs), such as the Hemispheric Social Alliance (HSA) and the Mexican Network of Action Against Free Trade (RMALC, by its Spanish acronym). Links with the second group led the government to send a new team of negotiators to the Universidad de Puebla (Mexico), to be trained according to anti-FTAA premises, and inviting members of RMALC to give seminars in the Ministry of Foreign Affairs.

Regarding the Venezuelan strategy in the negotiations with the EU as a CAN member, the government participated in the process leading to the joint document.[12] Before each of the evaluation meetings with experts from the EU, the CAN Secretariat met with the vice ministers in charge of the process in each Andean country, to discuss and amend the documents to be presented. The Venezuelan Vice-minister and Director of Integration of the Ministry of Commerce, Roger Figueroa, took active part in this process. From the beginning, however, Venezuela manifested a lack of interest in the trade component of the association agreement.

---

12   This information was gathered by the author in interviews with officers of the CAN Secretariat in Lima, Peru (September 2006). Persons Interviewed: Gladys Genúa (Coordinator, Section of Andean Integration and Trade Negotiations, CAN Secretariat, 7 September 2006), Nilsa Mújica (Coordinator of the ATR Program, CAN Secretariat, 7 September 2006), José Rivero (Officer of the CAN Secretariat, 8 September 2006).

Also Venezuela had been the last Andean country to sign the GSP-Plus in 2005 due to two objections: (1) provisions for unilateral revisions by the EU of Andean countries compliance with the terms of the agreement, and (2) provisions leading to sign the International Labour Organisation agreement regarding children labor, when Venezuelan law on that subject was more developed than those provisions.

For the Venezuelan government, the trade component of an agreement with the EU, together with the development of an Andean common external tariff, such as the EU insisted that CAN should have,[13] would mean the flooding of Andean markets by European goods. During the joint evaluation process, Venezuela emphasised that the existence of a common external tariff in CAN was not a *sine qua non* condition for the agreement, and tried to change 'the predominantly economic and commercial character of negotiations towards more political and social aspects' (Valoración Conjunta 2006: 394–95). In fact, the Venezuelan argument for rejecting the joint assessment document was that it did not incorporate concepts of solidarity and recognition of asymmetries between CAN and the EU.

In the last stages of the process, when Venezuela had the pro-tempore presidency of CAN, its government applied a strategy of stalling, already employed during FTAA negotiations. For example, the Venezuelan government did not call the CAN meeting scheduled for March 2006 in Margarita Island, where Andean governments were expected to approve the joint evaluation document. The Brussels meeting in April was called by the EU, and forced the Venezuelan government to disavow the document and announce its withdrawal from CAN. This prevented CAN and the EU from announcing a definite date for the launching of negotiations of an association agreement at the Vienna meeting in May, and the announcement was postponed until December 2006.

If we look at the political economy aspects of EU-CAN from the perspective of the Venezuelan economy, we find that Venezuelan imports from the EU in 2004 represented a little over 20 per cent of total imports to that country, while Venezuelan exports to Europe represented only four per cent (Rosales 2005: 131). Since July 2005 Venezuela benefited from the GSP-Plus regime. The GSP together with the Most Favoured Nation (MFN) clause, allow duty free treatment for almost 85 per cent of Venezuelan exports to the European market (EU-Venezuela relations 2006). The mainstay of Venezuelan exports to Europe are energy products (around 80 per cent in 2006), in spite of the stated objective of diversification. So the balance of trade between Venezuela and the EU depends mainly on the international price of oil and not on preferential tariffs.[14]

---

13   The EU wanted an Andean market in which European goods could freely circulate as Andean exports would circulate within the European market (Comisión Europea 2006).

14   The Colombian Minister of Commerce, Industry and Tourism has summarised the situation: 'To sell gas and oil you do not need free trade agreements. But if you depend on selling shoes, t-shirts, home appliances, light industry, and machinery, you need agreements'. www.laprensagrafica.com/economia/902003.asp, 20 October 2007.

We may conclude that, before 1999, the Venezuelan government had a positive outlook about the FTAA, formed a high level technical negotiating team, with little civil society participation except for the private sector, and political interest in the subject was moderate. After 2001, the government outlook turned negative, the negotiating team was supplanted by political appointees, civil society participation remained scant, the private sector was marginalised, and the political visibility of the FTAA for the government became high (Porcarelli 2005: 151). Venezuela left CAN before the start of formal negotiations with the EU, but by then it had made clear its lack of interest in the trade component of those negotiations.

Assessment of negotiations and of strategies

Positions in trade negotiations are the result of strategic decisions based on a combination of economic analysis (quantitative costs and benefits for sectors) and political analysis (electoral cost of labour restructuring, for example). But it is not exceptional that these decisions respond to one or other rationality. This seems to be the case of the decisions taken by the present Venezuelan government in the FTAA negotiations. Our assessment of the strategic decisions of Venezuela aims at answering these questions: What reasons led the government to change its strategic position in asymmetric trade negotiations? And how successful were those decisions in terms of reaching the objectives of the government?

Additionally, an assessment of Venezuelan participation and position in both the FTAA negotiation and the negotiation with the EU requires some previous definition of the changes that took place during those years, at different levels: (1) at that of the ideological and conceptual basis of regional integration; (2) at the level of the relationship of the government with internal and external actors; and (3) at the 'situational' level – defined as the combination of factors affecting the relative position of a nation in international relations at a given historical conjunction. From our perspective, the last one is probably the most relevant to explain the change of course in asymmetric trade negotiations, but some comments are necessary about the other two levels.

At the ideological and conceptual level, the concept of regional integration incorporated in the 1999 Venezuelan constitution places political matters in the forefront of commercial or productive forms of integration, and statements by government members established political and ideological affinity among governments as the basic structure of support for any type of decision (Méndez Romero 2004) – 'Economic integration is a consequence of political integration' (Chávez in Briceño Ruiz 2003–2004: 62) and, also, a necessary prerequisite is political affinity or 'Support for the Venezuelan government political project, as nothing could be done without it'. This affinity justifies the postponement of any other consideration of cost-benefit analysis, as demonstrated by the decision of Venezuela to become a full member of MERCOSUR.[15]

In support of this process of affirmation of the political basis of integration, the post 1999 Venezuelan government looked at historical projects of Latin American integration that have never constituted part of a unified proposal and had diverse origins and expectations. Thus, the political discourse was accommodated in order to provide a rational basis for a political project of regional integration. The government found a favourable regional environment when the governments of Brazil and Argentina echoed that discourse in defense of their own interests.[16] At the same time, the Venezuelan government used different platforms to spread this ideological discourse, especially favouring presidential addresses in national and international events and Venezuelan members of the Andean and Latin American Parliaments flagging proposals for political and supranational integration (Correa Flores 2005).

The relationship of the government with internal and external actors also changed during the process of negotiation of the FTAA. In the internal field, the administration of Caldera (1994–1998) was supported by a combination of traditional and leftist political forces, with a pro-Brazilian attitude, but also by members of the private sector interested in negotiating new trade links and attracting foreign investment. After 1999, the new administration was supported by leftist and nationalist political groups and by sectors of the armed forces with a similar orientation. These groups shared traits such as little experience and/or interest in trade matters and a clear anti-US position, thus making it relatively easier for the government to follow this line after 2001. At the same time, the political confrontation between the government and the private sector, since the employers' lockout of December 2001 and the oil strike, freed the Executive from the need to court their support by negotiating asymmetric trade agreements, an issue which in any case ran counter to the preferences of supporters in the armed forces and other political groups.

In the external field, after 2001 the government changed its perception of important external actors. The most obvious change can be seen in the enhanced importance granted to relations with MERCOSUR in detriment of relations with CAN, though at first this looked as the continuation of the emphasis on relations with Brazil inaugurated by Caldera. Soon, however, additional external actors, such as Cuba and anti-FTAA organizations, gained relevance. But still while the Venezuelan government openly employed a hard anti-FTAA and anti-US discourse, it never employed the same tone regarding the EU. This signals different perceptions of the Venezuelan government about the role that these two external actors can play vis-à-vis its own political process.

---

15   See Toro and Ruiz 2005, Klinkhammer 2005, Gutiérrez 2006 for an analysis of the negative effects on the Venezuelan economy.

16   Brazilian opposition to the FTAA is based on a cost-benefit analysis rather than on an ideological analysis (Chami Batista and Wagner de Azevedo 2002).

Though Venezuela tried to apply the same strategy in the FTAA negotiation and in the EU-Venezuelan negotiation through CAN, in the former the strategy was successful in stalling and then suspending negotiations, but its impact has been less in the latter. This might have been due to the fact that in the FTAA negotiations Venezuelan objectives coincided with those of other important players, such as Brazil and MERCOSUR, which were interested in stalling the process in order to have time for building its negotiating strength, and accelerate agriculture negotiations in the Doha round of the WTO. In the CAN negotiation with the EU, Venezuela achieved a smaller success because lack of Andean support for this position finally led to its abandonment of the group. Bolivia originally rejected the joint assessment document in Brussels, but approved it later, so the Venezuelan government failed in getting open support for its position. Also Colombian and Peruvian diplomacy managed to circumvent the Venezuelan delay of the approval of the document, when the EU sponsored the meeting in Brussels, in April 2006. Attacks made soon after by the Venezuelan government on President Toledo of Peru suggest that the Venezuelan government felt outsmarted.

At the situational level, the Venezuelan position in asymmetric negotiations was influenced by the change brought about by the incremental influx of oil money into the economy. Oil money changed the asymmetric perspective of the government vis-à-vis the US and the EU, by making Venezuela more immune to outside pressures by those actors. It also provided the Venezuelan government with almost unlimited resources to play a leading role in regional affairs, and in maintaining its association with its political-ideological partners, Brazil and Cuba, and later Argentina. Oil and oil money were important factors influencing MERCOSUR's decision to accept Venezuela as a full member, especially after the Venezuelan government bought the largest part of the Argentine external debt, allowing Argentina to repay its debt with the IMF. This development, together with the Venezuelan inability to swing Andean governments toward its position regarding free trade agreements, explained its exit from CAN and its entry into MERCOSUR.

But, what has not changed meanwhile is the structure of the Venezuelan economy, an important explanatory factor for its lack of interest in asymmetric trade agreements. Oil is still responsible for 30 per cent of GNP, 80 per cent of its exports,[17] and more than 50 per cent of the government's revenues. And, as long as Venezuela is the fifth producer of oil in the world and the international price of oil was high, its government did not feel the need to accept the conditions of more developed nations, which were basically dependent on its exports.[18] Also, Venezuela is still important for the EU, due to European investments in energy in

---

17 Most of the remaining exports concentrate on basic industries under State control – iron, aluminium, steel, and petrochemicals. For more on Venezuelan economic structure, see Toro and Ruiz (2005), Gómez (1991), Gutiérrez (2006).

18 In 2002, 64 per cent (US$188 million) of new investment in Venezuela came from Europe (Economic Commission 2006).

that country (European Commission 2006). In the end, to understand the pattern of Venezuelan negotiations with the EU, it is necessary to assess different scenarios.

Venezuela in EU-MERCOSUR negotiations

The process of EU-MERCOSUR negotiations has formally covered a lot of ground but has not moved on essential market access issues (see Botto and Bianculli in this volume). Nonetheless, incorporating Venezuela will lead to re-discuss most issues already settled. The most likely scenario is that future negotiations of Venezuela with the EU would take place within MERCOSUR, after the former acquires full status as member of this group. Full membership, however, has been delayed by a slow ratification process in which Paraguay remains amiss.[19]

How would Venezuela fit within MERCOSUR's strategy and interest representation in negotiating with the EU? The first observation is that major differences drive from structural factors, because roughly 80 per cent of Venezuelan exports are oil and oil derivatives, and the revenues these exports generate go straight into State hands, and are redistributed by the government. Additionally, Venezuela is a net importer of agricultural products. But this does not take into account that in the FTAA negotiations the Venezuelan government had already shifted the basis of its foreign trade position from a cost-benefit analysis to political-ideological considerations, so the same could be expected here. Even so, prospects are not good for the negotiation of the trade component of the agreement, because the negotiation incorporates points expressly objected by Venezuela in the FTAA process – trade in services, public procurement, and intellectual property rights.

In this case, the alternative to joint negotiation with the EU through MERCOSUR has two scenarios: (1) Negotiations of Venezuela with the EU, in preparation for full accession to MERCOSUR, in order to establish an agreement on political dialogue and cooperation but without the trade component. (2) No negotiations between Venezuela and the EU, but bilateral deals with some European nations in order to counteract US power and attract investments.

These scenarios are predicated on the fact that Europe is one of the biggest investors in Venezuela, with a high concentration in the energy sector.[20] This has important implications because, though there is no major trade interest, relations with the EU are seen as offsetting US power within the region. This explains

---

19   According to *Venezuela...Estrategia País 2007–2013:*.5, the European Commission's relations with Venezuela take place at a regional (EU-LAC and in the future EU-MERCOSUR) and bilateral level. European Commission. *Venezuela. Documento de Estrategia país 2007–2013.* [Online] Available at: www.europa.eu.int/comm/external_relations/la.

20   European oil companies have been affected by the decision of the government to reassume direct operations of oil fields. However, the government has paid them well for that right (Párraga 2007).

why, since rejecting the joint evaluation document, Venezuela has made positive gestures toward Europe, such as the visit of the Vice Minister of Foreign Relations for Europe to the European Parliament and the European Commission, in October 2006. The visit was presented by Venezuela as part of an effort to re-launch its relations with the EU, 'This launching includes the building of political, cultural, economic, and social mechanisms of interrelationship with Europe'. At the same time, European private sector representatives have been invited to Venezuela to explore business options.[21]

This approach, however, does not fall well with all members of the EU, which have claimed their disagreement with negotiations with individual nations, instead of regional groups[22]. And Venezuela's exit from CAN has 'shattered one of the historical objectives of the EU...: the development of integration processes in Latin America' (Dominguez 2007: 25). Some EU representatives have also warned about the erosion of democracy in Venezuela,[23] and the EU 'pattern of behavior shows a legacy of prudence' which does not agree with the radicalisation process in Venezuela (Roy 2007: 21). But, as long as Venezuela remains an attractive market, business may exert influence upon individual governments to negotiate with it, making the second scenario look plausible too.[24]

But these scenarios can be altered by pressure from the other four members of MERCOSUR, if they want Venezuela to participate in the negotiating process. In this sense, the existence of a common external tariff of MERCOSUR that covers 85 per cent of products points toward the need that all members of MERCOSUR jointly participate in external trade negotiations, mainly considering that in negotiations with the EU tariff bargaining is still the central issue.[25] Also, pressure from the EU may have an impact. These pressures would have to include some face-saving device for the Venezuelan government to accept the trade component of the agreement.

---

21 'Al Momento', a TV program sponsored by the government, announced a visit by German business for November 2006, with the objective of re-launching relations with Germany, and the EU.

22 This objection has disappeared, however, with the signing of the EU-Colombia and EU-Peru association agreements in 2010.

23 See statements of Benita Ferrero-Waldner, EU Commissioner for External Relations (Presentarán en Bruselas indicadores sobre Venezuela. El Universal, 19 octubre 2006) and Mikko Pyhala, *pro témpore* president of the EU (Peñaloza 2006).

24 Queiroz (2007) shows how Portuguese interests in energy security have favoured business with Venezuela.

25 Venezuela was granted additional time for joining MERCOSUR's external tariff, and this was not a pressing issue when the EU-MERCOSUR negotiations had slowed down, but the reactivation of the negotiation in 2010 may create distortions in trade between the two blocs if Venezuela does not become a member of a future EU-MERCOSUR agreement.

Conclusion

Summarizing, the conceptual basis and the political and economic interests in the asymmetric negotiation of the FTAA began to change after the accession of the Chavez administration in 1999, but negotiation objectives and strategies did not officially change until 2001. Regarding interest representation after that year, three facts are obvious: (1) Venezuelan business in industry and agriculture, who had developed closer links with the Andean region along decades, especially with Colombia, have lost out with the Venezuelan decision to leave CAN; (2) those same businesses are threatened by the decision to enter MERCOSUR, because Brazilian and Argentinian goods are more competitive than similar Venezuelan products (Klinkhammer 2005, Gutiérrez 2006) and (3) most businesses who may profit from Venezuelan membership in MERCOSUR are State owned or under its control – oil, petro-chemicals, iron, and aluminium –, although the official discourse emphasises the promotion of exports from small and medium size manufacturing enterprises and/or cooperatives. Meanwhile, the collapse of the FTAA negotiations does not represent a hardship for the Venezuelan private sector, except that it has postponed needed governmental reforms in terms of transparency in public procurement.

After 2001, oil money flowing into Venezuela has helped to create a business sector dependent upon government procurement. As most of these contracts are granted without public bidding, it has also increased the need for businesses to associate with the government in order to take part in the contracts. These links tend not to be transparent, and the secrecy that surrounds most subjects dealing with foreign policy and/or public procurement matters prevent a proper analysis of political and economic interests. The fact that decisions are highly centralised and dependent on the favour of the presidency complicate matters.

Asymmetric trade agreements are opposed by the current government due to a combination of political/ideological aspects, which emphasised integration agreements with Latin American nations, including political, social, and military elements, and its lack of interest in developing markets for the Venezuelan private sector in general. The only exception appears to be ALBA, in which Venezuela grants technical and economic aid to lesser economies (Bolivia, Cuba, Nicaragua, and nations of the Caribbean) and the resources of preferential trade in oil can be used by those countries to buy other goods in Venezuela. Most of the recent trade agreements signed by the government, with the stated objective of diversifying exports, have ended up with Venezuela exporting oil and oil derivatives and the other countries (Iran, Russia, etc.) increasing their exports to Venezuela, which means that only the sources of Venezuelan imports have been diversified.

In handling the question of asymmetries, Venezuela has openly sided with the position supported by anti-globalisation groups, and has practically employed the same language and the same arguments as the HSA, stressing ideological elements of its revolutionary process in support of this position. But, at the same time, the Venezuelan economy is atypical within the universe of developing nations, and a set of circumstances makes it less costly for Venezuela to sustain that position. So, not only ideology and politics provide support for what Venezuela has been doing in asymmetric negotiations. Behind this position we can point at, on the one hand, economic factors such as the high price of oil and a more active presence of China and Europe in the international economy, and, on the other, geopolitical factors such as an enhanced interest of the EU and other international actors in counterbalancing U.S. power.

In conclusion, there is little possibility that the position of the Venezuelan government in negotiating with the EU would deviate from that assumed in FTAA negotiations. The most important external elements that could alter this situation would be the strategies and interests of the other members of MERCOSUR and a stronger position of the EU in support of the negotiation. It is unlikely that a slowing down of the international economy *per se* may have the same effect, even if oil prices drop, because without those external pressures the Venezuelan government could still resort to a more radicalised, nationalistic and ideological position.

References

Adiwasito, E., De Lombaerde, P. and Pietrangeli, G. 2005. On the joint assessment of Andean integration in EU-CAN Relations. *Studia Diplomatica,* LVIII(3), 115–143.

Allegrett, E.E. 1999. *La Energía: Motor de Integración Brasil-Venezuela.* Venezuela: Analítica.

Briceño Ruiz, J. 2003–2004. La posición de Venezuela frente al ALCA y las relaciones de la CAN con Estados Unidos y la UE. *Aldea Mundo*, 8(16), 59–66.

CAN Secretariat. 2003. *Las negociaciones del ALCA y la CAN en acceso a mercados de bienes agrícolas y no agrícolas.* Lima : CAN. [Online] Available at: www.comunidadandina.org.

Cardozo, E. 2006. *La agenda de seguridad de Venezuela-Colombia en el contexto de la subregión andina.* Caracas: ILDIS.

CELARE. 2004. *America Latina-Unión Europea. Documentación de Base 2003.* Santiago de Chile: CELARE-CEPAL.

Chami Batista, J. and Wagner de Azevedo, J.P. 2002. El TLC y las pèrdidas de mercado de Brasil en los Estados Unidos, 1992–2001. *Revista de la CEPAL,* 78, 167–82.

Comisión Europea 2006. *Euronotas,* 36 (Bogotá: Delegación de la Comisión Europea para Colombia y Ecuador).

Correa Flores, R. (comp) 2005. *Construyendo el ALBA* (Caracas: Parlamento Latinoamericano).

Da Motta Veiga, P. 2001. *The Latin American and Caribbean Countries and Trade Negotiations: an Exercise in the Development of Scenarios* (Washington: Inter American Development Bank).

Dominguez, R. 2007. Between Vienna and Lima, in *After Vienna: Dimensions of the Relationship between the EU and the Latin America-Caribbean Region*, edited by Roy, J. and Dominguez, R. Miami: Jean Monnet Chair-University of Miami, 23–32.

Estevadeordal, A. and Ekaterina, K. 2000. *Negotiating Market Access between the European Union and Mercosur.* Occasional Paper 7, (Buenos Aires: INTAL).

European Commission. 2006. *Report on the Venezuela Strategic Paper 2001–2006.* [Online] Available at: www.ec.europa.eu/comm/external_relations/venezuela.

Genúa, G. 2001–2002. El ALCA y los patrones de comercio entre Estados Unidos y Venezuela. *Aldea Mundo*, 6(12), 30–38.

Giacalone, R. 1999. *Los empresarios frente al Grupo de Los Tres: Integración, intereses e ideas.* Caracas: Panapo.

Giacalone, R. 2005. Panorama de la posición empresarial venezolana frente al ALCA, in *El ALCA. Perspectivas desde Venezuela,* edited by Briceño Ruiz, J. and Bustamante, A.M. Mérida: CEFI-ULA, 257–277.

Gómez, E. 1991. *Dilemas de una economía petrolera.* Caracas: CEDICE-Panapo.

Grisanti, L.X. 2005. Muere SGP andino. *El Universal*, (July 21), 2–13.

Gutiérrez, A. 2006. Venezuela en el Mercosur: Oportunidades y amenazas, in *El ALCA frente al regionalismos sudamericano*, edited by Briceño R. and Gorodeckas, H. San Cristóbal: ULA, 137–82.

ICE. 1995. *Las preferencias andinas de la Unión Europea: Oportunidades para Venezuela.* Caracas: ICE, Instituto de Comercio Exterior.

ICTSD. 2005. *Puentes entre el comercio y el desarrollo sostenible.* [Online], 2(8). Available at: www.ictsd.org.

Klinkhammer, R. 2005. ¿Debería Venezuela ingresar a Mercosur?, in *Venezuela en el ALCA: entre realidades y fantasías,* edited by Giacalone, R. Mérida: Vicerrectorado Académico- Universidad de Los Andes, 187–209.

Méndez Romero, A. 2004. Entrevista especial al Viceministro de Relaciones Exteriores, Arévalo Méndez Romero, por Eduardo Rodríguez, in *TvPrensa 2000 Transcripción de Programas de Opinión, Monitoreo de Noticieros, Venevisión*, 15(73).

Mora Brito, D. 2004. La política exterior de Hugo Chávez en tres actos (1998–2004). *Aldea Mundo*, 8(16), 76–85.

Morales Manzur, J.C. and Naim Soto, N.N. 2002. La democracia y la integración latinoamericana: un análisis inconcluso. *Revista de la Facultad de Ciencias Jurídicas y Políticas*, (124).

Párraga, M. 2007. PDVSA pagó $250 millones por Jusepín. *El Universal*, (6 marzo), 1–10.

Peñaloza, P.P. 2006. Comisión Europea propone respetar libertad de ONGs. *El Universal*, (octubre 19).

Porcarelli, E. 2005. Venezuela en las negociaciones del ALCA, in *El ALCA. Perspectivas desde Venezuela,* edited by Briceño Ruiz, J. and Bustamante, A.M. Mérida: CEFI-ULA, 149–62.

Porcarelli, E. and Fidel, G. 2005. Evolución de la participación y la posición de Venezuela en las negociaciones del ALCA, in *Venezuela en el ALCA: entre realidades y fantasías,* edited by Giacalone, R. Mérida: Vicerrectorado Académico-ULA, 117–37.

Queiroz, M. 2007. *Venezuela refuerza su presencia en UE.* Lisboa, (October 3), [Online] Available at: www.domino.ips.org.

Rico Frontaura, V. 2004. *La coordinación y negociación conjunta de los países de la Comunidad Andina en el marco del ALCA y de la OMC.* Buenos Aires: INTAL-BID.

Rojas, L. 2005. Situación actual de las negociaciones para la formación del ALCA, in *Venezuela en el ALCA : entre realidades y fantasías,* edited by Giacalone, R. Mérida: Vicerrectorado Académico-ULA, 15–31.

Romero, N. 2003. Venezuela y el ALCA. *Cuadernos Latinoamericanos*, 14, 38–67.

Rosales, O. 2005. Economía política en la relación económica euro-latinoamericana, in *América Latina-Unión Europea. Documentación de Base 2004,* Santiago de Chile: CELARE, junio, 127–145.

Roy, J. 2007. Inertia and Vertigo in Regional Integration, in *After Vienna: Dimensions of the Relationship between the EU and the Latin America-Caribbean Region*, edited by Roy, J. and Dominguez, R. Miami: Jean Monnet Chair-University of Miami, 7–21.

Saguier, M. 2007. The Hemispheric Social Alliance and the Free Trade Area of the Americas process: the challenges and opportunities of transnational coalitions against neo-liberalism. *Globalizations*, 4(2), May-June.

Taccone, J.J. and Uziel, N. (eds) 2005. *Informe Andino, 2002–2004.* Buenos Aires: INTAL.

Toro, G.L.A. and Ruiz I.J.A. 2005. Efectos potenciales de la inserción comercial de Venezuela en el ALCA, in *Venezuela en el ALCA: entre realidades y fantasías,* Giacalone, R. Mérida: Vicerrectorado Académico-ULA, 75–91.

Chapter 6

Negotiating the Colombia-US FTA: A Colombian Perspective

Luis Jorge Garay, Philippe De Lombaerde and Fernando Barberi

Introduction

The Free Trade Agreement (FTA) between Colombia and the United States (US), signed by the parties at the end of 2006, is of particular interest from an analytical point of view because of the existing special political relationship between both countries.[1] It is well known that Colombia has been one of the strong bastions of the US in Latin America, especially during the Uribe administration. The country even supported the invasion of Iraq. In effect, traditionally, Colombia has collaborated closely with the US with respect to the eradication of illicit drugs and the struggle against drugs traffic and terrorism. On the other side, the US has supported the country with the Andean Trade Preference Act (ATPA) and, afterwards, the Andean Trade Promotion and Drug Eradication Act (ATPDEA), and with the so-called Plan Colombia with an important military component in the struggle against drugs trade and irregular armed groups framed in the strategy of the fight against terrorism.

In these circumstances, it was to be expected that the Agreement between the two countries, apart from being negotiated in conditions of obvious structural asymmetry, would have certain special characteristics, particularly in the negotiation of its agricultural chapter, given the important role the rural sector and agricultural production are playing for the political, economic and social stability of Colombia.[2]

Generally speaking, agriculture and intellectual property rights have been the most sensitive issues, not only in the negotiations of US trade agreements, but also in multilateral negotiations.[3] They were also the most problematic in the negotiations of the Colombia-US FTA. It is therefore that these two cases are analysed in this chapter in more detail (in sections four and five, respectively). These case studies are preceded by a discussion of the antecedents and Colombia's

---

1   The official title of the agreement is Trade Promotion Agreement (TPA).

2   According to a recent comparative cases-study (Genna 2010), the existence of asymmetries would be a contributing factor to the success of negotiating western hemispheric FTAs.

3   See, for example, Pugatch (2006) and Tsai (2006).

motivations to enter into the negotiations (in section two), and a general assessment of the negotiations (in section three). Section six concludes.

Motivations for Colombia's engagement in the negotiations

The market of the US is and remains very important for Colombia (Figure 6.1). Over the last 20 years, exports to the US have always oscillated around 40 per cent of total Colombian exports (Figure 6.2).[4] Their composition remains very traditional, however. Colombian exports are largely dominated by minerals, followed by agricultural products (coffee, fruits etc.) (Table 6.1). Colombia is also an important destination for American foreign direct investment (FDI) (Figures 6.4 and 6.5).

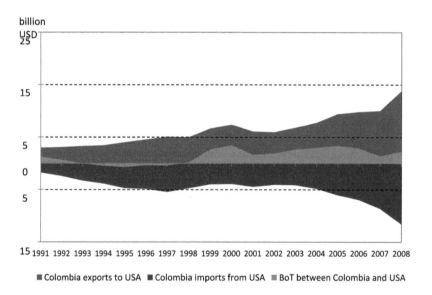

Figure 6.1 Bilateral trade between Colombia and the US (1991–2008)
Source: UNCOMTRADE Database, 2010.

---

4   Obviously in stark contrast with the importance of trade with Colombia for the US (Figure 6.3).

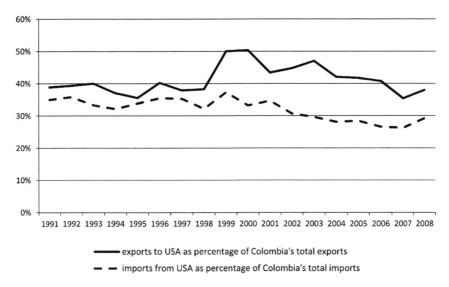

Figure 6.2 Relative importance of bilateral trade for Colombia (% of total)

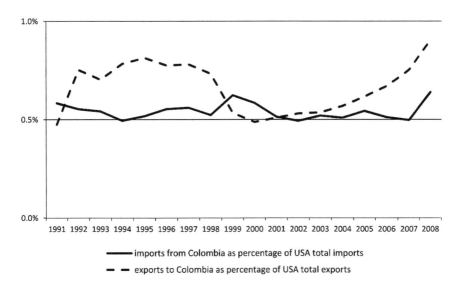

Figure 6.3 Relative importance of bilateral trade for the US (% of total)

Source: UNCOMTRADE Database, 2010.

Table 6.1 Structure of Colombia-US bilateral trade (2008)

	Colombia exports to USA		Colombia imports from USA	
	Product	percentage	Product	percentage
1	Mineral fuels, mineral oils and products of their distillation; bituminous substances; mineral waxes	63.5%	Nuclear reactors, boilers, machinery and mechanical appliances; parts thereof	18.6%
2	Coffee, tea, mate and spices	6.1%	Mineral fuels, mineral oils and products of their distillation; bituminous substances; mineral waxes	9.8%
3	Natural or cultured pearls, precious or semi-precious stones, precious metals, metals clad with precious metal, and articles thereof; imitation jewellery; coin	5.3%	Cereals	9.8%
4	Live trees and other plants; bulbs, roots and the like; cut flowers and ornamental foliage	4.7%	Organic chemicals	9.4%
5	Edible fruit and nuts; peel of citrus fruit or melons	1.9%	Electrical machinery and equipment and parts thereof; sound recorders and reproducers, television image and sound recorders and reproducers, and parts and accessories of such articles	6.1%
6	Articles of apparel and clothing accessories, not knitted or crocheted	1.5%	Aircraft, spacecraft, and parts thereof	5.4%
7	Articles of iron or steel	1.4%	Plastics and articles thereof	4.6%
8	Plastics and articles thereof	1.2%	Vehicles other than railway or tramway rolling-stock, and parts and accessories thereof	4.5%
9	Articles of apparel and clothing accessories, knitted or crocheted	1.1%	Optical, photographic, cinematographic, measuring, checking, precision, medical or surgical instruments and apparatus; parts and accessories thereof	4.1%
10	Salt; sulphur; earths and stone; plastering materials, lime and cement	0.7%	Articles of iron or steel	2.3%

Source: UNCOMTRADE database, 2010.

Notes: Product category based on HS-1996 classification.

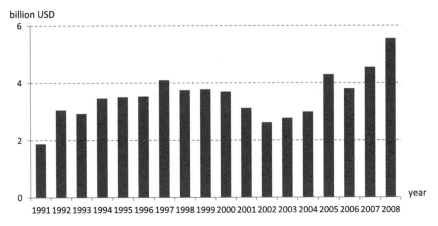

Figure 6.4 US FDI in Colombia

Source: Online database, Bureau of Economic analysis, U.S. Department of commerce. http://www.bea.gov/international.

Notes: data retrieved on 26 November 2010.

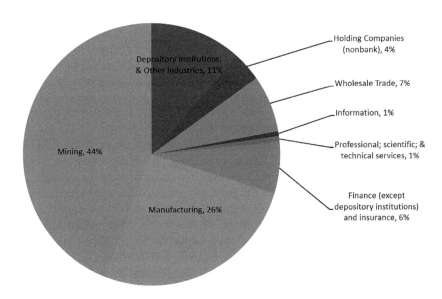

Figure 6.5 The composition of US FDI in Colombia, by industry groups (2008)

Source: Online database, Bureau of Economic analysis, U.S. Department of commerce. http://www.bea.gov/international [accessed 26 November 2010].

From the perspective of the Colombian government, the negotiation of the FTA with the US was based on the basic premise to deepen the integration of the Colombian economy in the international economy. This process started in the beginning of the 1990s, when tariff and related barriers were significantly and unilaterally lowered, the services sector was opened, the capital market was liberalised, foreign investment was allowed in most sectors of the economy, Andean integration was deepened, and the model of international integration was modified from an inward looking regional integration scheme towards a model of open regionalism.

In this context, it was decided to deepen the external relations of the Andean economies and, consequently, to engage in trade negotiations multilaterally, bilaterally or individually within the framework of Andean rules, preferably with Latin American and Caribbean countries, but also with third markets. By that time, the idea of negotiating a multilateral trade agreement among all countries of the American hemisphere, including the US, was gradually taking shape. And it was at the Summit of the Americas, held in Miami in 1994, that 34 heads of state agreed to start the negotiation of a Free Trade Area of the Americas (FTAA).

However, this negotiation failed at the beginning of this decade basically because of the US position with respect to agricultural subsidies, having a distorting effect on production and international trade, which led Brazil, followed by the Southern Common Market (MERCOSUR), to propose to exclude services and intellectual property rights from the agreement.

Nevertheless, since the Gaviria presidency (1990–1994) Colombia had initiated preliminary contacts with the US to seek the signature of an FTA. The country was then even named as the second country on the list, behind Chile, to strike a trade deal with the US. Since that time, the Colombian government considered necessary to consolidate the trade preferences that were unilaterally conceded by the US to the Andean countries, with the exception of Venezuela, basically in return for the fight against drugs.

The trade preferences offered on the basis of the Andean Trade Preference Act (ATPA) was a policy innovation re-shaping the relations between Andean countries and the US on the premise that if economic development and legal economic activity is stimulated, the fight against illicit drugs production would become easier.[5] The concession of such preferences by the US government meant that they openly accepted a joint responsibility in the fight against drugs. This explains why this concession was always subject to the accomplishment by the benefiting countries (Bolivia, Colombia, Ecuador and Peru) of a set of conditions imposed by the US with respect to the production and trafficking of illicit drugs.

The ATPA foresaw trade preferences that were wider than those under the Generalised System of Preferences (GSP), covering approximately 65 per cent of the tariff universe (Ramírez Ocampo 2007: 56). At the same time, rules of origin

---

5   The ATPA was enacted on 4 December 1991, and was in force until 4 December 2001.

were made more flexible. With a utilisation rate fluctuating between 13 and 16 per cent, the impact of the preferences was generally speaking rather modest, although for specific products like flowers the preferences allowed for a substantial growth in exports (Ramírez Ocampo 2007: 57).

During the Pastrana administration (1998–2002) the circumstances to extend ATPA were rather complicated, especially the political ambiance for its approval was rather difficult in the US Congress. This is why the government started diplomatic contacts with the US government seeking the negotiation of an FTA, without diminishing its efforts in the negotiations of the FTAA, to which Colombia was firmly committed. This informal phase culminated with the formal request of Colombia to negotiate the FTA. The request was rejected by the US government because the Bush administration channelled all its priorities towards achieving on agreement on the FTAA.

The trade preferences were extended by the ATPDEA, enacted in August 2002, in principle for a period of five years.[6] It included a number of new product categories, including textiles and petroleum derivatives.[7]

The first Uribe government (2002–2006) reiterated the request put forward by the previous administration. Different circumstances coincided and explain why the negotiation of an FTA now could take off. They should be seen against the background of a changing US foreign policy which inclined towards regionalism since the beginning of the 1990s (De Lombaerde and Garay 2008: 16–25), when the Initiative for the Americas was launched and NAFTA was signed, and also included the failure of the FTAA negotiations and the stagnation of the Doha Round. In the new situation, the US moved towards the signing of bilateral FTAs with various trade partners, on the premise that this strategy offered better chances to defend its interests and reach its objectives on the bilateral and plurilateral levels, with an eye on extending them to the multilateral level afterwards. In addition and importantly, for the Bush administration the FTAs were instrumented as part of its strategy of national security.

For Colombia, the negotiation with the US fitted with its policy of open regionalism, with the objective of integration in the large economic blocks, and with the necessity to find effective market access to third markets as a fundamental element of the country's development strategy. This identification of interests between the parties, together with the strategic role of Colombia in US foreign policy gave rise to the start of the negotiations.

Colombia formally requested the start of trade negotiations on 30 April 2003. The US government reacted positively in August of the same year but proposed plurilateral negotiations with all Andean beneficiary countries of ATPDEA, thus leaving Venezuela outside.

---

6   The ATPDEA had retro-active effects from 31 December 2001 onwards. It was later extended until 31 December 2007, on the condition of prior signing of an FTA.

7   The number of covered tariff positions increased from 5524 to 6500 (Pulecio 2005: 15).

Various factors explain why the Colombian government promoted the negotiation of the FTA with the US. At the general level, the negotiation was framed within the economic vision of the Colombian government, basically based on the mainstream economic views on the potential positive contribution of free trade and economic integration to the welfare of societies. It was also compatible with the political position of the government which emphasised the importance of the political and economic relations with the US, the size of its market, the level of per capita income of its population, and above all the fear of losing the ATPDEA preferences (which would in principle extinguish in December 2007) and end up in disadvantage with respect to other countries which signed FTAs with the US, and the position that such an agreement would constitute a fundamental factor for the attraction of foreign investment.

In this endeavour, the government was supported by the (majority) fractions in the Congress that supported the President (including the Conservative Party), and most of the sectoral employers' organisations (*gremios*) under the leadership of Luis Carlos Villegas, combining the presidencies of the umbrella organisations ANDI (National Business Association of Colombia-Asociación Nacional de Empresarios de Colombia)[8] and CGA (Consejo Gremial Ampliado).

Opposition came from the left-wing opposition in the Congress (Polo Democrático Alternativo), trade unions and other civil society organisations. The RECALCA-platform (Red Colombiana de Acción frente al Libre Comercio y el ALCA),[9] which was created during the negotiations of the FTAA, managed to play an effective coordinating role between the different opposition groups, effectively networked with similar organisations and movements in other countries in the region, and lobbied directly against the FTA in the US. The Liberal Party and the academic world were divided on the issue.

General assessment of the negotiations ... chronicle of a non-ratification foretold

The negotiation process formally started in May 2004 when the first Round took off in Cartagena (Box 6.1). The signature of the agreement in November 2006 thus took altogether two years and a half. Whereas initially, negotiations were started with Colombia, Ecuador and Peru together, by the end of 2005 the three countries opted for distinct strategies.[10] Colombia and Peru pursued the signing of bilateral agreements,[11] whereas the negotiations between Ecuador and the US were suspended in May 2006.

The negotiation process is not exactly an example of a smooth process. And as the whole issue of the Colombia-US FTA became gradually more and more politicised, it is not surprising that very different and contradictory readings of the

---

8   See, www.andi.com.co.
9   See, www.recalca.org.co.
10   Bolivia participated initially as an observer. Venezuela did not participate in this process.
11   Peru concluded negotiations on an FTA in December 2005.

results of the negotiations have been presented. The Colombian government has presented the outcome of the negotiations as a success and has strongly defended its contents in the Colombian Congress and before the public in general, but it was criticised by the opposition in the Congress, several sectors of civil society, certain producers' organisations, and certain sectors in academia.[12]

Box 6.1 Chronology of negotiations

I Round: Cartagena, Colombia (18–19 May 2004)
II Round: Atlanta, US (14–18 June 2004)
III Round: Lima, Peru (26–30 2004)
IV Round: Fajardo, Puerto Rico (13–17 September 2004)
V Round: Guayaquil, Ecuador (25–29 October 2004)
VI Round: Tucson, US (30 November–4 December 2004)
VII Round: Cartagena, Colombia (7–11 February 2005)
VIII Round: Washington, US (14–22 March 2005)
IX Round: Lima, Peru (18–22 April 2005)
X Round: Guayaquil, Ecuador (6–10 June 2005)
XI Round: Miami, US (18–22 July 2005)
XII Round: Cartagena, US (13–19 September 2005)
XIII Round: Washington, US (14–22 November 2005)
XIV Round: Washington, US (25 January–3 February 2006)
Closure of negotiation: Washington, US (28 February, 2006)
Signature of TPA: Washington, US (22 November 2006)

Araújo Ibarra, a consultancy company, presented a detailed matrix in which the negotiations were evaluated (Araújo Ibarra 2007). A summary matrix is presented in Table 6.2. In the matrix, the final outcome of the negotiations was compared with the 406 initial objectives of the Colombian negotiators. The conclusion of the authors is that 79 per cent of the initial objectives were fully obtained, amounting to around 85 per cent of those that remained valid during the negotiation process. Only 6 per cent of the objectives were not met, but those were never considered as threatening vital interests of the country. It was maintained that 'some' of these objectives were originally included for strategic reasons, in order to be given up in the final stage of the negotiations to achieve other more fundamental objectives. Nine per cent of the original objectives were partially reached, meaning that they were reached sufficiently in order to protect Colombian or that they were replaced by other objectives that better reflected the priorities of the negotiators.

---

12   Critical analyses include: Umaña (2004), Zerda et al. (2005), Sarmiento (2005), Oxfam (2006), and RECALCA (2006).

Table 6.2 Matrix of objectives and achievements of negotiations: Colombian perspective (Araújo Ibarra)

Negotiation table	Theme	# objectives	# objectives reached	# objectives partially reached	# objectives not reached	# other objectives
Market access	*Sub-total*	*69*	*61*	*4*	*2*	*2*
	Scope and coverage	2	1	0	0	1
	National treatment	1	1	0	0	0
	Elimination of tariffs	8	6	0	1	1
	Relation with WTO	1	1	0	0	0
	Special regimes	4	4	0	0	0
	Non-tariff barriers	5	5	0	0	0
	Other measures	1	0	1	0	0
	Institutional provisions	1	0	1	0	0
	TBTs	14	12	1	1	0
	Customs procedures	11	11	0	0	0
	Origin regime	10	9	1	0	0
	Textiles	11	11	0	0	0
Agriculture	*Sub-total*	*27*	*4*	*15*	*7*	*1*
	Market access	14	2	10	2	0
	Internal support	2	0	0	2	0
	Export competition	6	0	3	3	0
	SPS	2	2	0	0	0
	Agricultural committee	2	0	2	0	0
	Resources and objectives	1	0	0	0	1
Environmental issues	*Sub-total*	*16*	*13*	*1*	*0*	*2*
Institutional issues	*Sub-total*	*15*	*12*	*1*	*0*	*2*
	Institutional issues	11	10	0	0	1
	Transversal legal issues	3	1	1	0	1
	Legal issues	1	1	0	0	0
Labour issues	*Sub-total*	*9*	*9*	*0*	*0*	*0*
Competition	*Sub-total*	*15*	*10*	*3*	*1*	*1*
Government procurement	*Sub-total*	*11*	*10*	*1*	*0*	*0*
Cooperation – strengthening of trade capacity	*Sub-total*	*43*	*35*	*0*	*2*	*6*
	Participation in negotiation	2	2	0	0	0
	Implementation	11	10	0	0	1

	Adaptation – restructuring of agricultural sector	5	4	0	0	1
	Adaptation – Improving productivity and competitiveness	10	10	0	0	0
	Adaptation – Sustainable development	3	1	0	0	2
	Adaptation – logistics	2	2	0	0	0
	Adaptation – science and technology	5	2	0	2	1
	Participation of civil society	2	1	0	0	1
	Adaptation – services	2	2	0	0	0
	Adaptation – foreign investment	1	1	0	0	0
Trade remedies	*(Bilateral safeguards) Sub-total*	*23*	*20*	*1*	*1*	*1*
Investment	*Sub-total*	*29*	*25*	*1*	*3*	*0*
SPS	*Sub-total*	*21*	*20*	*1*	*0*	*0*
	Harmonisation	4	4	0	0	0
	Equivalence	3	2	1	0	0
	Evaluation of risks and adequate protection	5	5	0	0	0
	Transparency	3	3	0	0	0
	Regionalisation	2	2	0	0	0
	SDT	1	1	0	0	0
	Dispute settlement	1	1	0	0	0
	Cooperation and technical assistance	1	1	0	0	0
	Bilateral SPS Committee	1	1	0	0	0
Intellectual property	Intellectual property	54	37	4	3	10
Financial services	Financial services	13	12	0	0	1
Telecommunication services	Telecommunications services	28	26	1	1	0
Cross-border trade in services	Cross-border trade in services	17	13	2	2	0
Dispute settlement	Dispute settlement	16	15	0	1	0
	Total	**406**	**322**	**35**	**23**	**26**
	%	**100**	**79**	**9**	**6**	**6**

Source: Based on Araújo Ibarra (2007).

However, the exercise by Araújo Ibarra should be read with caution. Apart from the observation that a certain 'proximity' existed between the company and the government, from a methodological point of view, it should be observed that it is not clear which criteria are used to include a negotiation objective as such, nor is it made explicit which weights should be attached to each objective. Each objective should ideally be weighted by the potential benefits of reaching it, which in absolute terms equals the costs of not reaching it. In addition, a 'correct' calculation should take into account conditional benefits (costs) given the fact that the latter depend on whether other related objectives have also been reached (or not).

But even from this biased and unweighted quantified evaluation it becomes clear that in several areas, the outcome of the negotiations is not satisfactory. Agriculture and intellectual property are clear cases and will be looked at more in detail in the next sections. Also investment has been pointed out as a problematic sector.[13] These disappointing results have been related to two false premises on which the strategy of the government was based: the premise that Colombia would receive a preferential treatment as strategic ally of the US in the region (premise 1), on the one hand, and the premise that the United States Trade Representative (USTR) could be considered as the decisive interlocutor capable of manoeuvring the FTA through Congress (premise 2), on the other (Pulecio 2005). Other factors that should not be forgotten in explaining Colombia's apparently weak negotiation position include the fact that the initiative to negotiate came initially from the Colombian side (Garay, Barberi and Cardona 2006, López 2007) and the fact that the Andean countries did not succeed in adopting common positions throughout the process.

Because of premise 1, the weakness of its own negotiation position was apparently underestimated by the Colombian government in the beginning of the process and became only gradually clear in the course of the process. It was revealed when Colombia had to change its strategy after Round VI in December 2004 (accepting the WTO-Plus logic of the US FTAs and, more specifically, the precedents of the US-Chile and US-CAFTA-DR (US-Central America FTA-Dominican Republic) negotiations), when Colombia (together with the other Andean countries) had to formally request an extension of the ATPDEA in June 2006, and when President Uribe personally tried to lobby in Washington towards the end of the process. The corresponding strength of the US position was revealed by the fact that they were able to stick very closely to their initial negotiation positions and that they were able to clearly separate their commercial interests from their geo-strategic interests.

It is telling that the chief negotiator for Colombia stated in May 2008 that the main benefits from the FTA for Colombia were not to be expected from trade gains or Foreign Direct Investment (FDI) gains (sic), but were to be found in domestic policies (better regulation of government procurement, better labour regulations, better customs administrations, etc.), given the fact that countries like Colombia

---

13   On the investment chapter, see also, Maruyama and Rosenberg (2010).

have limited capacities to reform (Gómez 2008). And he argued that this (positive) effect on domestic regulation and policies could already be noticed before the end of the negotiations and was understood by the multinationals as a signal of modernisation and institutional strengthening, which reacted with increased FDI. He further suggested that investment and trade should also be seen in a different light. With respect to investment protection, according to the chief negotiator, Colombia did also have an interest in the proliferation of provisions on investment protection, because of its interests in protecting Colombian FDI in Peru, Ecuador and other countries. With respect to trade, he stated that pursuing an FTA with the US also allowed to pursue a new agreement with Peru, Chile and Mexico, as a way to replace the G-3.[14]

However, the major obstacle for the US-Colombia FTA at the end of the day appeared to be the ratification process in the US Congress. This was rather unexpected by most of the analysts. Thus, also premise 2 proved to be false. The Colombian government underestimated this aspect of the whole process and, in spite of stepped-up diplomatic and lobbying efforts, it did not succeed in taking this hurdle until today. This means that more than three years after closing the negotiations, there is still not even a perspective for ratification in the US Congress. This illustrates well the difficult and atypical trajectory of the negotiation and post-negotiation process of this FTA.

Indeed, after an improvised visit of President Uribe to Washington in February 2006, surmounting the remaining differences, and reaching an agreement on 28 February, the process did not follow the usual course of trade negotiations, i.e. the formal signature of the agreement and its smooth ratification by the respective parliaments. Soon after reaching an agreement, it became clear that in several chapters there were still a number of ambiguities and discrepancies between the English and Spanish versions of the text, which made it necessary to continue talks for several months. As a result, the government had to wait with the publication of the final texts for several months after the closure of the negotiations. This was heavily criticised by the opposition parties and social movements (RECALCA 2006: 181–215).

More importantly, because of the new democratic majority in the US Congress, the US government had to accept a negotiation with the Democratic Party (and the Republicans) in order to assure the ratification of the FTAs signed with Colombia, Panama, Peru and South Korea. As a result, several modifications to the four original texts were proposed, referring to investment, public procurement, intellectual property rights, environment, and resolution of environmental and labour-related controversies.[15]

---

14   The Group of Three (G-3) was a new generation FTA, established between Colombia, Mexico and Venezuela in 1995.

15   For an overview of the proposed modifications, see Rojas and Lloreda (2007: 399–405).

Ratification was further complicated when it became one of the issues during the presidential election campaign and the democratic primaries. Both Hilary Rodham Clinton and Barack Obama pronounced themselves openly against the FTA with Colombia. And when President Bush (finally) decided to submit the Act to Congress in the beginning of April 2008, in an unprecedented move House speaker Nancy Pelosi promoted and obtained a change in the House rules, thus avoiding a vote within 90 days after submission by the President. Voting on the Act was then first postponed until after the 2008 US Presidential elections, then until after the 2010 Colombian presidential elections, and then it was suggested that it would not happen before the end of Obama's (first) presidential period (Krugman 2010). The changed composition of the Congress after the November 2010 elections, with the Republicans re-conquering the majority – the House of Representatives was, however, a new element for US trade policy. Colombian lobbying and its strategy to negotiate parallel agreements with other trade partners, to put further pressure on the US Congress, did not succeed in bringing the ratification of the agreement between Colombia and the US on the Congressional agenda of the latter.[16] According to Krugman (2010), Obama does and should not use his political capital to push for a political consensus regarding the signature of new free trade agreements.

Assessment of the negotiation of the agricultural chapter[17]

The matrix in Table 6.2 already suggests the problematic negotiations of the agricultural chapter. Of the 27 initial objectives, the government achieved only four, 15 were only achieved partially and 7 objectives were not reached at all. A more detailed analysis of the rules and tariff elimination programmes with respect to bilateral trade, as written down in the text of the Agreement, only confirms that the objectives were not reached. The result was not only unequal and asymmetric in favour of the US, even more importantly than in the Central American FTA (CAFTA), but in addition it proved impossible to reach agreements on the elimination of or compensation for the NTBs in place in the US.

The unequal character of the negotiation of the agricultural chapter can be based on five principal arguments, being:

---

16 Colombia signed an FTA with Chile on 27 November 2006 (which entered into force on 8 May 2009), an FTA with Guatemala, El Salvador and Honduras on 9 August 2007 (the agreement with Guatemala entered into force on 12 November 2009), an FTA with Canada on 21 November 2008, and an FTA with EFTA countries on 25 November 2008. On 19 May 2010, on the occasion of the EU-LAC Summit in Madrid, the negotiations of an FTA with the EU were successfully and formally concluded. Finally, Colombia started to negotiate an FTA with South Korea in December 2009 and with Panamá in March 2010.

17 This section is to an important extent based on: Garay, Barberi and Cardona (2006).

Firstly, while the US maintained its protectionist and stabilisation policies by means of domestic production support (i.e. subsidies), Colombia accepted to give up the Andean System of Price Margins (*Sistema andino de franjas de precios*)[18] and the Public Mechanism of Quota Administration (*Mecanismo público de administración de contingentes*)[19] for imports originating in the US.

It should be specified that although it is true that both countries maintain the possibility to use internal measures to support production, it is also true that fiscal capacity in both economies is very different, leaving aside the fact that direct internal support to the sector are equivalent to 39 per cent of agricultural GDP in the US, compared to 3 per cent in the case of Colombia (Garay 2005). In addition, it should be observed that whereas for the US the Agreement does not have fiscal implications – given the fact that from a tariff perspective Colombia already benefited from preferences for the sector under ATPDEA since more than ten years and that its internal production support mechanisms are in place for several decades–, for Colombia its fiscal situation would be aggravated for two reasons: first, not only does it have to give up fiscal revenue from to-be-eliminated tariffs on imports originating in the US, but in view of the new competitive conditions imposed by the FTA, the government has already been obliged to increase domestic support to agricultural production for some time.

Secondly, it has not been possible to include in the Agreement a mechanism that replaces the system of price margins, as for example price safeguarding measures for the duration of the Agreement or until distorting production support in the US would be eliminated in the framework of the World Trade Organisation (WTO).

Although a quantity safeguard has been included in the FTA which could be considered as a means to compensate for the elimination of the system of price margins, in practice it is not an adequate substitute. A first reason is related to the fact that the objective of a price safeguard is to stabilise import prices and to protect domestic production against imports at unusually low prices, whereas a quantity safeguard, as its name indicates, aims at protecting production against excessive imports, not against low prices. A second reason has to do with the fact that the level of tariff restitution is not 100 per cent during the whole transition period and that it would only stay in force during this period, whereas the internal support in the US could continue indefinitely, i.e. beyond the transition period. In addition, the main sensitive Colombian agricultural products included in the system of price margins were not covered by safeguards (corn, sorghum, soy, pork meat).

Thirdly, no clause was foreseen that allows for a revision of the tariff reduction programme in case the US would decide to increase the levels of existing domestic support, which could lead to a further depression of US export prices in the future and to injury for import competing producers, independently of whether they managed to increase their competitiveness and reduced production costs. In

---

18   This is a system of flexible tariffs that inversely vary with the evolution of the international import price of a product with respect to a selected reference price.

19   This is an auction mechanism to allocate import quotas.

addition, domestic support could also be used by the US to substitute current border protection to sensitive products, thus negatively affecting the competitiveness of Colombian exports.

By way of contrast it should be observed here that in the Agreement between the US and Canada trade liberalisation was conditioned by the amount of domestic support. In effect, Canada was allowed to establish import permits for wheat, oat, barley and their derivatives when the level of internal support of the US for these products was higher than the Canadian level. It should also be mentioned that the Doha Round is currently on hold and that the US has not offered unconditional reduction of internal support (yet).

Fourthly, the US has excluded sugar and products with high sugar content not ready for final consumption from the liberalisation programme, whereas Colombia was not able to exclude any subsector or product from their tariff reduction programme in agriculture.

It should be pointed out that the fact that the US has offered the largest import quota for sugar and products with high sugar content not ready for final consumption to Colombia (in volume terms), does not take away the unequal character of the Agreement, if we consider that no single exclusion was accepted on the side of Colombia. Not only was Chile, in its Agreement with the US, allowed to technically exclude the whole sugar sector, including sugar substituting glucose and fructose syrup, but was Morocco, in its Agreement, allowed to exclude two important agricultural sub-sectors (beef and the wheat production chain). The same happened in other Agreements such as the one with Jordan which excluded the tobacco sector, the one with Canada which excluded poultry and milk products, and CAFTA which excluded potato and onion in the case of Costa Rica and white corn in the other Central-American countries.

It should also be noted that although the quota offered by the US to Colombia for sugar and products with high sugar content not ready for final consumption is the highest in volume terms, as a percentage of total national sugar production (2.0 per cent) it was only higher than the corresponding percentage for Guatemala (1.7 per cent), equal to the one in the Dominican Republic, but inferior to the percentages for Honduras (2.4 per cent), Costa Rica (2.8 per cent), Nicaragua (5.6 per cent) and El Salvador (6.1 per cent). In summary, the quota offered in CAFTA corresponded to 2.8 per cent of the sugar production in Central America, which suggests that access offered to Colombia should not necessarily be considered as the most generous in this sector.[20]

Fifthly, the US requested a non-reciprocal preferential clause, according to which Colombia committed itself to extend any additional preference, compared to the ones conceded in the FTA, that it might concede to any other country with which it would undertake trade negotiations after 27 February 2006.

---

20   Production data were taken from Food and Agriculture Organization (FAO), and correspond to the 2001–2004 period for Colombia and to the 2002–2003 period for the Central American countries.

The request of a non-reciprocal preferential clause does not seem to be an adequate compensation for the immediate tariff reduction that the US offered to Colombia, which corresponded to 100 per cent, given the fact that if we compare with duty free access conceded by Colombia to the US from day one of the entry into force of the Agreement through tariff contingents, we observe that this tariff reduction would effectively amount to 124 per cent, and if in addition potential trade diversion in favour of the US would be taken into account, total tariff reduction of Colombia towards the US would effectively be as high as 165 per cent.

On top of that, it should be observed that the US liberalised immediately 100 per cent of Central American exports without requesting the non-reciprocal preferential clause. It should not be forgotten that the said clause seriously limits the possibilities of market opening in future trade agreements because Colombia would find itself restricted when considering to offer wider preferential market access to other trade partners compared to the US, being obliged to automatically extend it to the latter.

The argumentation on the asymmetric treatment in favour of the US can be based on two criteria: the value of duty-free trade from the entry into force of the Agreement, and the difference in the levels of effective commitment as laid down in the exchange of notes between the countries (outside the Agreement) with respect to Sanitary and Phytosanitary (SPS) measures.

When valuing the offered quotas and the possibility of trade diversion from which the US can benefit in its bilateral agricultural trade with Colombia, taking into account the important preference margin that it receives compared to other trade partners with exception of the Andean countries, it follows that the US offered to Colombia a trade potential in the basket of immediate liberalisation equivalent to around 115 per cent of the average value of imports originating in Colombia in the period 2001–2004, whereas Colombia offered immediate liberalisation corresponding to about 165 per cent of the average value of imports originating in the US in the same period of time.

The commitments in the area of SPS by the US in a letter attached to the Agreement have a conditional language and are not effectively compromising, whereas the requests towards Colombia are very precise and peremptory.

This situation is especially relevant to the extent that the effective elimination of SPS restrictions in the US is a necessary condition for the realisation of opportunities for those products for which one could foresee better possibilities for the expansion of Colombian agricultural exports. However, this possible elimination of unjustified non-tariff barriers (NTBs) will depend on the good-will of the US administration.

Foreseeable impacts

Our estimation of the welfare impacts of the negotiation of the agricultural chapter of the FTA, including impacts on producers, consumers, tax revenue and the income of workers is based on the methodology developed in Garay (2005).[21]

The balance of costs and benefits for the country in terms of the production of import-competing goods, as result of the Agreement, is expected to be negative in the short term, corresponding to a value of around 357 billion USD per year, which is equivalent to 1.2 per cent of agricultural GDP in 2005. In the long run the net (negative) effect on the production of import competing goods would even amount to a figure between 2.6 per cent and 4.4 per cent of agricultural GDP per year, depending on the scenario.

The net balance for Colombia will depend on the expansion of exportables so that losses that would occur with respect to import-competing goods could be compensated or reduced. However, this expansion will greatly depend on the willingness of the US authorities to eliminate unnecessary or unjustified SPS measures which seriously affect the access of potentially exportable Colombian goods in the medium and long run (like fruits, vegetables, bovine meat).

If this reduction is not achieved, the risk that the Colombian agricultural sector becomes a clear loser of the FTA and with an even more substantial (negative) impact on the Colombian economy, would even become greater. Among other factors like the evolution of international prices of agricultural products, this depends also on the evolution of Colombian exports of ethanol and bio-fuel to the US, for which the country finds itself only in the beginning stages of studies, trials and installation for the production of ethanol based on sugar cane and bio-fuel based on palm oil, leaving still ahead the difficult task in the long run to reach sufficient production scales, competitiveness levels, quality standards and technical specifications to compete in the American market.

The negotiation of intellectual property and health-related issues

The WTO framework

The negotiation of the Agreement on Intellectual Property at the Uruguay Round proved complicated because of the possible implications derived from excessive protection of knowledge related to public health. The final deal in this regard was, on the one hand, to establish minimum standards of protection under the Agreement, as is clear from Article 1, which reads: '... members may, but shall not be obliged to, implement in their law more extensive protection than is required by this Agreement , provided that such protection does not contravene the provisions of this Agreement ....', and, on the other, to enable countries to adopt measures

---

21   See also, statistical annex of Garay, Barberi and Cardona (2006).

necessary to protect public health and the nutrition of the population or to prevent the abuse of intellectual property rights by the holders, provided that such measures are compatible with the Agreement, as it was referred to in Article 8 which relates to the Principles of the Agreement.

The Bilateral Trade Promotion Agreements signed by the US

US pharmaceutical companies were not satisfied with the achievements of the WTO and have constantly pressured their government to increase the protection of knowledge. The relationships between these companies and the Republican Party led to increase this protection in the Bilateral Trade Promotion Agreements between the United States and different countries worldwide.

The United Nations Economic Commission for Latin America and the Caribbean (ECLAC) argues that such agreements contain provisions that go far beyond the levels of coverage, protection and enforcement of intellectual property rights embodied in the TRIPs (CEPAL 2006: 47).

Not only in developing countries there is a concern about the implications of increasing the protection levels for medical drugs on health, but also for the Democratic Party of the US. According to a report for member of congress H.A. Waxman,[22] the granting and extension of patents are preventing developing countries to acquire affordable essential medical drugs. Moreover, a dozen senators, in a letter to Susan Schwab,[23] recalled that in 2001 the United States together with 142 countries adopted the Doha Declaration, which reaffirms the right of WTO members to protect public health, expressing their concern that FTAs may undermine this commitment.

The Colombia-US agreement

The FTAs signed between Peru and Colombia, and the US were no exception to this trend, although the government of the US has been arguing that the FTA negotiations did not increase the protection of intellectual property.[24]

---

22   US House of Representatives Committee on Government Reform – Minority staff Special Investigations Division. Trade Agreements and Access to Medications under the Bush Administration. prepared for rep. Henry A. Waxman (California, Democratic Party), June 2005, p. 18.

23   Third World Network (TWN) Info service on intellectual property issues. Key Congressional Democrats voicing concerns over TRIPs-Plus in FTAs, 16 March 2007. Signed by US members of Congress: Waxman, McDermont, Allen, Dodggett, Schakowsky, Stark, DeGette, Van Hollen, Lee, Blumneauer, Lewis and Emanuel.

24   The President of the Republic, as well as the Ministers of Trade, Industry and Tourism, and Social Protection announced to the country that 'the agreement on medical drugs was very difficult, but [that] in the end a text was reached which does not add anything to the way we have been protecting intellectual property. Because generics and

In the Treaty signed by Colombia four clear concessions were granted to improve the protection standards for American pharmaceutical companies, which will have an impact on the prices of medical drugs and on health expenditures of the population. These concessions were (a) the protection of test data with more restrictive modalities than those contained in Decree 2085 of 2002 which regulates these issues in the country, (b) the establishment of a link between the authority for the approval of patents and the health authority, (c) the extension of the term of the patents to compensate for the unreasonable delays in their concession and in the process of authorisation of the commercialisation permissions, and (d) the restriction of the use of the International Non-proprietary Names (INN).

According to Holguín (2007: 19), the protection of test data and the establishment of the link between the patent office and the sanitary office could impose restrictions on the right of the State to use the concept of compulsory licenses, which is constituted by one of the tools created by the WTO (Uruguay Round) and ratified by the Doha Declaration to ensure access to medical drugs and to achieve a balance between the commercial rights and majority public interest.

In addition to the above, the lack of clarity in some of the negotiated texts can lead to problems of interpretation, which could eventually lead to the granting of patents of secondary medical use, and to extending the duration of patents via minor modifications of products already in the market. The ambiguous nature of some of the texts will probably be interpreted in favour of the interests of the US. Finally, there are contradictory texts in the Treaty in relation to the so-called Bolar clause and the Treaty contains difficulties for Colombia to implement the rule of exhaustion.

The protection of test data

The protection of test data prevents the health authority, during a period of time, to grant registration for the commercialisation of a generic that is based on the security and effectiveness tests that are already public in most cases and requires the applicant to present their own effectiveness and safety tests of the substance. Taking into account the cost of conducting these tests, this becomes a barrier for local companies.

The FTA signed with the US consolidates the permanent and exclusive protection of test data that had been introduced in Colombia by Decree 2085 of 2002 and strengthens the protection standards, by establishing a protection term of minimum five years and by eliminating the pro-competitive exceptions and some other related to secondary medical uses of known substances that established the mentioned Decree to mitigate the economic and health effects of the measure.

These provisions prevented to recognise as new chemical substances the new or secondary uses and the new features or changes in the pharmaceutical forms,

---

public health were saved', Presidential Address, with the Ministers of Trade and Social Protection, in the Congress of the Republic, 27 February 2006.

indications or secondary indications, the new combinations of known chemical substances, formulations, dosage forms, modifications involving changes in the pharmaceutical kinetics, packaging and marketing modalities, and generally those involving new presentations.

Besides this, the decree exempted new chemical substances from the system of test data protection when in the process of supporting another application, the holder of the sanitary registration has authorised the use of undisclosed information, or when it had not been commercialised in the country one year after issuing the authorisation to commercialise. This exception was also foreseen in case it was necessary to protect the public interest, as evaluated by the Ministry of Health, and when the new chemical substance is similar to one that had been approved and commercialised in Colombia, provided its term of protection had expired.

In addition, the Treaty, unlike Decree 2085 of 2002, grants protection to the information on safety and effectiveness of a new pharmaceutical product and not of a new chemical substance, and extends the protection to the disclosed data.

The link between the patent and the registration

The Treaty establishes a link between the office responsible for the approval of the patents and those responsible for issuing sale permits.

When a company requests an authorisation to commercialise a competing medical drug, the rules foresee an obligation for the health authority to inform the alleged owner of the patent about the identity of the applicant, which enables the owner to act against the latter if necessary, apart from the obligation to implement measures to prevent the commercialisation of competing products during the term of patents.

Establishing this link would force the *Instituto Nacional de Vigilancia de Medicamentos y Alimentos* (INVIMA) to publish a list of products and people or companies that are applying for a permission to commercialise, which can delay the entry of competing products to the market, because that permission to commercialise cannot be granted until the competent authority has not resolved the objections that the patent holder presents.

The experience of the US, where this link is established since 1984, shows, according to the Federal Trade Commission (FTC), that between 1992 and 2001, the objections for alleged patent infringement caused that 72 per cent of the requests for commercialisation of competing medical drugs were suspended for 30 months or more, of which 73 per cent was decided in favour of the generic product (Holguín 2007: 44).

Extension of the term of patents

The FTA includes an increase in the duration of patents for pharmaceutical products. Article 16.9.6, subparagraphs a and b, introduces the obligation to compensate unreasonable delays in the authorisation of patents, as well as unreasonable reductions in the effective term of patents derived from the approval of the permission to commercialise. The unreasonable delay of the term is defined as any delay longer than five years of the patent, calculated from the moment of application or three years calculated from the date of the examination of the patent. On the contrary, there is no definition of unreasonable reductions with respect to the permission to commercialise. As long as the delays attributed to the applicant are excluded from the unreasonable delays in the authorisation process of a patent, no exclusion of any delay is allowed from the unreasonable reductions resulting from the granting of the permission to commercialise.

This extension of the patent term is not covered by WTO rules, nor by those of the Andean Community, and can lead to the paradox that the effective patent term is higher in Colombia than in the US, which would turn out to be unbalanced and asymmetrical in favour of the US.

Restrictions on the use of the INN

The use of the generic name in medical drugs is very important for consumers, the doctors and those responsible for procurement, because it allows them to choose between different pharmaceutical products that have the same active ingredient and can rationalise the health expenditures. If it would come to the point that branded goods do not contain information on the active ingredient, the consumer would be denied of the information required to compare a prescription and it would be an attack against their right to choose and this would force them to buy more expensive products. In Colombia, the Pan American Health Organisation has estimated that the medical drugs commercialised under the generic name cost on average 50 per cent of those which are sold branded (OPS-IFARMA 2005).

According to Holguín (2007: 64), Article 16.2.3 of the Treaty invokes Article 20 of the TRIPs on trademarks, with the only intention to include for the first time among the not permitted requirements, the provisions requiring the use of the common (non-proprietary) name, in a manner that it reduced the effectiveness of the brand, including requirements relating to size, location or style of use of the brand in related to the generic name.

The effect of this article will fundamentally depend on the interpretation and reach it will be given, given the fact that the decision on the extent to which conditions for the use of the generic name of a product diminishes the effectiveness of the brand, is highly discretional.[25]

---

25 Currently, under Decree 677 of 1995, on the labels of branded medical drugs the corresponding generic name must appear with similar size and character, which eventually can be seen as undermining the effectiveness of the brand.

Patents of secondary use

The problems of interpretation of the negotiated text do not allow to be sure that in the light of the Treaty, the patenting of secondary uses was excluded. On the one hand, there are indications that point in the direction of exclusion: (a) the absence of an explicit text in the Treaty allowing such patents, as enshrined in the agreements signed by the US with Morocco, Australia and Bahrain; (b) the withdrawal of a text from the negotiating table that proposed the concession of patents to any new use or method of use of a known product; (c) the letter of the director of the USTR, B. Portman, to congressman T. Allen, according to which in the negotiated text with Peru, there is no obligation to grant patents to new uses of patented products; and (d) the fact that the summary published by the USTR, including the improvements concerning patents achieved by the US, do not refer to patent use or secondary use.

However, on the other hand, the texts of some articles of the Treaty may raise concerns. For example, in article 6.10 3 (a), when establishing the obligation to implement measures to prevent others from commercializing a product covered by a patent shall include its method of use. Additionally, article 16.9.11, by claiming that an invention can be applied in the industry if it 'has a specific, substantial and credible utility', could lead to the granting of patents for therapeutic uses. It should be noted that this interpretation is shared by the Colombian patent authority (Superintendency of Industry and Trade) which said: 'The acceptance of the change of criteria for patentability from industrial application to utility would lead to expand the range of patentable subject matter.'[26]

Patents for trivial development of known molecules

Concerning the entrance of generic products to the market, it is necessary to warn about the danger related to the fact that in the text of the Treaty the parties can consider as synonymous the terms 'inventive activity' and 'not obvious', ignoring Decision 486 of the Andean Community, which defined that an invention is inventive if for a person with a normal professional background in the corresponding technical matter, this invention would not have been obvious or would not have been derived in a evident way from the existing techniques.

Unlike the US, where it is considered sufficient that an invention is the result of laborious research, of long exploratory research or of an incidental (not obvious) finding to comply with one of the conditions of patentability, in Colombia an invention needs to produce a surprising and unexpected effect in order to be patentable, in other words, to behave differently compared to what is already

---

26 Superintendency of Industry and Commerce (communication January 2006), cited by the Office of International Legal Affairs of the Ministry, memorandum of 2 February 2006.

known under the existing technical state of the art. For this reason, in Colombia, until now, there was no room for patenting minor changes to known products.

This way, if the US pressed Colombia to use the term 'not obvious' as synonymous for inventive activity, the entry of generic products on the market would slow down as multinational companies could extend the life of a medical drug, whose patent is about to expire, through trivial modifications of know chemical substances, by manufacturing a product that is virtually identical to the original by giving it another brand name.

The Bolar clause

The establishment of the link between the patent and the health registry, as mentioned before, could result in the elimination of the Bolar exception or the exception of early work, that allows the use of the protected substance of a patent to develop generic versions and to seek their approval to the health authority so that they can be commercialised immediately after the expiration of the patent.

In this respect the text of the Treaty is contradictory, because although on the one hand, article 16.10.3 only prevents the commercialisation of generics when the patent of the innovator is in force, thus maintaining the Bolar exception, on the other hand, article 16.9.5 suggests that the health registry should only be issued once the patent expires, which means the elimination of this exception. In this sense one could understand the statement incorporated in the agreements between the governments of Colombia and the US, as stated in a letter annexed to the Treaty, which says: "Each part recognises...that the measures that implement Article 16.10.3 (a) and (b) operate together in a way that they prevent the approval of a pharmaceutical product to enter the market during the patent term in its territory as foreseen provided in this Article." At this point the question would be whether this understanding prohibits the approval of the product during the term of validity of the patent or just the approval of the product to enter the market during the term of the patent.

The right of exhaustion

The Treaty empowers the parties to establish the so-called exhaustion of the data protection right, by stating that such protection should be requested in the territory of the party within five years after having obtained the approval of the commercialisation in the other territory.

This rule provides favourable and unfavourable aspects for Colombia, because, on the one hand, it allows in practice a commercial exclusivity of a product for a period of ten years or more, five years of exhaustion of the right plus five or more years of protection of test data; but on the other hand it prevents the further protection of 'old' chemical substances (older than five years).

It should however be noted that it is not clear to what extent the right of exhaustion can be applied, since the subscribed text, which is virtually identical to the Peruvian text, provides that this figure is only applicable if approved by the reference method, a method that is only used exceptionally in Colombia, because the normal procedure is used instead.

The report of the Washington meeting

Some of the concerns raised regarding the negotiation of intellectual property prompted a meeting with by President Uribe in Washington, on February 16, 2006, during which, according to a meeting report signed only by the president, parameters to minimise the impact of some of the rules incorporated in the Treaty were agreed with the USTR. According to this document the following agreements were reached: (1) Colombia could take the necessary measures to protect public health in relation to any area of the chapter on intellectual property, including patents and the protection of test data; (2) that within the frame of the Treaty, it was clear that Colombia would not be obliged to patent methods of use or second use; (3) that Colombia could continue to protect test data in the same way as it had been doing in the light of the provisions of Decree 2085 of 2002, and (4) that the figure of exhaustion could be applied in Colombia, without changing any of the procedures currently in force.

Without a doubt, to the extent that these commitments would have binding power, they would weaken the effects of the Treaty on the health of Colombians. The problem lies in the legal force that can be derived from a meeting report, signed by only one party, which is not part of the Treaty, since it only includes the text, annexes and letters of understanding.

The petition of the Liberal Party to the government

In the review process of the Treaty, the Colombian Liberal Party prepared a petition to the government that included questions that sought to clarify the government's interpretation of the negotiated text on intellectual property. In this regard it should be noted that the official response explained that the country did not lose the power to take necessary measures to protect public health. It is namely included in the understandings reached between the parties during the negotiation. As concerns the secondary uses, the full applicability of Decree 2085 of 2002 and the danger of restricting the use of a generic name remain. Concerning 'linkage', it became clear that the problem remains that unjustified opposition to granting health registration, slows down the entry of generics to the market. Finally, the interpretation of the government on the existing contradiction in the text on the Bolar exception suggests that it was removed.

The impact of the negotiation on Public Health in Colombia

The potential impacts of the negotiation of intellectual property which are presented in this section were calculated in the study Misión Salud-Ifarma (2006).

According to that study, the granted concessions would lead to increased market share of protected active substances that would reach 44 per cent after five years and 63 per cent after 15 years, the price index for medical drugs in Colombia would increase around 30 per cent after five years and 40 per cent after 15 years, and to maintain a constant level of consumption the health expenditure must be 500 million USD higher per year around year 5 further increasing to 1000 million USD per year around year 15. Finally, it should be noted that if it was not possible to obtain these resources, the consumption of medical drugs could be reduced up to 40 per cent in year 15.

If it would not be obligatory to concede patents to secondary uses and to trivial developments of known chemical substances, the corresponding increases for year 15 would be reduced by 8 percentage points and the health expenditure by 180 million USD per year.

The Letter of the chairman of the United States House of Representatives Committee on Ways and Means

The Democratic Party of the United States expressed its concern because the commitments by the US to countries with which it has negotiated Trade Promotion Agreements, including Colombia, have broken the balance between the protection of knowledge and the access to medical drugs at reasonable prices to protect public health, and conditioned its support to the ratification, among other things, on the following changes to the text on intellectual property:[27]

- The protection of test data should be granted only on new chemical substances and should have a duration of five years.
- The compensation for delays in the procedure of the patenting of a product or of its permission to be commercialised should no longer be mandatory but optional.
- The link between the health authority and the patent granting authority should be eliminated. It should be required, however, that the parties establish simple administrative and legal procedures that allow the adoption of sanctions in case a patent is violated and a transparent system that ensures that the patent holders have enough time and opportunities to effectively protect their rights.
- The letter on public health, attached to the Treaty and signed by the two governments in November 2006, should be incorporated in the text of the Agreement.

The position of the Democratic party seems beneficial for Colombia, as it allows to take measures to protect public health even if the protection of test data is in force and as it reduces the protection for branded medical drugs, by removing the link between the patenting authority and the health authority, restricting the

---

27   See communication of Senators Levin and Rangel to the Trade Representative of the United States, 10 May 2007.

exclusive protection of test data for new chemical substances and limiting the period of protection of such data to five years, among other things.

Conclusions

Our analysis of the outcome of the negotiations of the Colombia-US FTA clearly shows their asymmetric character. The case shows that the US has been able to separate these commercial negotiations from political relations and geo-strategic and security considerations. Colombia's political and diplomatic proximity to the US could not be played out as a factor strengthening its negotiation position. Other factors that weakened Colombia's negotiation position include: (i) the fact that the Andean countries were not able to negotiate as a group, and (ii) the fact that in sequential negotiations with a hub country, the latter uses specific outcomes of previous negotiations (Chile, CAFTA, Peru) as precedents when its suits its interest.

The case further illustrates that countries negotiating with the US should not under-estimate the importance of the ratification process in Congress which is sensitive to changing political and electoral circumstances, although Colombia is to some extent perhaps a special case because of its complicated internal political situation.

As we have shown, the outcomes of the negotiations on agriculture and intellectual property illustrate very well the degree of asymmetry in the negotiations.

With respect to agriculture, our assessment of the unequal character of the negotiations was based on five arguments:

- while the US maintained its system of subsidies, Colombia accepted to give up the Andean System of Price Margins and its mechanism to administer quotas, while having only very limited margins to organise production support mechanisms itself;
- price safeguarding measures were not included in the Agreement;
- no revision of the tariff reduction programme is allowed in case the US would decide to increase the levels of existing domestic support;
- sugar and products with high sugar content not ready for final consumption were excluded from the US liberalisation programme, whereas no subsectors or products were excluded from the Colombian tariff reduction programme;
- and a non-reciprocal preferential clause was requested from Colombia.

With respect to intellectual property, the following conclusions can be drawn:

- contrary to what the Colombian government is arguing, protection levels for branded drugs were raised because of the results of the negotiations on test data, compensations for delays in administrative procedures concerning patents and commercialisation permits, the establishment of a link between patent and public health authorities, and the restriction of the use of the common international denomination;

- certain parts of the text of the chapter are confusing, which can lead to patenting of secondary uses and of trivial developments of known chemical substances;
- as a consequence of the agreement, it is estimated that the price index for medical drugs in Colombia would increase around 30 per cent after five years and 40 per cent after 15 years, and that health expenditure would be 500 million USD higher per year around year 5 and further increasing up to 1000 million USD per year around year 15;
- if the interpretation of certain sections of the chapter would avoid the obligation to concede patents to secondary use and to trivial developments of known chemical substances, the corresponding increases for year 15 would be reduced by 8 percentage points and by 180 million USD per year;
- the introduction of the modifications suggested by the democratic members of the US Congress would significantly reduce the impact of the Agreement on the public health sector in Colombia.

References

Araújo Ibarra. 2007. *Matriz de intereses de Colombia en la negociación del TLC con Estados Unidos*. Bogotá: Araújo Ibarra.
CEPAL. 2006. *Los derechos de propiedad intelectual en los acuerdos de libre comercio celebrados por países de América Latina con países desarrollados*. CEPAL, División de Comercio Internacional e Integración.
De Lombaerde, P. and Garay, L.J. 2008. El nuevo regionalismo en América Latina, in *Del regionalismo latinoamericano a la integración interregional*, edited by De Lombaerde, P., Kochi, S. and Briceño Ruíz, J. Madrid: Siglo XXI, 3–35.
Garay, L.J. (ed.) 2005. *El Agro Colombiano Frente al TLC con Estados Unidos*. Bogotá: Ministerio de Agricultura y Desarrollo Rural.
Garay, L.J., Barberi, F. and Cardona, I. 2006. *La negociación agropecuaria en el TLC. Alcances y consecuencias*. Bogotá: Planeta Paz-Ediciones Ántropos.
Genna, G.M. 2010. Economic Size and the Changing International Political Economy of Trade: the Development of Western Hemispheric FTAs. *International Politics*, 47(6), 638–658.
Gómez, H.J. 2008. 'New' Issues in the FTAs in the Multilateral Order, presentation at *the dialogue on global trade challenges and research priorities*. Barcelona: University of Barcelona-ICTSD, 28–29 May.
Holguín Zamorano, G. 2007. *TLC y salud: la verdad*. Bogotá: Publicaciones Misión Salud.
Krugman, P. 2010. El TLC no está en la agenda. Entrevista con Paul Krugman. *La República*, 12/07.

López, C. 2007. *Ponencia para el proyecto de ley 178/2006 Senado, 200/2007 Cámara, por medio del cual se aprueba el Acuerdo de Promoción Comercial entre la República de Colombia y los Estados Unidos de América, sus cartas adjuntas y sus entendimientos.* Bogotá, radicada en mayo 4/2007.

Maruyama, W.H. and Rosenberg, C.B. 2010. The Investment Chapter of the US-Colombia FTA: New protections for US Investors. *The Journal of World Investment and Trade*, 11(3).

OPS-IFARMA. 2005. Determination of the impact of strengthening the Intellectual Property rights as a consequence of the negotiation of a Free Trade Agreement with the United States. Bogotá: OPS-IFARMA.

Oxfam. 2006. Cantos de sirena. Por qué los TLCs de Estados Unidos con los países andinos socavan el desarrollo sostenible y la integración regional. *Informe de Oxfam*, (90).

Pugatch, M.P. 2006. The International Regulation of IPRs in a TRIPs and TRIPs-Plus World, in *Trade and Investment Rule-making: The Role of Regional and Bilateral Agreements*, edited by Woolcock, S. Tokyo: UNU Press, 177–207.

Pulecio, J.R. 2005. La estrategia Uribe de negociación del TLC. *Colombia Internacional*, (61), 12–32.

Ramírez Ocampo, J. 2007.*¿No TLC? El impacto del tratado en la economía colombiana.* Bogotá: Norma.

RECALCA. 2006. *De la indignidad a la indignación. La verdad sobre las negociaciones del TLC*. Bogotá: Recalca.

Rojas Arroyo, S. and M.E. Lloreda, P. 2007. *¿TLC? Aspectos jurídicos del Tratado de Libre Comercio entre Colombia y Estados Unidos.* Bogotá: Norma.

Sarmiento, E. 2005. ¿Por qué no firmar el TLC? *Colombia Internacional*, (61), 136–145.

Tsai, C. 2006. Rule-making in agricultural trade: RTAs and the Multilateral Trading System, in *Trade and Investment Rule-making: The Role of Regional and Bilateral Agreements*, edited by Woolcock, S. Tokyo: UNU Press, 27–50.

Umaña, G. 2004. *El juego asimétrico del comercio. El Tratado de Libre Comercio Colombia-Estados Unidos.* Bogotá: Universidad Nacional de Colombia.

Zerda, Á. et al. 2005. *Impactos del Tratado de Libre Comercio Colombia – Estados Unidos en el sector salud del Distrito Capital.* Bogotá: CID-Alcaldía Mayor de Bogotá.

Chapter 7
Negotiating the Thailand-US Free Trade Agreement

Wisarn Pupphavesa, Ludo Cuyvers,
Santi Chaisrisawatsuk and Philippe De Lombaerde

Introduction

Thailand and the United States (US) have had strong political and economic relations for over 175 years. Official Thai-US relationships began with the Treaty of Amity during the reign of King Rama III (1824–1851). The Thai-US relations have grown deeper and more comprehensive over the years and could be characterised as being relations of 'shared interest and friendship' (Thiparat and Phetcharatana 2005: 10). In the early years of these relations, Thais generally placed a high value on American friendship. During the period of colonialism, Thais did not perceive Americans as a threat. On the contrary, Americans were regarded as modernisers and even entrusted to be official negotiators and advisors for the Siamese Government. Both countries had shown willingness to support each other on several occasions. For example, King Rama IV offered assistance to President Lincoln during the Civil War; Thai and American soldiers fought side-by-side each other in both World Wars and the Korean War; the US safeguarded Thailand's sovereignty after World War II thus allowing Thailand to proceed with its socio-economic and political development ever since.[1]

Given a common interest in fighting and containing the communist threat, Thailand and the US formalised their military alliance by the 1954 Manila Pact. After the Vietnam War, however, as the communist threat subsided there was a 'dilution of shared concern' (Thiparat and Phetcharatana 2005: 12) and hence, the alliance was somewhat weakened. While the US took time out from the region, China emerged as a 'new' regional power (Thiparat and Phetcharatana 2005: 10–12).

Bilateral economic and trade relations have ascended in importance over the last decades with a considerable trade surplus for Thailand (Figure 7.1). The structure of bilateral trade is shown in Table 7.1. The asymmetric character of the bilateral relationship is clear when looking at the relative importance of the trade flows (Figures 7.2 and 7.3). However, whereas the importance of Thai exports as

---

1   See, for example, Warr (1993).

a percentage of total exports was always around 20 per cent in the 1990s, it has
fallen continuously since then (i.e. well before the start of the negotiations).

The importance of bilateral relations is also visible when looking at FDI flows
(Figures 7.4 and 7.5).

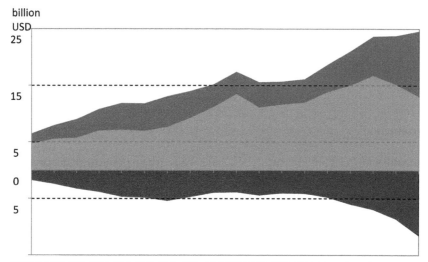

Figure 7.1 Bilateral trade between Thailand and the US (1991–2008)

Source: UNCOMTRADE Database, 2010.

Note: All figures are import figures CIF.

Table 7.1 Structure of Thai-US bilateral trade (2008)

	Thailand exports to US		Thailand imports from US	
	Product	percentage	Product	percentage
1	Electrical machinery and equipment and parts thereof; sound recorders and reproducers, television image and sound recorders and reproducers, and parts and accessories of such articles	23.5%	Electrical machinery and equipment and parts thereof; sound recorders and reproducers, television image and sound recorders and reproducers, and parts and accessories of such articles	18.8%
2	Nuclear reactors, boilers, machinery and mechanical appliances; parts thereof	20.2%	Nuclear reactors, boilers, machinery and mechanical appliances; parts thereof	17.4%
3	Rubber and articles thereof	6.7%	Iron and steel	6.3%
4	Natural or cultured pearls, precious or semi-precious stones, precious metals, metals clad with precious metal, and articles thereof; imitation jewellery; coin	4.9%	Plastics and articles thereof	4.6%
5	Preparations of meat, of fish or of crustaceans, molluscs or other aquatic invertebrates	4.6%	Optical, photographic, cinematographic, measuring, checking, precision, medical or surgical instruments and apparatus; parts and accessories thereof	4.5%
6	Articles of apparel and clothing accessories, knitted or crocheted	4.2%	Natural or cultured pearls, precious or semi-precious stones, precious metals, metals clad with precious metal, and articles thereof; imitation jewellery; coin	4.4%
7	Fish and crustaceans, molluscs and other aquatic invertebrates	3.9%	Mineral fuels, mineral oils and products of their distillation; bituminous substances; mineral waxes	3.2%
8	Articles of apparel and clothing accessories, not knitted or crocheted	3.0%	Miscellaneous chemical products	3.2%
9	Optical, photographic, cinematographic, measuring, checking, precision, medical or surgical instruments and apparatus; parts and accessories thereof	2.0%	Articles of iron or steel	3.1%
10	Plastics and articles thereof	2.0%	Organic chemicals	3.1%

Source: UNCOMTRADE Database, 2010.

Notes: Product category based on HS-1996 classification.

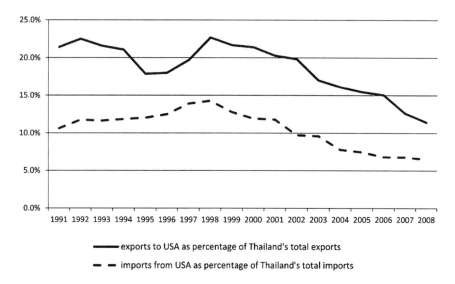

Figure 7.2 Relative importance of bilateral trade for Thailand (% of total)
Source: UNCOMTRADE Database, 2010.

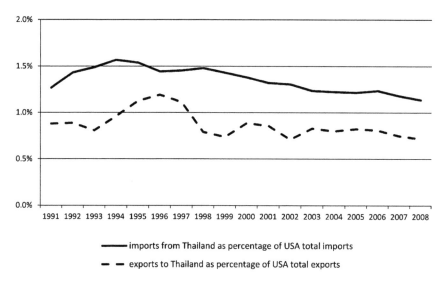

Figure 7.3 Relative importance of bilateral trade for the US (% of total)
Source: UNCOMTRADE Database, 2010.

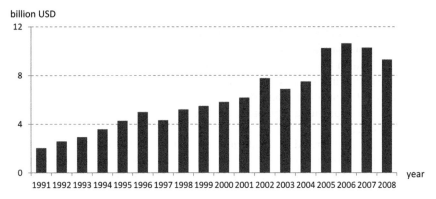

Figure 7.4 US FDI in Thailand

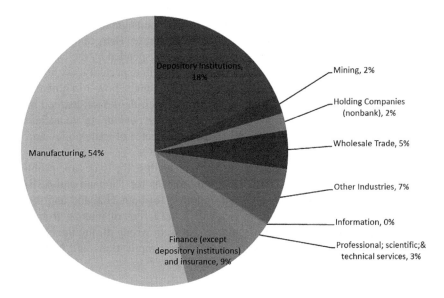

Figure 7.5 The composition of US FDI in Thailand, by industry groups (2008)

Source: Online database, Bureau of Economic analysis, U.S. Department of commerce. http://www.bea.gov/international [accessed 26 November 2010].

At the same time, some conflicting interests emerged between Thailand and the US. Although Thais appreciated the important contributions of the US to Thailand's economic development, they were later disappointed by the US trade remedy measures such as the use of anti-dumping and countervailing measures to protect domestic industries and the import ban on shrimp and shrimp products on the ground that the catching method was harmful to sea turtles.

The US threat to remove the Generalised System of Preferences (GSP) privileges from Thailand for failing to implement intellectual property rights (IPR) protection to its satisfaction also troubled Thai exporters.

Since Thailand has been an export-led-growth economy, continuing and improving export market access is vital to its economic stability and sustainability.[2] Like many other developed and developing, large and small countries, Thailand became active in pursuing regional and bilateral FTA as the Doha Round failed to make progress.

One year after President Bush announced his desire to pursue a series of bilateral free trade areas under the 'Enterprise for the Association of South East Asian Nations (ASEAN) Initiative' (EAI) during the 10th Asia-Pacific Economic Cooperation (APEC) Leaders Meeting in October 2002, Prime Minister Thaksin and President Bush announced their intention to negotiate a Thailand-US Free Trade Agreement (TUSFTA). Over the course of the next two years, the US and Thai trade negotiation teams conducted six formal negotiations. The sixth and last round of negotiation was held on 13 January 2006 in Chiangmai, Thailand without any progress but marred with protest and political unease. Then came the *coup d' état* on 19 September 2006 and the negotiation was suspended by the US.

Although the negotiation ended shortly and unexpectedly without any progress, it was a major trade policy undertaking by a mega power in global trade and a small dynamic developing economy from which the lesson learned might have interesting implications and be useful for other developing countries and particularly ASEAN member countries in their pursuance of trade policy and the realisation of the ASEAN Economic Community (AEC).

This chapter, therefore, intends to identify and analyse the issues and problems in the negotiations and draw lessons and implications for Thailand and ASEAN. The next section deals with motives and rationale for both Thailand and the US to negotiate a TUSFTA. Section three surveys the issues of interest from each party's perspective. Section four discusses what went wrong during the course of negotiations. Lastly, the concluding section draws implications and lessons for Thailand and ASEAN.

Motives and rationale for TUSFTA

According to Naya and Plummer (2005: 2–5), the EAI did not really come as a surprise. First, the US policy changed in the 1980s from merely supporting multilateral liberalisation under the General Agreement on Tariffs and Trade/ World Trade Organisation (GATT/WTO) framework to actively pursuing FTAs with developing countries, starting with an FTA with Israel (goods) in 1985, followed by an FTA-like agreement with the Caribbean Basin (1986), the US-

---

2 On Thailand's export-led growth, see for example, Akrasanee et al. (1991), Herderschee (1993), De Lombaerde (2008).

Canada FTA (1989) and North American Free Trade Agreement (NAFTA) (1994). After the Bush Administration received Trade Promotion Authority in 2002, it negotiated bilateral FTAs with a number of countries throughout the world.[3] Second, since one of these FTAs was with Singapore, a key member of ASEAN member, agreements with other ASEAN members could sensibly be expected. In fact, it was explicitly mentioned in the EAI announcement that the US-Singapore FTA (USSFTA) would be used as a 'model' for the other bilateral US-ASEAN member FTAs. Third, ASEAN is a natural priority target because they are many times more important trade partners of the US in proportion to their size, and their commitment to create an AEC makes it an even more attractive region. Fourth, the US has long pondered means to promote closer bilateral and regional relations with the ASEAN countries since the late 1980s, for which the study entitled the ASEAN-US Initiative (AUI) by Naya and a group of both ASEAN and American scholars funded by the State Department and the United Nations Development Programme (UNDP) recommended that a framework agreement be developed under which the US and ASEAN could eventually form an FTA, provided that ASEAN deepened economic integration significantly (Naya et al. 1989). As ASEAN subsequently deepened its integration and the US renewed its interest in bilateralism, 'supply' and 'demand' for an agreement appeared to be in place.

In the notification letter sent to the Speaker of the House and the Senate Majority Leader, the US Trade Representative Robert Zoellick identified several potential commercial and foreign policy gains from an agreement as well as certain sensitive issues (CRS 2007). It is argued that agricultural producers would benefit from increasing export sales to Thailand as a result of eliminating or reducing Thailand's high tariffs and other barriers. An FTA would also boost US exports of goods and services in sectors such as information technology, telecommunications, financial services, audiovisual, automotive, and medical equipment.

Under the 1966 Treaty of Amity and Economic Relations (AER) Thailand accorded national treatment to US citizens and companies to own and operate in Thailand, which became preferences extended to US investors and thus violated Thailand's WTO obligations to the Most Favoured Nation (MFN) treatment. Thailand received an exemption from the WTO for ten years which would expire in January 2005. Thus, maintaining preferential access for US investors in Thailand under an FTA was also a top priority for US business.

Regarding US foreign policy interests, an FTA would strengthen Thailand's position as a key military ally, particularly in the war on terrorism. Regionally, an FTA would advance the EAI. Multilaterally, an FTA could encourage Thailand to cooperate with the US in supporting multilateral trade negotiations under the Doha Development Round, particularly in agricultural liberalisation.

Naya and Plummer (2005: 5–8) also tried to clarify the US motives for a bilateral (rather than a regional) FTA with ASEAN members. First, technically,

---

3   For a comparative analysis of US trade bilateralism, see e.g. Heydon and Woolcock (2009).

the US could not negotiate with ASEAN as a region due to membership problems. It has imposed strict economic sanctions on Myanmar. Laos and Vietnam were not yet members of the WTO. As such an agreement would not be entirely regional but rather a '10-x'. Second, because of tremendous socio-economic and political diversity among ASEAN members, a regional agreement would not be possible unless it would be 'loose' or 'flexible', which the US does not agree to. Third, the US wanted to move forward quickly with its FTA agenda and Singapore would be relatively easy and allow the US to fashion a basic model for the other ASEAN countries. Besides, Singapore's economic structure made it easy to sell politically and economically in the US with strong support from the business community as well as enable the US to show that it still intends to be highly engaged in Asia. Fourth, according to certain critics, the US turns to bilateralism to 'divide and conquer'. Naya and Plummer, however, argued that it is not the case. The US still continues to be active at the WTO and has not always chosen to go bilateral. They argued that the Free Trade Area of the Americas (FTAA) was always the biggest FTA priority of the first Bush Administration. Also an FTA with Central America (CAFTA) had been negotiated and was being debated in the US Congress.

As for Thailand, the motive and rationale for a bilateral FTA with the US is more straightforward. First, the US is the largest market for Thailand's exports. As the US keeps expanding its FTA network throughout the world, Thailand cannot afford to stay out of it. Indeed, the sooner Thailand can become one of the US FTA partners, the better Thailand can maintain its competitiveness in the US as well as the rest of the world markets.[4] Second, since Singapore has already had an FTA with the US, other members of ASEAN including Thailand would be under pressure to have an FTA with the US to neutralise the competitive advantages that Singapore would gain through the USSFTA. Thailand has to race not only to catch up with Singapore but also not to fall behind other ASEAN members especially, Malaysia, Philippines and Indonesia. Third, the Thai government at the time was very proactive on bilateral FTAs as a trade policy strategy to improve the competitive advantages and diversify export markets.

Finally, ex ante simulations of the potential impact of a Thai-US FTA on the Thai economy gave further support to the intentions of the Thai government. At the time of the negotiations, data were available from the Institute of International Economics (De Rosa 2003) and from the Thailand Development Research Institute (TDRI 2003) (Table 7.6). Both CGE models showed small net positive effects on Thai GDP.[5] The effect is larger in the TDRI model because NTB's are kept in place, thus leading to a smaller increase in Thai imports and less 'leakage'

---

4   It should be noted in this respect that in the years prior to the start of the negotiations (1998–2002), Thailand's share in US imports was falling (Table 7.3). This was mainly due to a specialisation in commodity categories with a below-average demand growth in the US (TDRI 2003: 19–23).

5   One should in addition take into account that it may take a few years before these impacts are fully realised (TDRI 2003: 33).

from the economy (TDRI 2003: 31). De Rosa's GTAP model reduces NTB's and produces probably more plausible effects if the negotiations would have led to an outcome close to the one in the case of the Singapore-US FTA. According to TDRI, the agricultural sector would be gaining more than proportionally from the agreement. The impact on trade flows according to the CGE models contrast starkly with the corresponding figures from de Rosa's gravity model. According to the authors, these should interpreted as upper bounds as they only show trade creation effects and fail to show trade diversion effects. The contradicting results with respect to tariff revenues are explained by the fact that in the TDRI model, the increase in imports is (rightly) considered to be mainly imports from the US.

Table 7.2 Ex ante simulations of the impact of a Thailand-US FTA on the Thai economy

% change	Gravity model (De Rosa 2003)	GTAP model (De Rosa 2003)	TDRI CGE model (TDRI 2003)
Exports		3.46	3.46
Exports to US	118		5.41
Exports to RoW			2.91
Imports		4.68	1.82
Imports from US	118		4.99
Imports from RoW			1.37
Real GDP			1.34
Agriculture			2.25
Industry			1.70
Services			0.85
Nominal GDP		0.72	2.71
Tariff revenue (mill. USD change)		1531	-226

Mapping the interests and conflicts of interests in TUSFTA

As explicitly mentioned in the EAI announcement that the USSFTA would be used as a 'model' for the other bilateral US-ASEAN FTA accords, Thailand would have to prepare to negotiate with the US on those issues competently. Although the USSFTA is regarded as one of the most modern FTAs in the world today (Naya and Plummer 2005: 2), it does not necessarily mean that it suits the interest of Thailand. Certain provisions might not even be acceptable to Thailand. However, Thailand was ready to negotiate a comprehensive FTA including trade in goods and services, agriculture, investment, intellectual property rights, government procurement, competition policy, and custom procedures among other issues (CRS 2007).

Concerning trade in goods, the US is concerned with the relatively high tariff rates on autos and auto parts, alcoholic beverages, fabrics, footwear and headgear and some electrical appliances. Besides, the US would raise issues on import licensing, opaque custom procedures and excise taxes. Thailand's interest is related to tariff reduction for textiles and apparel, light trucks and transparency in trade remedy measures such as anti-dumping and countervailing.

Concerning agriculture, both Thailand and the US impose higher tariff rates than on non-agricultural goods. While Thailand would seek improved market access for processed seafood, frozen shrimp, rubber, rice, tapioca, sugar and fruits and vegetables, the US would ask for liberalisation in meat and dairy products, fresh fruits and vegetables, sugar, and tobacco.[6]

Regarding intellectual property rights, the US is critically concerned with deficiency in Thai protection of US IPR. The US would push for longer protection for pharmaceutical products and more effective protection on copy right and trade mark.

With respect to trade in services, the US would press for improvement in access for US providers of financial, telecommunications and professional services and other sectors. The US would also push for a negative list approach in liberalisation of trade in services.

Concerning investment, the US would want to retain the privileges for US companies and nationals under the AER Treaty.

Development of FTA negotiations[7]

The first round of talks took place in Honolulu, Hawaii from 28 June until 2 July 2004 in a positive atmosphere. The meeting was generally and mostly on getting to know each other between members of both negotiation teams and exchanges of information and ideas on various issues. The meeting split into 23 groups,[8] each dealing with an issues package, including: Market Access for Industrial products, Market Access for Agricultural products, Market Access for Textiles and Apparel Products, Trade Remedies, Sanitary and Phytosanitary measures (SPS), Technical Barriers to Trade (TBT), Rules of Origin, Customs Administration and Procedures, Cross-Border Services, Financial Services, Investment, Mobility of Business

---

6   See Table 7.2 on the composition of bilateral trade.

7   Based on the summary made available to the public on the Ministry of Foreign Affairs website (http://www.mfa.go.th/tusfta/index) and Fiscal Policy Research Institute Foundation's website (http:///www.ftamonitoring.org/data3/2006%20Jan20060117/ftaus_round6.pdf) (in Thai language).

8   Science and Technology and SMEs were added subsequently at the suggestion of the Thai Team in the first Meeting.

Persons, Labour, Environment, Intellectual Property Rights, E-Commerce, Telecommunications, Government Procurement, Competition Policy, Science and Technology/R+D, Capacity Building/Small and Medium-sized Enterprises (SMEs, Dispute Settlement, and Transparency.

The negotiations continued with five subsequent meetings between October 2004 and January 2006 (Box 7.1).

Box 7.1 Chronology of negotiations

First Round, Honolulu, Hawaii, 28 June–2 July 2004
Second Round, Honolulu, Hawaii, 11–15 October 2004
Third Round, Pataya, 4–9 April 2005
Fourth Round, Great Falls, Montana, 11–15 July 2005
Fifth Round, East-West Centre, Honolulu, Hawaii, 26–30 September 2005
Sixth (and last) Round, Chiangmai, 9–13 January 2006

The subsequent meetings mainly focused on further exchanges of information, experiences from earlier FTAs and ideas of both sides and consultation on various issues, including modalities, scope, definitions, relevant rules and regulations and related issues.

Talks on market access for agricultural products and industrial products went smoothly and made good progress. Both sides made initial requests and offers at the Sixth Meeting. The US offered to open up the market for 8,100 industrial export items of Thailand constituting 74 per cent of total annual US import value from Thailand. Among the major export products are products made of wood and rubber, glass/ceramics, plastic products, jewellery, processed food, steel products, textiles and apparel etc. Thailand offered market opening for imports from the US covering 71 per cent of Thailand's annual total imports value from the US.

The US offer also covered more than 1,300 products constituting 65 per cent of the US's agricultural import value from Thailand. Major items include rice and rice products and fresh and processed fruits and vegetables. Thailand, on the other hand, would open the market for cotton and chicken breeds but would take 10–20 years for adjustment before completely opening the markets for meat, dairy, corn, potatoes and onions.

On rules of origin, both sides were still working on the preparation of the offers/requests.

On customs procedures, both sides agreed to consult on more technical details to facilitate exports and imports but still differed on the length of the adjustment period.

On SPS, both sides agreed to set up a joint committee on SPS under an FTA.

On trade remedies, Thailand and the US still differed on the exemption of Thailand from Global safeguard although the US made exemption for earlier FTA partners. Also Thailand wanted a Proof of causal link between imports and injury but the US did not.

On trade in services, both sides agreed to adopt a mutually agreed list for market access.

On telecommunications, Thailand was still not ready and needed more time to develop a clear policy on satellite services and submarine cable system connections.

On e-commerce, Thailand wanted a reservation on certain sensitive content while the US insisted on freedom of medias.

On financial services, Thailand was considering the US request for liberalising investment advisory services and mutual funds.

Regarding labour, both countries still differed on various points including the use of labour rights for protectionist purposes, commitment on effective enforcement of labour laws and application of an agreement to states government. Besides, Thailand, from the beginning, did not want to include a labour issue in the FTA.

Regarding the environment, it was still inconclusive whether to include an environmental clause in the FTA. However, both countries intended to prepare a Memorandum of Understanding (MOU) for cooperation. Also, Thailand was considering the US request on the effective enforcement of environmental laws.

With respect to intellectual property rights, the US would consider Thailand's request related to geographical indication protection for Thai Hom Mali rice and Thai silk, as well as to the protection of local bio-resources and wisdom and sharing of the benefits derived from use of such bio-resources. Thailand, on the other hand, still resisted the US demand for protection for pharmaceutical and agricultural chemicals test information for five and ten years respectively because of its sensitivity.

On competition policy, both countries agreed to exchange information and to clarify each other's laws and practices. The US would provide capacity building assistance on the enforcement of competition laws to Thailand.

Regarding government procurement, Thailand was not yet ready for market opening while the US explained its system of public procurement and made the case for liberalising this market.

Finally, the US was also willing to cooperate with Thailand on science and technology as well as to provide capacity building for SMEs.

Conclusions

Thai-US negotiations on a free trade agreement took place between June 2004 and January 2006. And although they were not finalised successfully, they constitute an interesting case, which has relevance for other negotiation scenarios. It is clearly a case of negotiations between trade partners with asymmetric negotiation positions, the Thai economy to an important (although decreasing) extent being dependent on the US economy. Market access to the US market and inflows of American FDI were and are indeed of crucial importance for the Thai economy. In addition, the negotiations cannot be seen as completely separated from geo-political considerations and the political alliance between both states. The asymmetric character of the negotiations was further also visible in terms of the negotiation capacity of both sides; on issues like telecommunications, financial services or the environment Thailand did not have a clear position yet in the early phase of the negotiations.

For the US, the negotiations with Thailand were part of a new strategy of bilateralism that sought to keep a number of issues on the international and multilateral trade agenda (IPR, government procurement, protection of FDI etc), while making optimal use of its relative economic and political power in striking deals with individual countries. In addition, the US carefully sequenced the negotiations in such a way that negotiation outcomes from negotiations with certain countries (Chile, Mexico, Singapore, ...) were systematically used as precedents for subsequent negotiations with countries where initially less convergent negotiation positions existed.

In the case of Thailand, the shadow cast by the previously reached US-Singapore agreement was very clear. Not only was its outcome used as a benchmark by the negotiators, but ASEAN member states were effectively manoeuvred in a situation of competition in their relations with the US. Strengthening its negotiation position through coordination at the level of ASEAN was therefore not an option for Thailand. However, it should be observed that this was not only because of the strategy of the US but also because of the lack of political will and converging economic interests within ASEAN.

It is difficult to pronounce ourselves on the chances of success of these negotiations but it is clear that the negotiators still had many hard nuts to crack and that civil society and certain sectoral interest groups were stepping up their opposition to the negotiations. Particularly problematic for Thailand were, for example, the liberalisation of certain agricultural imports, rules of origin, e-commerce, labour clauses, IPRs, and government procurement.

References

Akrasanee, N., Dapice, D. and Flatters, F. 1991. *Thailand's Export-led Growth: Retrospect and Prospects*. Bangkok: TDRI.

CRS. 2007. *US-Thailand Free Trade Agreement Negotiations*, Congressional Research Service, Report RL32314, 16 January.

De Lombaerde, P. 2008. The Paradoxes of Thailand's Pre-crisis Export Performance. *Global Economic Review*, 37(2), 249–264.

De Rosa, D. 2003. *US Free Trade Agreements with ASEAN*. Washington: Institute for International Economics.

Herderschee, H. 1993. Incentives for Exports: The Case of Thailand. *ASEAN Economic Bulletin*, 9(3), 348–363.

Heydon, K. and Woolcock, S. 2009. *The Rise of Bilateralism. Comparing American, European and Asian Approaches to Preferential Trade Agreements*. Tokyo: UNU Press.

Naya, S.F. and Plummer, M. 2005. *The Economics of the Enterprise for ASEAN Initiative*. Singapore: Institute of Southeast Asian Studies (ISEAS).

Naya, S., Plummer, M., Sandhu, S. and Akrasanee, N. (1989), *ASEAN-US Initiative*. Singapore: ISEA.

TDRI. 2003. *A Study on the Impacts of Thailand-US Free Trade Agreement*. Bangkok: TDRI.

Thiparatana, P. and Phetcharatana, N. (ed.) 2008. *Thai-US Relations: Forging a New Partnership in the 21ˢᵗ Century*. Thailand: Ministry of Foreign Affairs.

Warr, P. 1993. *The Thai Economy in Transition*. Cambridge: Cambridge University Press.

Websites

http://www.mfa.go.th/tusfta/round1.htm
http://www.mfa.go.th/tusfta/round2.htm
http://www.mfa.go.th/tusfta/round3.htm
http://www.mfa.go.th/tusfta/round4.htm
http://www.mfa.go.th/tusfta/round5.htm
http://www.ftamonitoring.org/Data3/2006%20Jan/20060117/ftaus_round6.pdf

Chapter 8

Postscript: Asymmetric Trade Negotiations After the Turn-of-the-decade 'Global' Financial Crisis?

Timothy M. Shaw

To oversimplify a little, the performance of the world economy in 2011 depends on what happens in three places: the big emerging markets, the euro area and America. These big three are heading in very different directions, with very different growth prospects and contradictory policy choices. Some of this divergence is inevitable... (Economist 2010b)

For a long period the study of regions and regional orders occupied a small if not insignificant place in international relations theory and scholarship. Now we have...books which argue that regions are central to our understanding of world politics. (Acharya 2007: 629)

...we set out some of the benefits for EU studies scholars of a better dialogue "across the EU studies-new regionalism frontier" ... EU studies cannot afford to rest on its laurels. Much recent work in the field has been somewhat introverted ... it is common for EU studies scholars to ignore the advent of global governance or to integrate globalization fully into their own studies ... (Warleigh-Lack and Van Langenhove 2010: 542)

Introduction

The global 'financial' crisis of the turn of the decade has accelerated changes in the relative standing of major regions, especially the global South. This is particularly undeniable in the case of the 'rise' of Asia. We can argue about the definition of 'Asia' as other regions. But we cannot down-play its ascendancy in the new decade, exacerbated by the relative decline in the established trans-Atlantic nexus whether narrow, bilateral Anglo-American or broader multilateral EU-NAFTA: a further shift towards the Pacific. In turn, the divergence between, say, the EU and NAFTA on the one hand and ASEAN+3 on the other, further encourages not just 'inter-regional' analyses (Gaens 2008, Laursen 2010) but also 'new regionalisms', reaching beyond the inter- to non-state actors and relationships (Shaw, Grant and Cornelissen 2011).

In short, trade negotiations in the second decade of the 21st century are likely to take place among increasingly asymmetrical national and regional partners.

Together these directions encourage 'revisionism' in regional studies as the established EU 'model' is devalued or discredited in a world of PIIGS,[1] reflected in the euro crisis (Lorca-Susino 2010), while innovations in East Asia cannot be decried (Ravenhill 2010 a, b). EU studies are beginning to recognize and incorporate insights from new regionalism (Warleigh-Lack and Van Langenhove 2010, Warleigh-Lack et al. 2011). In short, the current conjuncture compels innovative regional analysis and explanation which serve to confront established hierarchies in frameworks/explanations and inter-/intra-regional interactions; in a world of 200 states, ironically, global relations/studies may be becoming regionalized? (Van Langenhove 2011). In turn, such work impacts established approaches and debates as indicated in the final section (De Lombaerde et al. 2010).

In terms of broader debates, first, this cross-regional analysis reinforces claims for a variety of perspectives: Fareed Zakaria's (2008) rise of the 'rest', in this case neither other states or other actors, but rather regions other than the established trans-Atlantic ones. Similarly, secondly, a focus on the emerging middle is compatible with the notion of a 'second world' from Parag Khanna (2009): the new 'middle' is neither rich nor poor in aggregate. And thirdly, debates about forms of IR (Tickner and Waever 2009) and IPE (Phillips and Weaver 2010) outside the old centres of trans-Atlantic, intellectual hegemony, especially American, British and French, are supported by such an approach as suggested at the end of this chapter.

Attention to divergent regionalisms also encourages renewed analysis of state-non-state relations, especially private companies and civil societies, including diasporas and hence forms of transnationalism (Khagram and Levitt 2007), particularly 'transnational governance' (Brown 2011, Dingwerth 2008). It encourages further attention to and recognition of varieties of capitalisms/ companies/societies etc. And it also reinforces distinctions between 'emerging markets' and emerging states/companies/powers. In short, new regionalism which includes attention to divergent regional directions at the turn of the decade is increasingly heuristic for several disciplines and discourses as indicated in the final section. It also reinforces the imperative of open, 'network' rather than closed 'club' diplomacy (Heine 2006), again treated at the end.

This postscript focuses on neither regions in decline – the EU and NAFTA – nor those clearly on the rise – ASEAN+3 – but rather on the spill-over of both onto the rest of the global South, especially Africa, the Caribbean and Latin America. This trio of regions is differentially impacted, leading to new forms of inter- and non-state inequalities within the emerging second world. These are reflected in the proliferation of formal regions in all three areas: compatible and/or competitive regionalisms (Mace, Cooper and Shaw 2011)?

In turn, inter-regionalisms constitute a growing sub-field, historically around the EU – Asia-Europe Meeting (ASEM) (Gaens 2008) and Euro-Med (Zank 2009)

---

1   PIIGS refers to the economies of Portugal, Ireland, Italy, Greece and Spain.

etc – but now increasingly around ASEAN, the Shanghai Cooperation Organization (SCO) etc. Interestingly, the Middle East is marked by underdeveloped regional institutions (Harders and Legrenzi 2008, Legrenzi and Momani 2011) yet current anti-government movements seem to have distinctive regional dimensions? And regions can be brought together by pipelines (Kuzemko, Goldthau, Keating and Belyi 2011) as well as containers and couriers. Such inter-regional relations are advanced by 'emerging powers' seeking to reinforce their 'emerging' status.

In the 'Asian' crisis of the late 20th century (Robertson 2008), Asia was blamed as the cause. By contrast in the current crisis, Asia is the savior, keeping the global economy afloat (Moschella 2010). ASEAN+3 was one response to the regional crisis of the mid-1990s; now it is symbolic of Asia's rise and ability to play a global role given the fall-out in the Anglo-American world. In the 'new' world of the G20 and multi-level governance (Cooper 2010), regions may come to play an important role in representing the other 150 countries in terms of global issues, especially if emerging powers so animate and connect (Payne 2010).

I turn first to the most marginal of continents – Africa – but one which has enjoyed significant, sustained growth since the turn of the century, largely because of demand for its energy, mineral and other resources by BRICs like China and India.[2] The other pair of regions overlap in the Western Hemisphere and like Africa is characterized by a proliferation of regionalisms on offer. Interestingly, one or two other regions tend to be overlooked in such discourses, such as the Gulf and MENA, although they feature in notions of kick-starting the global economy through SWF etc (Harders and Legrenzi 2008, Legrenzi and Momani 2011).

Africa

> …Africa has outgrown the gloom and doom…Africa, in fact, is now one of the world's fastest growing regions… (Door, Lund and Roxburgh 2010: 80)

Africa may contain over a quarter of the world's states; as indicated at the end of this section, it certainly is a centre for the proliferation of formal inter-governmental regional organizations. And in part because, like Central Asia and Central Europe, it contains a significant percentage of land-locked countries, the extent of informal and transnational regional relations is also significant. This impacts its 'international relations' which tend to be non- rather than inter-state in character whether analysts so recognise or not. As Douglas Lemke (2003: 117) laments:

> …political power is exercised by a variety of states and non-state actors in Africa. Because standard international relations research theorises about and collects data only for official states, much of Africa's international relations are left out.

---

2   See www2.goldmansachs.com.

Thus far, the new century has been good for the continent, especially for those countries which have energy and mineral reserves which have attracted the attention of and investment from China and India (Cheru and Obi 2010). At the start of this decade, the Boston Consulting Group (BCG) identified 40 African corporations which are competing with the world; the Center for Global Development (CGD) pointed to 17 burgeoning economies (Radelet 2010); and The Economist recently reported on six African states being among the ten to have grown fastest this century (2011); indeed the continent's growth rates are likely to exceed those of Asia over the next five years. Others have attracted demand for land and agricultural commodities, especially from the Gulf states. Even the skeptical Economist (2008: 20) has had to express some revisionist optimism:

> After four decades of political and economic stagnation...the continent's 48 sub-Saharan countries have been growing for the past five years at a perky overall rate of 5% or so...Once described by this newspaper, perhaps with undue harshness, as 'the hopeless continent', it could yet confound its legion of gloomsters and show that its oft-heralded renaissance is not just another false dawn prompted by the passing windfall of booming commodity prices, but the start of something solid and sustainable...Africa has a rare chance to break out of its poverty trap.

However, it has yet to rationalise its seven regional groupings and agree EPAs with the EU despite EU pressure and a variety of partial accords. Europe's difficulties with the PIIGS and eurozone have changed the balance of power; the EU is less hegemonic, reflected in Africa's reluctance, approaching resistance, to sign any EPAs thus far:

> The overlap of membership between regional integration arrangements in the wider southern and eastern African region is without parallel anywhere else in the world...seven regional economic communities are effectively operating in parallel within the region (SADC, COMESA, EAC, SACU, IGAD, ECCAS and CEPGL). (Braude 2008: 7)

And Africa's pair of emerging powers – Nigeria and South Africa – is less hegemonic than, say, India in South Asia: more second world than BRICs despite China's invitation to the Republic of South Africa (RSA) to join the next BRIC summit in 2011. South Africa's status is in part a function of its hosting of major multinational companies (MNCs) such as Anglo American, de Beers, MTN, SABMiller etc (www.bcg.com) and its franchises and supply chains increasingly define the region as does its need for electricity, water etc (www.tralac.org). Since the anti-apartheid era, it has hosted some leading global conferences, the path-breaking World Commission on Dams (Dingwerth 2008) and INGOs like Civicus. Meanwhile, Africa's distinctive transnational relations are likely to continue despite sustained growth in some of its economies (Cornelissen, Cheru and Shaw 2011).

The Caribbean

What constitutes the Caribbean? …Among scholars, 'the Caribbean' is a socio-historical category…it embraces the islands and parts of the adjoining mainland and may be extended to include the Caribbean Diaspora overseas. As one scholar observes, there are many Caribbeans…

> In short, the definition of the Caribbean might be based on language and identity, geography, history and culture, geopolitics, geoeconomics, or organisation. (Girvan 2005: 304)

The Caribbean however defined consists of many small states most, but not all, of which are independent. So it has been the focus of a series of regional experiments by both colonial and independent authorities along with international agencies like the United Nations (UN) and Organization of American States (OAS). Its most extensive and inclusive institution is the Association of Caribbean States (ACS), with the Caribbean Community (CARICOM) being meso- and the Organization of Eastern Caribbean States (OECS) micro-level. But these now compete with Venezuela's Bolivarian Alternative for the Americas (ALBA) initiative. The Caribbean Forum (CARIFORUM) (CARICOM plus the Dominican Republic [DR]) is the only region thus far to sign an Economic Partnership Agreement (EPA) with the EU, albeit with marginal impact to date despite being very asymmetric?

And the Caribbean economy has several dimensions to it which impact formal and informal regionalisms: from informal and illegal to the diaspora. Transnational relations, both legal and otherwise impact, such as offshore financial centres along with money-laundering, in theory regulated by the Caribbean Financial Action Task Force (CFATF).[3] Likewise, the diaspora constitutes an important market for goods and services, including Carnival. But transnational gangs undermine established tourist and other sectors as well as increase the cost of doing business. So CARICOM now has an agency in Trinidad and Tobago dedicated to treating crime and guns: the Implementation Agency for Crime and Security (IMPACS).[4] In terms of a distinctive, organic definition of regionalism in this region, Alejandra Bronfman (2007: 5–6) offers a compelling perspective:

> …the circulation of commodities is one of the unifying aspects of Caribbean history…Globalization has not just happened to the Caribbean. The Caribbean has participated in the making of globalization…four things circulate: people, capital, drugs and information.

---

3   See www.cfatf-gafic.org.
4   See www.caricomimpacs.org.

Latin America

Despite all the attention placed on globalisation and its processes, regional integration mechanisms continue to hold a pivotal position in world affairs... Although the debates surrounding the European approaches and concepts maintain a privileged position, variants located in other regional projects deserve closer examination. This requirement is no more apparent than in the America where the process of regionalisation has a long history and is currently becoming increasingly complex, contested and fluid...

> In terms of intensity, inter-American regional projects bring out the contrast between the familiar and the novel components. (Mace, Cooper and Shaw 2010: 1)

With the demise of the dream of an ambitious neo-liberal Free Trade Area of the Americas (FTAA), several alternative regional schema have been proposed by emerging economies like Brazil. The status of the OAS is increasingly problematic because of the presence as well as decline of the United States (US). And the ambitions of NAFTA are under threat from the war around drugs and gangs on the Mexico-US border (Morales 2011). Aside from ALBA and Mercosur, then, Brazil has animated UNASUR, a hemispheric grouping without the two gringo countries to the north (Mace, Cooper and Shaw 2010).

Brazil as a BRIC is impacting the Southern Cone and its neighbours as well as the US and Canada and its own growth trajectory is impacted by Chinese demand. Such demand has transformed large-scale agriculture in both Argentina and Brazil. Brazil's foreign policy has increasingly global reach, including links with other emerging democratic powers – India, Brazil and South Africa (IBSA) – and around the December 2009 Copenhagen Climate Change conference (COP 15) – BASIC.[5] And its larger companies are also global players: Embraer, InBev with Belgium's Interbrew, Petrobras, Vale etc.[6] In terms of civil society, Porto Alegre is home to the World Social Forum (WSF). As the region celebrated its bicentennials in 2010, *The Economist* (2010: 13) suggested that

> ...something remarkable is happening in Latin America. In the five years to 2008 the region's economies grew at an annual average rate of 5.5%...While Latin American squabbling politicians blather on about integration, the region's business are quietly getting on the with job – witness the emerging cohorts of *multilatinas*...

Two things lie behind Latin America's renaissance. The first is the appetite of China and India for raw materials with which the continent is richly endowed. But the second is the improvement in economic management...

---

5   BASIC refers to Brazil, South Africa, India and China.
6   See www.bcg.com, www.research.hsbc.com.

New regionalisms in the second decade of the 21st century

The G20 is without question the new game in town in respect of global governance. All 192 countries in the current world system have concerns about and perspectives on contemporary global governance after the financial crisis of 2008–2009, and are seeking to participate in its resolution in a variety of ways and in a number of different diplomatic and institutional arenas…

> …global governance – around whatever set of issues – will become even more complicated as more and more countries come to recognize the need to pursue development diplomacy as effectively as they can on the global stage. (Payne 2010: 729, 738, 740)

The shake-up in the hierarchy of global regions given the interrelated factors of the global crisis and the related rise of the BRICs poses the question about whether the second decade of the 21st century will be characterized by more or less divergence/ convergence? In part this question about direction is a function of which emerging markets/companies/powers continue to rise. In turn, it will be impacted by which varieties and combinations of capitalisms/companies/civil societies are best suited to the competitive, post-neoliberal world of the second decade of the new century beyond the Washington Consensus. Aside from the impact of the G20 nexus, one other major variable determining trends in the second decade will be the balances in the northern hemisphere among the EU of 27, including the PIIGS, NAFTA and ASEAN+3. In turn these will be influenced by the state of the economy of their leading powers – i.e. Germany, US and China, respectively – another definition of the G3? In short, there are likely to be a set of emerging asymmetries.

As Tony Payne suggests in the opening citations to this concluding section, 'development diplomacy', what Jorge Heine (2008) would term 'network diplomacy', is ever more imperative at both global and regional levels: advancing ideas and interests among a heterogeneous set of actors, not just states. Such a perspective is compatible with notions of new regionalisms as these seek to identify and include non-state regional relations, from micro-to macro-level, in their analysis. So development or network diplomacy can be advanced from the local to the global given the presence of non-state actors at all levels, including the regional. Such correlates of new regionalisms will be featured in an imminent state-of-the-field *The Ashgate Research Companion to Regionalisms* (Shaw, Grant and Cornelissen 2011). And they should impact comparative analyses of regionalisms as advanced through UNU-CRIS and interlocking networks etc (De Lombaerde and Schulz 2009, www.cris.unu.edu, www.csgr.org, www.garnet-eu.org, www. giga-hamburg.de, www.netris-acp.org). They were already placed into comparative conceptual context at the turn of the decade (De Lombaerde et al. 2010).

Finally, let me conclude by way of reflecting on some of the implications of such divergent regionalisms and associated asymmetrical negotiations for established approaches/disciplines/policies:

- *development studies* – proliferation of issues and institutions, especially around Asian drivers, developmental states, second world etc, increasingly 'the rest';
- *emerging economies/markets/powers/societies/states* – how compatible/ competitive as reflecting set of divergent 'disciplines'/assumptions?
- *environmental studies* – impacts on different regions of climate change to resource wars around water and land as well as energy and minerals;
- *gender studies* – from women and development to gender dimensions of crisis and rebalancing;
- *global governance/multilateralisms* – beyond inter-governmental law to the 'rest': global coalitions (Dingwerth 2008: 628–30) around blood diamonds (Kimberley Process), landmines (Ottawa Process), fisheries and forestry certification (Gale and Haward 2011), but minimal momentum around, say, child soldiers or small arms;
- *global studies* – beyond homogeneous inter- or non-governmental relations to emerging heterogeneous global structures, such as the Global Redesign Initiative (RDI) of the World Economic Forum (WEF) (www.weforum.org);
- *international political economy* – beyond assumptions of American existential and intellectual hegemony to identification and recognition of varieties of sources and types (Phillips and Weaver 2010);
- *international relations* – recognition of plurality as well as diversity of states – developmental as well as fragile or failed – and hence salience of development or network diplomacy; and
- *security studies* – treating both 'old' and 'new' security issues including the high price of energy, food, resources etc (Sneyd 2011, Richardson 2009) along with diverse forms of privatisation of security and civil-military relations.

References

Acharya, A. 2007. Review Article: the Emerging Regional Architecture of World Politics. *World Politics*, 59(4), 629–52.

Acharya, A. and A.I. Johnston (eds) 2007. *Crafting Cooperation: Regional International Institutions in Comparative Perspective*. New York: Cambridge University Press.

Braude, W. 2008. SADC, COMESA and the EAC: Conflicting Regional and Trade Agendas. *IGD Occasional paper*, (57).

Bronfman, A. 2007. *On the Move: The Caribbean Since 1989*. Halifax: Fernwood.

Brown, S. (eds) 2011. *Transnational Transfers and the State*. London: Palgrave Macmillan. (forthcoming)

Cheru, F. and C. Obi (eds) 2010. *The Rise of China and India in Africa: Challenges, Opportunities and Critical Interventions*. London: Zed for NAI.

Cooper, A.F. 2010. The G20 as an Improvised Crisis Committee and/or Contested "Steering Committee" for the World. *International Affairs*, 86(3), 741–57.

Cornelissen, S., F. Cheru and T.M. Shaw (eds) 2011. *Africa and International Relations in the Twenty-first Century: Still Challenging Theory?* London: Palgrave Macmillan. (forthcoming)

De Lombaerde, P. et al. 2010. The Problem of Comparison in Comparative Regionalism. *Review of International Studies*, 36(3), 731–53.

De Lombaerde, P. and M. Schulz (eds) 2009. *The EU and World Regionalism: The Makability of Regions in the 21st Century.* Farnham: Ashgate.

Dingwerth, K. 2008. Private Transnational Governance and the Developing World: A Comparative Perspective. *International Studies Quarterly*, 52(3), 607–34.

Dorr, N., S. Lund and C. Roxburgh 2010. The African Miracle: How the World's Charity Case Became its Best Investment Opportunity. *Foreign Policy*, Dec., 80–81.

Economist 2008. Briefing: Africa's Prospects – Opportunity Knocks. 389(8601), 20 and 33–6.

Economist 2010a. Nobody's Backyard. The Rise of Latin America, 396(8699), 13 and Special Report (1–18).

Economist 2010b. The World Economy: Three-way Split: America, the Euro Zone and the Emerging World are Heading in Different Directions. 9 Dec.

Economist 2011. A More Hopeful Continent: the Lion Kings? 398 (8715), 72–3.

Gaens, B. (ed) 2008. *Europe-Asia Interregional Relations: A Decade of ASEM.* Aldershot: Ashgate.

Gale, F. and M. Haward 2011. *Global Commodity Governance: State Responses to Sustainable Forest and Fisheries Certification.* London: Palgrave Macmillan.

Girvan, N. 2005. Reinterpreting the Caribbean. in D. Pantin (ed). *The Caribbean Economy: A Reader.* Kingston: Ian Randle, 304–18.

Harders, C. and M. Legrenzi (eds) 2008. *Beyond Regionalism? Regional Cooperation, Regionalism and Regionalization in the Middle East.* Aldershot: Ashgate.

Heine, J. 2006. On the Manner of Practising the New Diplomacy. *CIGI Working Paper*, (11).

Khagram, S. and P. Levitt (eds) 2007. *The Transnational Studies Reader.* New York: Routledge.

Khanna, P. 2009. *The Second World: How Emerging Powers Are Redefining Global Competition in the 21st Century*, New York: Random House.

Kuzemko, C., A. Goldthau, M. Keating and A. Belyi (eds) 2011. *Dynamics of Energy Governance in Europe and Russia.* London: Palgrave Macmillan. (forthcoming)

Laursen, F. (ed) 2010. *Comparative Regional Integration: Europe and Beyond.* Farnham: Ashgate.

Legrenzi, M. and B. Momani 2011. *Shifting Geo-Economic Power of the Gulf: Oil, Finance and Institutions.* Aldershot: Ashgate.

Lemke, D. 2003. Review Article: African Lessons from International Relations Research, *World Politics*, 56(1), 114–38.

Lorca-Susino, M. 2010. *The Euro in the 21st Century: Economic Crisis and Financial Uproar*. Farnham: Ashgate.

Mace, G., A.F. Cooper and T.M. Shaw (eds) 2010. *Inter-American Cooperation at a Crossroads*. London: Palgrave Macmillan. (forthcoming)

Morales, I. (ed) 2011. *National Solutions to Trans-Border Problems? The Governance of Security and Risk in a Post-NAFTA North America*. Farnham: Ashgate.

Moschella, M. 2010. *Governing Risk: The IMF and Global Financial Crises*. London: Palgrave Macmillan.

Payne, A. 2010. How Many Gs are There in 'Global Governance' after the Crisis? The Perspectives of the "Marginal Majority" of the World's States. *International Affairs*, 86(3), 729–40.

Phillips, N. and C. Weaver (eds) 2010. *International Political Economy: Debating the Past, Present and Future*, Abingdon: Routledge.

Radelet, S. 2010. Emerging Africa: How 17 Countries Are Leading the Way. Washington DC: CGD.

Ravenhill, J. 2010a. Understanding the New East Asian Regionalism. *Review of International Political Economy*, 17(2), 173–77.

Ravenhill, J. 2010b. The New East Asian Regionalism: a Political Domino Effect. *Review of International Political Economy*, 17(2), 178–208.

Richardson, B. 2009. *Sugar: Refined Power in a Global Regime*. London: Palgrave Macmillan.

Robertson, J. (ed) 2008. *Power and Politics after Financial Crises: Rethinking Foreign Opportunism in Emerging Markets*. London: Palgrave Macmillan.

Shaw, T.M., J.A. Grant and S. Cornelissen (eds) 2011. *The Ashgate Research Companion to Regionalisms*. Farnham: Ashgate. (forthcoming)

Sneyd, A. 2011. *Governing Cotton: Globalization and Poverty in Africa*. London: Palgrave Macmillan.

Tickner, A.B. and O. Waever (eds) 2009. *International Relations Scholarship around the World*. Abingdon: Routledge.

Van Langenhove, L. 2011. *Building Regions: The Regionalization of the World Order*. Farnham: Ashgate.

Warleigh-Lack, A. and L. Van Langenhove 2010. Rethinking EU Studies: The Contribution of Comparative Regionalism. *Journal of European Integration*, 32(6), 541–62.

Warleigh-Lack, A. et al (eds) 2011. *New Regionalism and the European Union: Dialogues, Comparisons and New Research Directions*, Abingdon: Routledge (forthcoming)

World Bank 2011. *Global Economic Prospects 2011*. Washington DC.

Zakaria, F. 2008. *The Post-American World*. New York: Norton.

Zank, W. (ed) 2009. *Clash or Cooperation of Civilizations? Overlapping Integration and Identities*. Farnham: Ashgate.

www.bcg.com
www.cris.unu.edu
www.csgr.org
www.ec.europa.eu
www.ecdpm.org
www.economist.com/theworldin/2011
www.garnet-eu.org
www.giga-hamburg.de
www.hdr.undp.org/en/reports/global/hdr2010
www.netris-acp.org
www.research.hsbc.com
www.tralac.org
www2.goldmansachs.com

Index

Locators shown in *italics* refer to figures, tables and boxes.

THE INTERNATIONAL POLITICAL ECONOMY OF NEW REGIONALISMS SERIES

Other titles in the series

Development and Security
in Southeast Asia
Volume III: Globalization
Edited by David B. Dewitt
and Carolina G. Hernandez

Development and Security
in Southeast Asia
Volume I: The Environment
Edited by David B. Dewitt
and Carolina G. Hernandez

Development and Security
in Southeast Asia
Volume II: The People
Edited by David B. Dewitt
and Carolina G. Hernandez

Thailand, Indonesia and Burma in
Comparative Perspective
Priyambudi Sulistiyanto

For Product Safety Concerns and Information please contact our
EU representative GPSR@taylorandfrancis.com Taylor & Francis
Verlag GmbH, Kaufingerstraße 24, 80331 München, Germany